JESSICA VITKUS
AND MARJORIE INGALL

SMART SEX

Illustrations by Michiko Stehrenberger
Designed by Red Herring Design

NEW YORK · LONDON · TORONTO · SYDNEY · TOKYO · SINGAPORE

POCKET BOOKS

This book was produced in association with Melcher Media, Inc.
170 Fifth Avenue, New York, NY 10010
Charles Melcher, Publisher

Editors: Genevieve Field, Sarah Malarkey, Gillian Sowell, and Elizabeth Ward
Editorial Assistant: Emily Donaldson
Photography Editors: Gillian Sowell and Russell Cohen
Research Assistants: Amanda Block and John-Ryan Hevron

Illustrator: Michiko Stehrenberger

Designer: Kristina DiMatteo at Red Herring Design
Diagrams and map by Adam Chiu at Red Herring Design

MTV's Sex in the 90's created by Lauren Lazin

Special thanks to:
Kye Bennett, Brian Blatz, Duncan Bock, Erin Bohensky, Eduardo Braniff, Gina Centrello, COLORS Magazine,
Julie Davidson, Michael Dubb, Tina Exharos, Twisne Fan, Lisa Feuer, Janine Gallant, Kate Giel, Robin Eichel
and Stacey Lisheron at FPG, Nina Justman, Greer Kessel, Dr. Lyuba Konopasek, Rachel Kranz, Andrea LaBate,
June O'Leary, Donna O'Neill, Ortho-McNeil Pharmaceutical, Ed Paparo, Pharmacia & Upjohn, Renee Presser,
Francis Ramos, Dr. Mark Schuster, Robin Silverman, Donald Silvey, Liate Stehlik, Jennifer Stipcich,
David Terrien, Van Toffler, Kara Welsh, Ray Whelan, Jr. at Globe Photos, Joe Wittkop, Megan Worman,
Wyeth-Ayerst Laboratories, and to all the helpful people at the many organizations we contacted who
were so generous with their time in assisting us with our research.

An *Original* Publication of POCKET BOOKS

POCKET BOOKS, a division of Simon & Schuster Inc.
1230 Avenue of the Americas, New York, NY 10020

ISBN: 0-671-01910-4

First Pocket Books trade paperback printing March 1998

10 9 8 7 6 5 4 3 2 1

Printed in the U.S.A.

CONTENTS

INTRODUCTION

INTRODUCTION

Whether you are having sex or not, you are a sexual creature. Every adult is—the bus driver who took your fare this morning, the bored-looking cashier at the convenience store, your cookie-baking Aunt Mavis. Sexuality goes along with being human. So why can't people talk about it? You *do* hear bragging from friends, endless rock and rap lyrics about wanting and needing and getting action. You go to movies and see people swept off their feet for a choreographed moment of ecstasy where no one bumps noses and nobody's arm ever falls asleep.

Despite what you see on the screen and hear in locker rooms, sex doesn't just happen. Real sex is a lot of work—including a lot of brainwork. Sex involves a series of choices, and the best plan is to get all the facts. We have assembled the essential and most up-to-date info here—the basics of consent, birth control, safer sex, sexually transmitted diseases, pregnancy and more. You'll also find interviews with people who can get real and talk about what works and what doesn't. You might not agree with everything they say—issues surrounding sex are often emotionally charged and highly debatable—but armed with these facts and opinions you can figure out what's best for you.

So dive right in and meet our panel of opinionated young men and women who are speaking from the front lines, telling you about their desires, mistakes, strategies and shining moments between the sheets. Turn the page and make your sex a little smarter.

THE DISCUSSION PANEL

We wanted to hear firsthand what's going on—what you're thinking, feeling and facing. So we gathered a group of people with different stats and different ideas about sex. This book grew out of the panel's discussion and concerns. Meet the inquiring minds and honest confessors who will dish about their experiences, fantasies and views. The few, the proud, the panelists.

CATHERINE, 19
BALTIMORE, MD
STUDIES BUSINESS, MUSIC
LIKES TO: *Play violin*
LISTENS TO: *Prodigy, Beck, Oasis, Dave Matthews Band, Edwin McCain*
THINKS: *"Sex has a lot to do with how you see yourself. And if you think you're sexy, you are. Different acts make you feel dirty or sexy depending on how you perceive them."*

TODD, 22
LITTLE ROCK, AR
STUDIES THEATER
LIKES TO: *Rollerblade, take road trips, camp, draw, read*
LISTENS TO: *Madonna, Sarah McLaughlan, everything but country and rap*
THINKS: *"I just like things to go where they will. I don't like to force them*
to happen. I've had everything go faster than planned, and afterward I didn't feel comfortable with that person. The starting point was sex, so we didn't have anywhere further to go. It started with the physical before the emotional."*

SIMON, 17
SOUTH BRONX, NY
SENIOR IN HIGH SCHOOL
LIKES TO: *Play football and basketball, see movies with friends*
LISTENS TO: *Lost Boyz, Offspring, KoRn, Soundgarden, Silverchair, Smashing Pumpkins*
THINKS: *"When you have sex, you just think about the present, you don't think about the outcome. It's, 'I love you right here and now.' It seems like if you think about babies and STDs, it'll ruin the moment. But when I stop, afterward—that's when I think about it."*

GINA, 24
WESTMINSTER, CA
WORKS IN A BOOKSTORE
LIKES TO: *Read, shop, take spur-of-the-moment road trips*
LISTENS TO: *Chris Isaak, Fiona Apple, Natalie Merchant, TLC, Saturday Night Fever soundtrack*
THINKS: *"You think nothing's ever going to happen to you, that you're untouchable. Since I had had only one boyfriend, I never worried. I had all the information, but it didn't matter to me. I turned a deaf ear. Then I faced my own virus [HPV, or genital warts]. The reality is it's not AIDS, but to me, this is my life. Now I'll tell someone, 'If we're going to have sex, there will always be a condom.' "*

DAVID, 20
DETROIT, MI
INSTALLS TELEPHONES
LIKES TO: Go to clubs, write, hang
   with his girlfriend, party
LISTENS TO: Bob Marley, The Fugees,
Tupac, Tori Amos, Roots
THINKS: "I wish I hadn't started having
   sex so young, because now I'm not
   really impressed with it. I feel like
   I've been having sex for a while.
   It's old, and I'm only twenty."

VIRGINIA, 20
ATLANTA, GA
STUDIES BUSINESS
LIKES TO: Participate in student
   government, hang out with
   sorority sisters, go hiking
LISTENS TO: The Police, Widespread
   Panic, No Doubt, Sheryl Crow
THINKS: "Sex is fun and sex is really
   special, but it's taken me a long
   time to learn responsibility. I'm still
   not always a responsible person."

ANDREW, 25
WASHINGTON, DC
HEADHUNTER FOR CONSULTING FIRM
LIKES TO: Watch sports, smoke
   good cigars and drink fine beers
LISTENS TO: Rancid, Oasis, The Specials,
   PJ Harvey, Sublime
THINKS: "Sex is a spiritual thing. I was
   a virgin until I was twenty-four. I
   did have the urge to get the thing
   over with, but I'm so glad I didn't.
   A year or two out of school it dawned
   on me: I'm ready now."

CHARLIE, 17
PHILADELPHIA, PA
HIGH SCHOOL STUDENT,
WORKS AT A GROCERY STORE
LIKES TO: Work on car, ski, lift weights
LISTENS TO: Pearl Jam, Soundgarden,
Bush, The Beatles, Silverchair
THINKS: "I just want to chill right
   now. I don't want to have sex at all.
   I'll miss it, but I just don't want to
   make any mistakes I'll regret."

RYAN P., 20
COLUMBUS, OH
STUDIES LITERATURE
LIKES TO: Go to clubs, exercise,
   talk on the phone, see movies,
   go to coffeehouses
LISTENS TO: The Chemical Brothers,
   Depeche Mode, Alanis Morissette,
   all kinds of techno and rave
THINKS: "For most kids who are straight,
   it's easier to get to know someone,
   to learn the steps to love, because
   you see it around you every day, even
   in your household, your parents.
   You've basically been coached by
   society. If you're gay, you don't
   have that kind of role model."

KARLEY, 17
PORTLAND, OR
HIGH SCHOOL STUDENT, MOTHER
LIKES TO: Go to movies, talk to friends,
   take her baby to the park
LISTENS TO: Tupac, Mary J. Blige, Brandy,
   Snoop Doggy Dogg, Keith Sweat,
   Bone Thugs N. Harmony, Toni Braxton
THINKS: "Since I've had my daughter,
   right now I'm trying to finish school
   and do other things. For me, if sex
   happens, it happens. If it doesn't,
   it doesn't."

KATIE, 23
PHILADELPHIA, PA
ACTIVIST WHO SPEAKS OUT AND
EDUCATES PEOPLE ABOUT DATE RAPE
LIKES TO: Read, play piano and tennis,
   do outdoor stuff like hiking,
   camping and water-skiing
LISTENS TO: Tori Amos,

Harry Connick, Jr., Rusted Root, Ani DiFranco, George Winston

THINKS: "*Someone has to do something (about date rape), and I feel like I can. How many women do I have to see who have suffered, who can't come forward? It's too much. All those stories I hear. Ten to twenty every day. It's too much.*"

PRIY, 23

BROOKLYN, NY

ACTIVIST, UP-AND-COMING WRITER

LIKES TO: *Read, shop, watch foreign films, go out with friends*

LISTENS TO: *Mary J. Blige, ABBA, Madonna, Beck, Fugees*

Thinks: "*Ultimately I'd like to see a world where sexual labels aren't important or necessary, where we can think beyond things as simple and defining as gender.*"

CHAD, 20

HOUSTON, TX

STUDIES POLITICAL SCIENCE

LIKES TO: *Fish, camp, hang out with fraternity brothers, go out to bars and clubs*

LISTENS TO: *Pearl Jam, Nirvana, George Jones, Hank Williams, Jimmy Buffett*

THINKS: "*During sex, say, 'That felt good.' Let her know.*"

LENA, 21

DALLAS, TX

STUDIES ART AND LANGUAGES

LIKES TO: *Read the classics, take dance classes, sit with friends in coffeehouses*

LISTENS TO: *Hootie and the Blowfish, Depeche Mode, U2, Radiohead*

THINKS: "*Casual sex does not build self-respect, self-esteem. It's one way of trying to get attention, using your body instead of your brain. We*

can all do that, but we don't have to. With non casual sex, you can get emotional and physical pleasure."

THOMAS, 18

SAN FRANCISCO, CA

HIGH SCHOOL STUDENT

LIKES TO: *Play basketball, play baseball, hang with friends*

LISTENS TO: *Souls of Mischief, U2, Snoop Doggy Dogg, Tupac, Bob Marley, KoRn*

THINKS: "*My rep is totally messed up right now. I'm considered a dog. I guess I used to get around or something. I think that I'm totally changed in that regard, but the girls don't. There are girls I'd want to be with, but they're going on what they've heard.*"

CRYSTAL, 18

BROKEN ARROW, OK

HIGH SCHOOL STUDENT,

MEMBER OF TRUE LOVE WAITS

LIKES TO: *Work out, participate in the school leadership program, go out on dates, go out with friends*

LISTENS TO: *Jars of Clay, Amy Grant, Michael Bolton, Mariah Carey, LeAnn Rimes*

THINKS: "*People who have sex outside of marriage are losing the fullness of how wonderful sex can be.*"

ALLISON, 22

NASHVILLE, TN

STUDIES POLITICAL SCIENCE, PSYCHOLOGY

LIKES TO: *Work out, read, paint*

LISTENS TO: *D'Angelo; Sarah McLachlan, Rollins Band, Nine Inch Nails, Portishead, Peter Gabriel*

THINKS: "*I think that if you're having sex, you're always relying on someone else for your happiness, and that's not something you should ever do. That's primarily why I'm a virgin. Sometimes I feel like I've missed out on a lot of the education* that my peers have gained, but then in some ways I feel like I have a lot of self-respect, self-reliance and independence because of it."

BRADFORD, 21
CHARLESTOWN, WV
STUDIES PSYCHOLOGY
LIKES TO: *Jog, bike, surf the Net, read, play cards*
LISTENS TO: *Ween, Nine Inch Nails, Primus, Pink Floyd, Dave Matthews Band, classical*
THINKS: *"I can catch AIDS. I can catch an STD. I can bring a life into this world. Every time I have sex, all that comes into play."*

ESTHER, 17
PITTSFORD, NY
HIGH SCHOOL STUDENT
LIKES TO: *Sing in folk band, write*
LISTENS TO: *Ani DiFranco, Smashing Pumpkins, Melissa Etheridge, Indigo Girls, Sinead O'Connor*
THINKS: *"Being gay is not a status symbol in my school. Since I'm a lesbian, for me sex is entirely the opposite of being cool and accepted."*

KIM, 20
SAN ANTONIO, TX
STUDIES ENGLISH
LIKES TO: *Watch basketball, talk and watch TV with friends*
LISTENS TO: *Tupac, The Pharcyde, Mary J. Blige, Snoop Doggy Dogg*
THINKS: *"Catching an STD was almost a blessing, because it made me stop my behavior before I got something even worse. I don't enjoy it, but I think that it's taught me a lot quickly."*

RYAN S., 19
RODEO, CA
GOES TO COMMUNITY COLLEGE

LIKES TO: *Go to The Rocky Horror Picture Show, make home horror movies*
LISTENS TO: *Pearl Jam, Nine Inch Nails, Nirvana, Hole, Beck*
THINKS: *"I wouldn't go so far as to say that sex is a goal, but it's something that I would like to have in my life. I think it's an important part of life."*

MELISSA, 23
SAN FRANCISCO, CA
MODELS, STUDIES PSYCHOLOGY
LIKES TO: *Ride her motorcycle, work out, read*
LISTENS TO: *PJ Harvey, Mozart, Guns N' Roses, Cowboy Junkies, Fiona Apple*
THINKS: *"I've had friends get pregnant before. Safe sex to us was making sure we didn't get pregnant. That's definitely what was most scary to us. HIV—it never occurred to me as being a problem at all. When I was practicing safe sex, I didn't factor HIV in at all. Up until I tested positive, I didn't think heterosexuals were in danger."*

With cameos by:
Trevor, 20; Eddie, 22; Andre, 25; Tom, 25; Julia, 25; Jonah, 24; Leeta, 20; Ellen, 21; Natasha, 19; Tino, 17; Lola, 21

And interviews with:
Billie Joe Armstrong
Bill Bellamy
Janeane Garofalo
Idalis
Dave Navarro
and
Steven Tyler

1

No doubt you already know how sex works—tab *A* goes into slot *B*. In fact, you're probably past that. But just when you think you've got this thing pinned down, along comes a new study, a new virus, a new person in your life who's got you asking questions. It's time to muddle through the mixed messages, the taboos, the hype and the misinformation. Smart sex definitely involves your body, but it starts in your mind. See if you have bought into any of the following myths.

BUSTING THE MYTHS

b

Smart Sex Poll

•More than 50 percent of females
and 75 percent of males surveyed
in the U.S. had sexual intercourse
before their 18th birthday.

•Among nonvirgins between ages
16 and 24, 82 percent have had
sex within the last six months.

•90 percent of young adults
between the ages of 16 and 24
think they are fairly well or
very well informed about sex.

*The *Smart Sex poll* results in this book were
compiled by a public opinion polling organization
between December 12 and 17, 1995. The survey
was conducted by telephone among 1,201 adults
between the ages of 16 and 24 throughout the U.S.

If you are trying to impress a crowd, you are forgetting to impress yourself. You are the one who has to live with the STD or the broken heart. Figure out what's good for you. Then go for it. The kind of status you get from sleeping with someone is pretty superficial. If you say okay to sex to please another person, keep in mind that he or she probably doesn't have your best interests as a top priority.

KIM, 20: When I came to college, I saw how people could get respect, and how men could like women even if they didn't have sex. I had thought the whole time that you had to have sex for guys to like you. I used to think. If they sleep with me, that means they like me.

MYTH #1: HAVING SEX WILL MAKE ME MORE COOL, ACCEPTED.

BRADFORD, 21: In high school, the guys who talked about having sex needed to show off in front of their friends. A good-looking girl was the same to them as a car—a status symbol.

In order to have good sex, considerate sex and (these days) safer sex, you have to do a little homework. One of the best ways to learn is to do a lot of talking—with your partner or with more-experienced friends. If there's a parent, teacher, medical pro or clergy-type you trust, he or she can answer questions and steer you toward accurate info. You can also read books, brochures and health magazines. But despite the good resources out there, most of us learn about sex from TV shows and films. Which leads to myth #3.

MYTH #2: SEX IS A NATURAL BEHAVIOR THAT COMES AUTOMATICALLY.

ALLISON, 22: I thought I knew about sex. I used to make my Barbies have sex. I'd put them in bed and walk away, and that was having sex to me. I knew that Ken put his penis in Barbie's vagina, but I had no idea there was any motion involved.

Even your cousin the chimpanzee, who doesn't have the Playboy channel or biology class, must learn about sex from watching others. Sex is a learned behavior. Sure, humans have primal instincts that drive the species toward sex—and hormones are powerful—but we are not preprogrammed with the hows and whats and whens. We have to gather that from observation and experience.

It's easy to get caught up in this myth, due to the sheer volume of film and videotape that passes before your eyes all the time. How many sex scenes have you watched onscreen? How many have you lived out firsthand? Confusing the two may raise your expectations unrealistically.

MYTH #3:
SEX IN
REAL LIFE
IS LIKE
SEX IN
THE MOVIES.

RYAN S., 19: In the movies, they make it seem like it's really easy to get laid. You go out, meet a girl, and *boom*, the next thing you know, you're laying on top of her, grunting and screaming. In my experience, that just doesn't happen.

Which leads to the next misconception.

KATIE, 23: In movies, everything works the right way the first time, and nobody has to talk to figure out how it's done, and everyone seems to know what they're doing through some kind of eye movement or something. It gives a false sense of romance and very little in the way of learning about how to communicate with a partner about sex.

Nearly all the sexual images around us feature young bodies with washboard abs rubbing up against other super-sculpted specimens. Remind yourself: This is fantasyland. Most sexual imagery is somehow chasing your dollar (at the box office, on a billboard, on the cover of a magazine, in a fashion layout, even in rock videos aiming to get you to buy the CD). These things are designed to push your buttons. We get trained to think that sex means two under-twenty-five, hunky bodies groping, and nothing else.

CRYSTAL, 18: I think it's worse for girls. We'll work ourselves to death to look beautiful, and guys expect it. I think guys get pictures of perfect women and that's what they want.

CATHERINE, 19: I'm not as judgmental about boys' bodies as I used to be. The guy I'm dating now is pretty hairy. I always thought that would bother me, but it doesn't. He's a nice, honest, caring guy—that's what I want.

What's more, it's easy to turn these unrealistic standards inward and say, "He/she will never like me until I lose ten pounds, gain ten pounds, get my nose fixed, get clearer skin," or what have you.

ANDREW, 25: The other day I was imagining myself with a woman at work who's a hottie, but I'm like, My belly is huge right now.

The size of your butt or breasts or thighs or nose has nothing to do with the amount of sexual pleasure you can feel or give. Look at the people walking down the street. They are not all Calvin Klein models, and they are all more or less capable of good sex.

MYTH #4: ONLY GOOD-LOOKING PEOPLE HAVE GOOD SEX.

KIM, 20: Sometimes I just feel so fat or ugly and want to wear my baggy clothes and not even eat.

TODD, 22: A nice body is good, but if they don't have a brain and can't keep up a conversation, there's nothing there for me.

There's nothing wrong with being turned on by the visual, but there are, obviously, many other things that matter. If you are messing around with someone just because of his or her looks, start digging, because you might want to get a little deeper.

MYTH #5: SAFER SEX DOESN'T APPLY TO ME.

You may think, I'm fine, my partner is fine, but most people who are spreading sexually transmitted diseases don't know they have them. STDs can remain asymptomatic—without visible symptoms—for months and even years. STDs can affect anyone regardless of class, sexual orientation, skin color. And age. Just because you are young and lively, this does not mean you are a superhero who can't get hurt. See Chapter 8 for a full-on explanation of safer sex and what it entails.

Safer sex applies to anyone who is sexually active. And STD prevention is cheaper, easier and much more pleasant than sickness and treatment. See next myth.

•Each year, about one quarter of all sexually active teenagers become infected with an STD.
•These three million teenagers account for one quarter of all STD cases annually.
•One in four new HIV infections occurs in people under 22.
•Rates of infection with sexually transmitted diseases in the U.S. exceed those of every other developed country.

KIM, 20: I think that you can know every fact in the world, but when it comes down to being worried about a disease, you think, Well, it probably won't happen to me. You just figure you're going to be the lucky one.

MYTH #6: SAFER SEX IS A DRAG.

By the way, the it's-like-wearing-a-raincoat mythology has gotten so built up that you might expect a condom to make you feel like you're barely in the same room with your partner. While some people feel a muting of sensation with condoms, others don't feel much difference at all. You will probably be pleasantly surprised with the results. And if you get into the rubber-donning habit from the start, sex with condoms will simply feel normal. Condoms provide maximum relief from anxiety. Worries about pregnancy, HIV and other STDs go out the window, so you can concentrate on bringing pleasure to your partner and feeling pleasure yourself. And condoms often make sex last longer.

PRIY, 23: I think that it's the most fun to use condoms and other protection when you act like they're toys—and not when you use them furtively, like, let's pretend that neither of us knows this is going to happen. You know, that quiet lull when he's tearing up the wrapper, or she's getting out the plastic wrap. When it's been stated from the very outset that, yeah, this is gonna transpire, then you kind of talk about it, joke about it.

TODD, 22: I really believe that half of the act of sex is mental. When I am safe, there's more of a sense of relief, so you can relax and enjoy it more.

A parallel to ponder: In the '60s, seat belts became mandatory safety equipment in cars. At first, people found them awkward, annoying, invasive. Now it's hard to imagine driving without one. Condoms have a similar story. They are the new standard safety equipment. Or you can think of them as sex-play accessories. Just the act of reaching into the drawer for protection can become an enticing ritual that means, I am about to have fun.

MYTH # 7: I AM NOTHING WITHOUT A BOYFRIEND/ GIRLFRIEND.

KIM, 20: I've definitely felt that I had to have a boyfriend. It's like having a little sign saying, you know, I'm desirable because here's someone who wants me. But now I don't feel that pressure at all. I'm pretty happy by myself, and if I want to date somebody, I'll date them.

Valentine's Day, love seats and tickets sold in pairs can easily make you feel like half of something waiting to be whole. It really works the other way around: You need to feel whole before you can be a good half. Otherwise you'll look to someone else to solve all your problems and make you feel valuable. Then what happens if that person ditches? You may fall apart. And worse, what happens if that person starts telling you that you're lame or wrong or fat or dumb? You may believe it.

Your self-esteem is too precious to be entrusted to someone else. Develop it on your own—and hold on to it. Do you believe that you are a kind, responsible, honest person? That you have talents? That you are worthy of respect? Everyone has flaws—but can you see past yours to recognize that you deserve attention and consideration from others? If you are not so sure about your answers, you might want to hold off on dating and sex. If you don't value yourself, you are in danger of not taking good care of yourself emotionally or physically. Spend time with friends who are proud of you and who care about you. Spend time alone and revel in the joys of your own company. The real remedy to low self-esteem is not found in the arms of a lover.

MYTH #8: SEX AUTOMATICALLY GUARANTEES LOVE AND AFFECTION.

8

Not that sex and love don't go together. They make an ideal combo platter. But sometimes your soul, ego and heart crave love, and sex is the nearest thing—and it's often easier to find than love. Maybe you're just looking for hugs and cuddling and companionship. If that's what you want, then you don't need sex (and all the responsibility that goes with it) to make it happen. Figure out what you're looking for before you find something you don't want.

VIRGINIA, 20: I've definitely felt like sex was really love. I'm not saying that that's a good thing. I'm just saying that there are a lot of times when I've been in a relationship where the only thing left was the sex. You would rather believe that all the emotions and the loving and the caring are there just because the sex is still there.

KARLEY, 17: I've had sex with quite a few people. I thought that was the right thing to do—to be loved and to get attention and affection. If I could get attention for that moment, then I was loved, and then with the next person it would be even more love. And if that relationship lasted, it would be more and more love, and hopefully it would progress into something more. But it never did.

Some people believe the polar opposite of Myth #8, that sex is just a physical act and it won't affect them emotionally. If you believe myth #9, but your partner doesn't, hurt feelings will likely follow. And if you both believe myth #9, you're missing out. Sex can be the sweetest, most intimate thing that two people share, a way of expressing love beyond words, a priceless gift. People who care about each other usually share more than sex—they share secrets, rides home, jokes, dinners, fears, advice, favorite sweaters. Sex works very nicely in the context of a relationship, but relationships are more about feelings than body fluids. Lovemaking between folks who care deeply about each other feels more like a spiritual experience than a bing-bang-boom, get-your-rocks-off deal.

MYTH #9: SEX IS ONLY PHYSICAL.

SIMON, 17: If you have sex and you don't care about the person, then it's like nothing, just a hobby. If you put your emotions in there, and you really understand the other person, and both people feel the same way—that's very special.

Casting yourself (or your partner) in a fixed role is extremely limiting. Forget the studly hero in the action movies or the blushing ingenue on the cover of a bridal magazine. Guys don't have to feel like it's their job to make all the passes, and it's certainly not their job to push sex play as far as possible. Fellas, ask yourself, How do I feel about this partner? Do I really want more action, or am I just going through the motions as programmed? And here's a news flash: women are not doomed to wait passively for something to react to. Nor is it always the gal's job to play

MYTH #10: MEN HAVE TO BE AGGRESSIVE; WOMEN HAVE TO BE SHY.

naysayer and gatekeeper. Girls are entitled to pleasure as much as guys are. Ladies, you can lunge for that goodnight kiss instead of expecting it. Guys, you can be the one to say, "Enough for tonight." A guy can treat a girl with respect and not be called *pussy-whipped.* A girl can make the first move or have condoms in her purse and not be called *slut.*

KATIE, 23: I say somehow we women have got to break through the idea that we're a slut, a tease or a prude. And the only way we're gonna overcome these stereotypes is not just by telling people not to call us these things but by surmounting these ideas ourselves—by doing exactly what we want, being proud of the choices we've made, understanding the mistakes we've made and moving forward.

SIMON, 17: I would like it if girls were more aggressive. I'd appreciate it if the girl came up to me—at least half of the time—because I hate rejection. It should be both of our jobs to make the moves, but I'm usually doing everything. You wanna kiss me? You gotta pull me over and kiss me, 'cause I'm usually the one who's pulling her over.

RYAN S., 19: There's a big old macho image that guys have to uphold. I guess you could say: If you're not having sex, you're a wuss.

MYTH #11: SOMETIMES YOU FOOL AROUND AND STUFF "JUST HAPPENS."

GINA, 24: I remember the first time I had sex with my boyfriend. Afterward, we said, "It just happened," but we really did know what we were doing. I remember thinking, This is happening, we're doing this. But later I said, "It just happened," to make it okay with myself.

Be clear with yourself and your partner about what decisions you're making every step of the way. It's true that you often don't know what you want or how you feel until you get there, but you can think through future consequences of present actions. Pay attention to the voice asking, "Is this really what I want?" "Am I going to be bummed tomorrow?" "Is anyone in danger of getting hurt (physically or emotionally)?" "Do we have protection?" Think about the answers. And if that voice is drowned out by drink or drugs, you are making yourself very vulnerable.

Make no mistake, talking about sex is a good thing. It shows that you care for the other person. It fosters openness and trust, which can help you get comfortable sexually. It's also fun, and adds more of your senses to the mix. It's another way to connect mentally while you are connecting physically. It may feel awkward at first, but you can't get what you want unless you ask. You can't refuse what you don't want unless you pipe up. Few people are equipped with ESP. That's why we talk.

Slang

Speaking of communication, sex is one of the richest areas of slang in our language (or any language). People use slang and humor to ease their discomfort with the topic. The proper words for sex can be a bit clinical anyway. Would you rather hear "I'm ready to have sexual intercourse, could you purchase some prophylactics?" or "Honey, I think Friday night might be crazy-friction night. Pack your love gloves"? Anything that smoothes communication about sex is a good thing. So embrace slang. Make up your own. Just try not to use it to make others uncomfortable ("Hey, Mama, let's bump uglies right here and now") or to put people down ("He's such a prick").

BRADFORD, 21: Before this year, about 95 percent of the time I never talked about sex past, "Should I or shouldn't I wear a condom?" The reason I'm so attracted to my girlfriend is that we have an unwritten rule—talk about everything. Before we even got to the bedroom we talked about sexual history, condoms, fantasies, kids. With other girlfriends, if you mentioned condoms, faces got red. But with my current girlfriend, everything flowed naturally.

GINA, 24: I used to avoid talking about sex. It's putting yourself out there on the table, and I wasn't comfortable with that.

MYTH #12: TALKING ABOUT SEX KILLS THE MOMENT, KILLS THE MYSTERY.

Among your best resources and advocates might be the very people who laundered your socks and taught you manners. Parents can come through for you in a crisis, and they can be good allies in normal times, too. It's a historical fact that they were once your age. Although they didn't have to worry about AIDS or female condoms or explicit-lyrics warning labels on CDs, they still felt their hormones kick into high gear, they still thought about sex and they still had to negotiate their own moral dilemmas and health issues. Plus, parents probably care more about your safety and well-being than anyone else.

MYTH #13: PARENTS WILL NEVER UNDERSTAND.

If you are sexually active and tell your parents about it, here are the benefits you may reap:

•Advice about relationships. Sometimes Mom or Dad will have insight and understanding that your peers just can't deliver.

•Access to health care, including exams, birth control, STD prevention. Hopefully this includes financial help, because doctors can be expensive.

•More respect and privacy. If you live at home, you might not have to sneak around as much to be alone with your loved one. Your parents may trust you more if you're more open with them.

•Someone to turn to if you face an unplanned pregnancy, STD or other crisis. Parents might be shocked or upset initially, but they may also be able to look at the larger picture and see that you need help and support more than judgment.

KIM, 20: I was sixteen. I had a boyfriend and I told him about something I had done with another guy in the past and he freaked out (like he had never done anything before he met me). I was upset about it and I told my mom. Even though she was probably freaking inside to hear that I'd done something sexual, she pushed her shock aside and tried to help me through it. She explained things, let me cry and gave me advice. She was there for me, not just like a mom, but also like a friend.

If there's just no way you feel you can talk with your parents, don't write off all adults. Look around for someone older who is understanding and responsible—an aunt, uncle, sibling, teacher, clergyperson or counselor.

DAVID, 20: My mom told me about the birds and the bees when I was younger. We talk openly. She was seventeen when she had her first kid, so she knows what's going on. I had an STD when I was fifteen. I told her about it in the aisle of the grocery store. I asked her, "Why does it hurt when I pee?" and she was like "Oh, David," and she helped me. I was scared.

Smart Sex Poll

Only about half of young males surveyed discussed sex facts and issues with a parent, compared with three quarters of young women.

ANDREW, 25: I think about sex all the time. We all do. If my mind wanders, it's gonna wander first to sex.

RYAN P., 20: I'm twenty and I'm at my sexual peak. I think about sex as much as every other twenty-year-old does. The one thing that's very interesting in college is that the guys around me talk about girls all the time, "pussy, tits," that's all we hear about. But when I say something about a guy, people are like, "You're obsessed. You're so horny." It's like, "Hello, I'm just as horny as you are."

VIRGINIA, 20: Class is the worst. I get so bored, and next thing I know, I'm like, Oh, gosh, why am I thinking about this right now? It's the most inopportune moment to be thinking about sex.

MYTH #14: I'M A PERVERT BECAUSE I THINK ABOUT SEX A LOT.

You'll go through phases that are more sexual or less sexual your whole life. But it's totally natural to think about sex—people do it much more than they admit. Thoughts and fantasies are harmless as long as you keep them in your head (or if you only act on them when you are sure that no one will be physically or emotionally hurt). Sexual fantasies—and sexual frustration—can be great inspiration for songwriting, jogging, dancing, drawing, journal writing. Much of our civilization was built on rerouted sexual energy.

DEFINING MOMENT: SEX

For a word people use and think about all the time, *sex* can actually mean different things.

For most people (and in this book) sex is "the act of the penis penetrating the vagina." And it's safe to assume that most of the advice about vaginal sex applies to anal *sex* (need a condom, need to be emotionally ready), minus the pregnancy issues. To some, sex includes oral sex, because there is penetration involved—a penis entering a mouth, a tongue entering a vagina. Plus, oral sex definitely includes some of the STD risk that a totally abstinent person need not worry about. Manual (hand-to-genital) sex can feel very intimate and can bring a partner to orgasm.

So, the boundaries of the word *sex* can be fuzzy.

WHAT IS

The answer is bigger than just "using a condom." The answer is subjective, personal and, hopefully, well-pondered.

KIM, 20: Smart sex would be a situation where you feel comfortable with everything you're doing and with the person you're with. A situation where you're not being forced or feeling embarrassed about doing or not doing certain things. If you feel good enough about yourself, and you have the strength of character to say, "This is what I want and this is what I don't want," then I think it's very smart sex.

RYAN S., 19: Smart sex? Caring about the person you're with, because if you don't care about the person, it's pretty empty and there's no point to it. I would also have to say knowing when it's your time to do it, and when it's not your time. If you don't feel it's right, you shouldn't jump into anything.

SO

LENA, 21: Smart sex is safe sex that you can still enjoy.

KATIE, 23: It's sex that's consensual, sex that's equal in terms of power. It's protected sex. It's sex with someone you can trust and know well. It's honest, it's sober. It's discussed.

CRYSTAL, 18: Smart sex is within a marriage—preferably where both are virgins when they get married. Then there's nothing to worry about as far as emotional commitment, as well as STDs.

PRIY, 23: Smart sex involves using your brain. It's beyond just the sensual.

ALLISON, 22: Smart sex? No sex. Well, it has been no sex for me.

SMART SEX?

VIRGINIA, 20: This sounds pessimistic, but I don't know if people my age know there's a thing called smart sex. I definitely believe that caring and knowing one another is extremely important, also being safe. It's really sad that I know that I should be safe, and all my friends know that they should be safe and we're just not.

If only sex were simple.

But interesting things never are.

VIRGINITY | 2

Everyone starts out with their virginity. Some are in a rush to lose it. Some are content to wait for sex. Many fall somewhere in the middle. Almost every virgin feels both curious and anxious about facing sex. Virginity can be frustrating. Virginity can breed self-confidence. One thing is certain: Virginity deserves respect. You only get to lose it once so consider how and when you want that to happen.

DEFINING MOMENT: VIRGIN

Virgin means someone who has never experienced sexual intercourse. Most people still consider themselves virgins even if they've had oral sex or experienced sex play other than the penis-in-vagina variety. Technically speaking, they can still call themselves virgins, but they can also get a sexually transmitted disease and can certainly get emotionally hurt from nonintercourse intimacy. (Chapters 8, 9 and 10 will explain more about STDs.) In the gay world, a virgin can refer to a gay person who hasn't had a sexual experience with someone of the same gender.

CRYSTAL, 18: I'm a member of True Love Waits. I made a commitment to stay sexually pure until I get married. We had a banquet and I repeated the vow that I had made to my parents, to my friends, to my future spouse and future children, to stay sexually pure. A lot of people get into a relationship, get physically involved, and then try to make their decision about wanting to have sex. If you truly make a decision about whether or not to have sex, you need to make it outside of a relationship, so you can be more objective.

ALLISON, 22: For me it has nothing to do with religion. It has nothing to do with ethics or even morality. I have two reasons why I haven't had sex yet. Number one: The first time you have sex it's gonna suck, right? Given all the physical discomfort that I'm going to experience, I want it to be with someone I really feel something for. If I'm in love, then the emotional part of it will make up for the physical part. Number two: I think that sex requires self-esteem and pride. I'm not sure if I'm at that point yet.

TREVOR, 20: I am a virgin. I find it really hard not to immediately offer explanations like "I could've, but . . . ," "I came real close one night when . . . ." Like I somehow need to justify it. Which in a way I'm still doing by even mentioning that I think about justifying it. To be even more truthful, I never let people know. I don't lie, but people usually assume that I have lost my virginity, so I just let them. It's far less hassle, because inevitably there'd be some roundtable discussion, and there's really nothing to it. I'm not antisex. I don't have religious hang-ups. I just haven't done it. Blah, blah, blah. So far I've just never been in a relationship that I thought could go past that point. Each time, I've decided that either it would destroy the relationship or really hurt somebody if things fell apart. Basically, I don't feel like doing it just to do it.

RYAN P., 20: I think virginity can't be defined just by penetration, especially in the gay community—it's a myth that all gay men have anal sex. So it's really once you get to an obviously intimate level, where it's not just kissing and hugging, but you're naked and you're close. Oral sex, I'd say, could be losing your virginity.

10 REASONS TO DELAY THE DEED

There are a number of good ones. You are wise to wait if . . .

You know that abstinence is the only guaranteed way to protect yourself against AIDS, STDs and pregnancy and for you, that's reason enough.

Very true. But make a commitment that if and when you do have sex, you'll use latex. Or better yet, latex plus backup birth control. (For more, see Chapters 7 and 8.)

You are not in love.

Wouldn't you prefer some romance, which you are more likely to get from someone you truly love? Better to be alone than to settle for someone unworthy of you.

You think premarital sex is morally wrong.

If so, then just say no. Explain to any potential partner that you believe that this is not just a physical and emotional choice but a matter of principle, and that you take it very seriously.

You're scared.

4 That's enough of a reason.

You don't feel ready for the responsibility.

5 Sex is like a credit card: Having it doesn't automatically make you an adult; what makes you an adult is using it wisely.

Someone's pressuring you to give it up, even though you're hesitant.

6 It's your decision, your body, your right. Anyway, how enjoyable will it be if you're going in with more trepidation than enthusiasm?

You don't feel comfortable having serious conversations about sex with the prospective Mr./Ms. First.

7 If you can't talk about the act with this person, how can you communicate your needs and desires? Better to wait for someone you're more in sync with.

You're not sure if you prefer girls or boys.

8 No rush to decide. You have some thinking to do. (See Chapter 6.)

You are not of legal age.

9 The age of consent is eighteen across most of the U.S., but a few states go as young as fourteen or as old as twenty-one. Sometimes the key issue is age difference—like if one party is a teen and the other is three (or more) years older, then sex is not legally okay. (Your local Planned Parenthood or rape crisis center will know the laws for your area.) These laws exist for your protection. Your judgment and sense of self gets stronger as you get older. Sex requires a great deal of responsibility, so let yourself grow up before you take it on.

You don't know why, you just don't want to have sex.

10 Go with that feeling.

CRYSTAL, 18: Giving up your virginity is a conscious decision you make. You don't lose it, you give it away. My boyfriend was telling me he was in eighth or ninth grade when he first did it. He said, "I didn't give it away. I threw it away."

ALLISON, 22: When you let someone enter your body, then you let them invade that sort of very private space you have on the planet. Hey, I've had rejection before and I've been dumped before. But at least I have that feeling of, "Well, he never got inside of me." And that way I can handle it that much easier.

REGRETS

If you feel the least bit uneasy, why not wait? Few people regret the delay, and quite a few people regret the rush.

CATHERINE, 19: I was fifteen. I was totally not ready. It was my first serious boyfriend. One night we were out, and he was like, "I have to stop by my friend's house," which was to get a condom. Then it just kind of happened. Afterward I was crying, he was crying. We talked about it a little. We decided we needed to save sex for later or it would get out of hand. I wish I could have had an experience that was ten times better. The mistakes I've made, they've cost me a lot emotionally. The problem with being younger is that the mistakes are more liable to stay with you the rest of your life.

TODD, 22: I was eighteen years old when I lost it. I was at a party, drinking. The girl I was dating kind of dragged me off. At the time I was kinda drunk. I didn't give it much thought. We didn't use protection. I remember asking around, but I didn't have anything. I didn't last very well at all, to be honest. Afterward, I guess it was kind of a feeling of guilt and I-can't-believe-I-did-that. That's not how I saw it happening. At the time I thought I was ready for it, but I wasn't completely ready for the after-effects. I went and talked to the girl later. We went our separate ways.

ONLY

GINA, 24: I wish I had waited longer. I should have been worrying about passing biology, not about birth control. To me, I was being adult about it. I thought that so long as I didn't get pregnant, nothing else mattered. But I wasn't ready for the emotional side. That's a very important component. It was very easy to let go of it. No one ever taught me that this is a special gift, this is valuable. I never saw it that way, as something I should hold on to.

BEING A VIRGIN ISN'T EASY

To be realistic, there are potential difficulties with remaining a virgin. You might take some flack for being a prude, a lightweight, immature (of course, who in this scenario is really immature?). There is the risk of losing a boyfriend or girlfriend who won't wait around. You could feel bad about yourself. In a culture obsessed with sex, it's easy to feel like you're missing out.

RYAN S., 19: It's a drag not knowing what sex is. It's a drag hearing people say, "You can't want sex that bad, because you don't know what you're missing—you've never had it." But that's the main point: I have never had it. I guess people say that eighteen, nineteen is the sexual prime of a man's life, and I'm, like, in my sexual prime right now, and I'm not having sex. So that's kind of why it's a big deal, besides the fact that now a lot of my friends are more open about talking about their sex lives, and I have no sex life to talk about.

ALLISON, 22: I'm kinda the virgin queen here on campus, and it really hurts my social life. People know that I'm not gonna hook up on a first date, and they know that I'm not even gonna hook up on a fifth date, and so I get the whole, "Why should I bother?" The funny thing is, you think, Well, I don't want these guys anyway. But I feel pressure from myself sometimes, because I feel odd.

RVES RESPECT

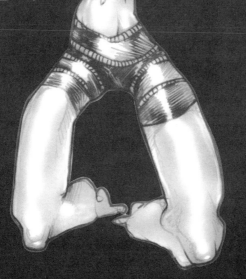

IMPORTANT THING TO REMEMBER

You can have a sex life without technically having intercourse. Sometimes people call this everything-but sexual activity "outercourse." There are certainly emotional risks that come with these other forms of sex play. And you should check out the chart on page 142 to find out about any risk of sexually transmitted disease. But if you are skipping full-on sex, you are definitely lowering the danger of disease and pregnancy —which should help you relax and enjoy the experience. That in mind, there are plenty of things to do on a rainy day (or sunny day, or wintry night) that do not include vaginal penetration.

LENA, 21: I can get a lot more excited about foreplay than actual sex. It gives you a better chance to learn about another person, all the little spots to concentrate on. I believe it's more intimate. With this one guy, we spent at least forty-five minutes on foreplay alone—with our clothes on. He was touching me all over. Arms, legs, ears. He didn't want to miss a part. He kissed every finger and every toe to show that they're there. It was the greatest thing. It was overwhelming.

SIMON, 17: Kissing could be considered sex—as long as the emotions are there.

More suggestions: You can massage each other. You can nibble, lick, breathe on and caress each other's earlobes, fingers, toes and other spots. As long as you agree ahead of time on how far to go and what STD precautions you want to take, you have endless options.

SECONDARY VIRGINITY

There are a growing number of people out there—men and women—who have had sex but choose to return to celibacy. In some ways it's difficult, because they know how good sex can feel. In some ways it's easier, because they know about all the anxiety that can go with sex, and they'd rather do without for a while.

LOLA, 21: You can kiss for five hours straight. You can watch porn together or read sex scenes aloud to each other. You can share smutty fantasies in graphic detail. You can masturbate, or masturbate the other person. You can cover your lover in whipped cream and lick it off. Um . . . I like to strip for my boyfriend.

ALLISON, 22: My old boyfriend and I had a very healthy sex life, even though we didn't have sex. It was basically based on oral sex. I am a huge proponent of oral sex. For me, it's very intimate, but the fact that there's no [vaginal] penetration—that's the issue. You're not allowing someone into you.

CRYSTAL, 18: The guy I'm dating has been abstinent for more than four years, even though he had sex before that. I respect him, because it's hard to go back once you've been there.

FOOD
FOR
THOUGHT

ALLISON, 22: Sex is not something that I don't want to ever happen. But when it does happen, I'll be totally okay with it. I'll always be able to look myself in the mirror.

CRYSTAL, 18: I'm not gonna lie. It is hard, especially when you love someone so much that you just want to express it with physical contact. But if you truly love each other and set limits, the best way to prove that love is to respect those limits.

INTERVIEW

INTERVIEW WITH DAVE NAVARRO
Guitarist, Red Hot Chili Peppers

SMART SEX: WHEN YOU TALK TO YOUR PARENTS ABOUT SEX?

Dave: I know in my heart of hearts that I could've gone to them and talked to them about anything. However, I didn't. I think a lot of that had to do with a self-centered

fear

of "What are they going to think about me if I approach them with this?" But at the same time, I knew I could. For example, when I was about thirteen or fourteen, my mother and I had a discussion about drugs in which she was very informative and open.

SMART SEX: HOW DID TV SHAPE YOUR VIEW OF SEX?

Dave: Well, we had cable [laughs] when I was younger. You know, I never, ever thought about it until now, but I learned from television that there were two types of sex. I learned that sex was either a very passionate, loving activity or a really raunchy recreational activity. And somehow I recall thinking that the later it gets at night, the more **raunchy** it is—basically because that's when the raunchy films came on.

SMART SEX: WHAT DO YOU THINK NOW?

Dave: I think that it can be raunchy at any time of the day. And it can be romantic and loving and emotional at any time of the day. It depends on the frame of mind that you're in and who you're with and what it is you want out of the experience.

SMART SEX: WHEN DID YOU LOSE YOUR VIRGINITY?

Dave: I basically lost my virginity at the age of twelve or thirteen. It was very scary, because I was afraid of not being very good at it, I was afraid of letting her down, I was afraid of letting myself down and I was afraid of what it may feel like. I was afraid about what that meant about our relationship. I didn't understand the ramifications. I was fortunate enough that I already loved that girl, and she was certainly ready and comfortable with the act and I was definitely intrigued and interested enough that we went through with it.

I had a positive experience.

But then again, I ejaculated immediately, and that was not so positive for me. I felt kind of bad about it.

Dave: When I am in *love* with somebody and engaging in sexual interplay—because it's not necessarily all about intercourse—it becomes an emotional exchange. It's a very warm and loving process that is sacred, between you and your partner. And for that time, it creates a sacred bond that's impenetrable by the outside world. It's a way to give and receive love at the same time. The other thing is that it can be an incredible tension reliever, which is a gift. You can relieve the tension of your day-to-day life or the tension between each other. And it helps you realize that yes, there is something higher and more important than the fact that she left the cap off the toothpaste.

Dave: For me, kissing, cuddling, caressing, massaging and even verbal expressions of love are all part of the sexual experience. To me, the sexual experience, basically, is everything that there is in the book and more—stuff that only you and your partner invent, in a romantic, loving sense.

Dave: I think that what could possibly be bad is being misinformed about the dangers of sexually transmitted diseases and being misinformed about birth control or protection. Also, in terms of one-night stands, we don't take into consideration the emotional frame of mind of the other person. People can be emotionally hurt, and that's why, for me, I'm not comfortable with random one-night stands. I don't want to mislead anybody, I don't want anybody to get hurt and I certainly don't want to get hurt. I think that it's very difficult and awkward to put your cards on the table and say, "I'm really just interested in doing you, and I don't want to talk to you after this," which is a painful thing to hear anyway.

Dave: I think that's a wide misconception. I can tell you that I've been touring in rock bands for maybe ten years now, and yes, there have been instances that finding a partner for an evening has been *easier* than if I was still living at home. But if someone is offering themselves to me openly and plainly, I'm not attracted to that. I tend to focus on the person rather than the body or the act. Someone with self-esteem of that caliber is not someone I'm interested in creating that kind of a sacred bond with. That's not to say I haven't done that—obviously I have done that, and that's how I'm able to know the difference. I think there is also something to be said for having done this for a long time and growing through that adolescent stage of trying to make as many conquests as possible.

SMART SEX: HAVE YOU EVER BEEN PRESSURED TO HAVE SEX WHEN YOU DIDN'T WANT TO?

Dave: Well, I've ended up regretting it, I've ended up resenting my partner and myself and I've ended up walking away feeling much worse about the relationship and the experience than if I had said, "You know what, I'm just not interested in this right now."

SMART SEX: WHAT ADVICE WOULD YOU GIVE ABOUT EXPERIMENTING WITH DRUGS AND ALCOHOL AND SEXUALITY AT THE SAME TIME?

Dave: [long pause] That's a tough one for me, because my whole experience with drugs and

alcohol have been of a very addictive nature. I'm now four years sober. Tips on how to use drugs and alcohol safely... I really don't know how to do that.

SMART SEX: HOW DID DRUGS AND ALCOHOL, WHEN YOU WERE USING THEM, AFFECT YOUR SEX LIFE?

Dave: Well, that I can answer. When I would get drunk, I think that I would be less *inhibited* and I would be much more willing to seek sexual relations with strangers, much more comfortable with myself, more confident. Now, being somewhat of a grownup, I know that I was basically giving myself a false sense of security. When it came right down to it, I know that drugs and alcohol detensified—is that a word?—detensified my sexual experiences. I either didn't remember them or I couldn't get an erection or I couldn't sustain an erection. There was a general sloppiness. Now that I'm sober and free of all mind-altering substances, my sexual experiences are better than they have ever been in my entire life. They're more intense, they are much longer lasting, the memories are more clear and sharp. I am able to involve my emotional side in the experience, which is something I wasn't able to do when I was chemically altered. And I am in a much better place physically and mentally to give and receive pleasure.

SMART SEX: DID YOU EVER STRUGGLE WITH YOUR SELF-ESTEEM?

Dave: Oh, I struggle with self-esteem daily, to this day. It took me a long time before I learned that whether or not I sleep with the girl of my choice, I'm still **okay.** And my self-worth doesn't come from my sexual conquests; my self-worth has to come from within. And I can also say that the more self-worth I gained through the years, the better my sexual relations became. I think it's important to understand that sexual conquests do not a man make.

SMART SEX: HAVE YOU EVER BEEN TESTED FOR HIV?

Dave: To this day I get tested every six months.

SMART SEX: HOW DO YOU BRING UP DISEASE PROTECTION?

Dave: When I am with a new mate and things are getting heavy, I put on a condom. Actually, with my present girlfriend, we discussed it long before I put a condom on, long before we had intercourse. She was very concerned; she knew my history as a touring rock musician and a former intravenous drug user, and she was very concerned And for good reason. And so I assured her I was HIV-negative and went so far as to go get tested the very next day to show her that she had nothing to worry about. I think that **condoms** and regular HIV testing are your best bet.

SMART SEX: WHAT KIND OF REACTION DID YOU GET FROM THE PICTURE OF YOU KISSING FLEA ON THAT MAGAZINE COVER? AND KISSING ANTHONY IN THE "WARPED" VIDEO?

Dave: Mixed. It was kind of odd, because a lot of the people in the homosexual community had a problem with it because they thought that we were making fun of their lifestyle. And then a lot of people in the heterosexual community had a problem with it because they thought that we were gay. Really bizarre. And the truth of the matter is, I think, that apart from being simply a shock-value visual, it was more an expression of **love** for one another. Which is actually something I did with Perry Farrell in the Jane's Addiction video. It was an expression of openness. It was an expression of being in touch with one's feminine side. However, it was neither a gay nor antigay statement. It actually wasn't a statement at all. I still think it's cool. And I stand by it.

MASTURBATION ⓜ 3

Sometimes the greatest love of all can be the art
of self-love. If you're still a virgin, masturbation
provides a way to make your sexuality and virginity
work together in one body. Many people (mostly
women) don't begin masturbating until after
they start having partner sex. But the benefits
of dimming the lights and exploring one's own
body may be worth checking out sooner.

DEFINING MOMENT: MASTURBATION
Masturbation is self-stimulation of the
genitals for sexual pleasure. That is,
using hands, sheets, pillow, sex toys
or whatever's handy to excite yourself
in a private moment. It doesn't have
to go all the way to orgasm to count.

KIM, 20: I've known some girls who are very open about masturbation, but I've also known some girls who are like, "Eww, gross, never." I think it just depends on how comfortable a person is with their sexuality. I think that society teaches women to be afraid to explore their own sexuality, to touch themselves. If masturbation can help a woman feel more comfortable with herself or with a man, then I'm all for it.

PRIY, 23: Masturbation is key. Only if a woman masturbates does she know what kind of orgasms she can have. Only with herself is she going to feel comfortable enough to experiment.

SIMON, 17: People have a hard time talking about masturbation, because when you're with a group of your friends, they'll be like, "Oh, I got laid last night, I got her quick, I got her easy." And if you're masturbating, it seems like you can't get any girls. If you get laid, you're kind of higher than the people who don't get girls and have to masturbate. But even the person with the most girls can masturbate.

RYAN S., 19: Around eighth grade I was reassured to find out that there were other people masturbating. It wasn't just me, and there wasn't anything wrong with it. If you're making out with a girl and you can't have sex—which happens to me a lot—then it's just a way to release all the pressure and make yourself feel better.

BRADFORD, 21: I think there's sexual tension that builds up and you have to relieve it. There was a Roseanne episode where D.J. started to masturbate, and they were like, "We never see him anymore." Everybody does it. I have a friend who's like, "I'm gonna go home and jerk off and go to bed," and we laugh because it's so honest.

ANDREW, 25: Masturbation is preferable to gratuitous sex.

THE SAFEST SEX AROUND

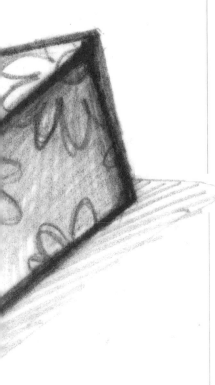

Masturbation could be dubbed "the safest sex," because it doesn't carry any of the risks of partner sex. When unplanned pregnancy, AIDS, herpes and other diseases are an enormous problem, masturbation offers an anxiety-free alternative to intercourse. And you don't have to take any of the emotional risks that come with an outside relationship. (Note also the savings on cologne, flowers, candlelit dinners, concert tickets, birth control and other expenses that often go with partner sex.) Masturbation makes you more comfortable with your naked body, which in turn can make it easier and less stressful to insert a diaphragm or roll on a condom. Masturbation helps you learn exactly what kind of touch turns you on; it teaches you the rhythms and sensitivities of your own body, perhaps even how to have an orgasm more reliably—useful knowledge that you'll be able to pass on to your future or present partner. It serves as a pleasing release of sexual tension so you don't get cranky. It can help you shed your inhibitions and enjoy sex more. Also, it can replace having sex with the wrong person.

FANTASY— THE THEATER INSIDE YOUR BRAIN

Masturbation goes hand-in-hand (so to speak) with fantasy. How else can you be the queen of France, Brad Pitt's lover, a firefighter—or any combination of those all at once? Replay scenes from movies, videos, books that turned you on, and rewrite them. It's amazing how your imagination can turn on your body's physical reaction before you even move a muscle.

RYAN P., 20: I think about movie stars. Also on *My So-Called Life*, Jordan Catalano. And the model Ethan Browne is hot.

ESTHER, 17: I have a cowgirl fantasy. Out west in the 1800s. Marauding Indians are involved, and a young woman. I'm riding bareback. There's no violence. I rescue her and take her away to my cabin, where I have my way with her, and she shows me how grateful she is.

RYAN S., 19: I think about people I'd like to have sex with, I guess. Sometimes I just imagine a stranger out of the blue. I've always thought sex in outer space would be cool, no gravity, just kind of floating around.

PRIY, 23: I recently fantasized about Bruce Willis.

THE GUILT FACTOR

Many religions and cultures discourage or forbid masturbation. Some believe that sexual activity is meant only for making babies, and that sexual stimulation for any other reason is wasteful and/or wrong. There is also a belief that masturbation means giving in to our most animal instincts, and that we should be more civilized and self-disciplined. If you were raised with this kind of thinking, you first need to decide if avoiding masturbation is healthy or realistic for you. If you were raised with this kind of thinking and you still masturbate, you might feel guilty and dirty. You are not alone.

Over the last few centuries, people have been given all kinds of warnings and told all kinds of myths to keep idle hands from wandering below the belt. If masturbation makes you feel guilty, you might want to let yourself off the hook or at least discuss the matter with a clergyperson or counselor to clarify your stance. From a medical standpoint, masturbation is harmless unless maybe you start to miss school or work or skip meals in order to partake.

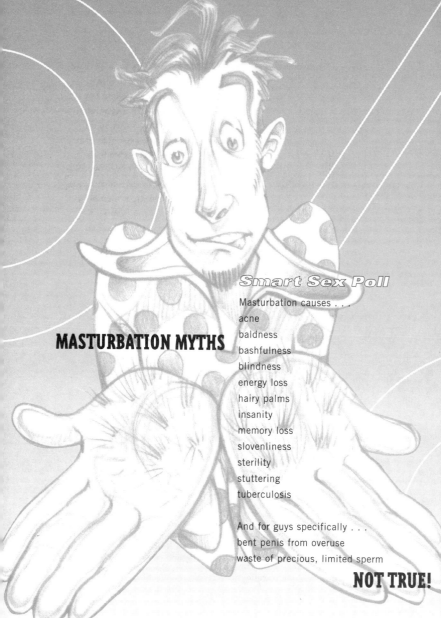

MASTURBATION MYTHS

Smart Sex Poll

Masturbation causes . . .
acne
baldness
bashfulness
blindness
energy loss
hairy palms
insanity
memory loss
slovenliness
sterility
stuttering
tuberculosis

And for guys specifically . . .
bent penis from overuse
waste of precious, limited sperm

NOT TRUE!

THESAURUS MOMENT: MASTURBATE

(BOYS:) Spank the monkey, whack off, wax the dolphin, beat the meat, polish the pole, choke the chicken, boot up the hard drive, slam the ham, stretch the turtleneck, feed the Kleenex, seed the rug, play the single-string air guitar, beat off, jerk off, have a date with Rosie Palm and her five beautiful daughters, shake hands with the president, make soup for one, give the tadpoles a swimming lesson, congratulate the bald-headed champion, paint a small Jackson Pollock, relieve the pitcher. (GIRLS:) Polish the pearl, pet the kitty, dig in, flick the switch, strum the big open C, buff the bead, hone the stone, make kitty purr, do the sweet slide, have ladyfingers and cream, juice it up, brush your Afro, Jill off. (Both:) Wank, go solo, take a trip down south, self-pleasure, jack off, kill time, fire the surgeon general, play solitaire, diddle, honeymoon in your hand.

A crucial step in making sex and sex play good is confirming that both parties want it. Sounds obvious, right? You'd be surprised. There is much room for confusion and poor judgment. Crossing the line from foreplay and experimentation to intercourse is a very big deal. Both people need to be sure they know where they're going. And there's no tidy map. Here are some tales of bumpy rides.

4 | CONSENT

Smart Sex Poll

Top three reasons given for why people might have sex when they feel reluctant to do so:
1. They think they will be liked or loved more if they have sex (44 percent).
2. They just don't know how to say no (29 percent).
3. They don't want to hurt the person's feelings (15 percent).

RYAN S., 19: I've had some bad experiences. My girlfriend now plays a lot of head games. I never really know what she wants, when she wants it. It's like, she'll say she wants to do something, then we'll start to get into it, then she'll say, "No, I was just joking." It really messes with my head, because I don't know what she wants. She's never really made it clear, so I still don't know.

According to one study, 74 percent of women who had had intercourse before age 14 and 60 percent of women who had had sex before age 15 report that that sex was involuntary.

KIM, 20: When I was younger and fooling around with a guy, I'd think, Well, I'm this far, I have to keep going. You know, I got them this hot, I can't really stop now. And what's the big deal? It's just sex. I didn't used to attach much importance to sex or think it was a very big deal. There were times when I was just not in the mood, but because I got in the situation, I'd just go along, even though I didn't even want to at all.

Just because somebody's kissing you back and letting you grope doesn't mean that you have a big green light to go further. Silence does not automatically mean yes. Do yourself and your partner a favor and check in with each other and make sure that everyone is comfortable. There are many ways to be sensitive to your partner's limits without totally wrecking the mood. Paying attention to body language helps. Tense shoulders, total passivity, arms and legs that "happen to be in the way" of where you were headed, hands stopping your hands, might all be signs that you need to slow down or back off. Murmuring, "Does this feel good?" is perfectly clear, as well as hot. And don't forget, ladies, that you, too, can be guilty of pressuring guys and ignoring signals, so give them the same kind of room to back out that you would want.

THE RULES, THE BOUNDARIES

ANDREW, 25: I had a friend who every time we went to the next step said, "May I?" I thought that was really considerate. Sometimes you get the body language that says, "This shouldn't happen." Or sometimes a hand put on my hand is a gentle way of saying, "That's fine where it is."

CRYSTAL, 18: My boyfriend and I were fooling around, and I was caught up in the moment. Those feelings are real and those feelings are strong. I was thinking about having sex. I rationalized it was okay because I was choosing it. It would have been easy for him to take advantage of me or for me to let him. But he's the one who stopped. It wasn't what he wanted. It's hard, but that's how he showed his love for me.

ALLISON, 22: I say, "I'm really uncomfortable with this; you're making me feel uncomfortable." Usually that scares them, because they start thinking about that whole rape subject and think, Whoa, I'm no rapist.

CHAD, 20: It's body language—if they're responsive, you can tell that they're enjoying it. If a girl tells me she wants to stop, I don't get upset. I'd much rather have a girl say something than end up regretting it or doing something she doesn't want to do.

It's one thing to say "Slow down" or "Here are my limits." It's another to say no. It's not always easy, but it is always your right.

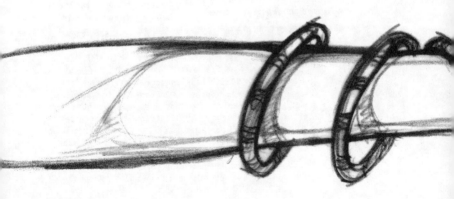

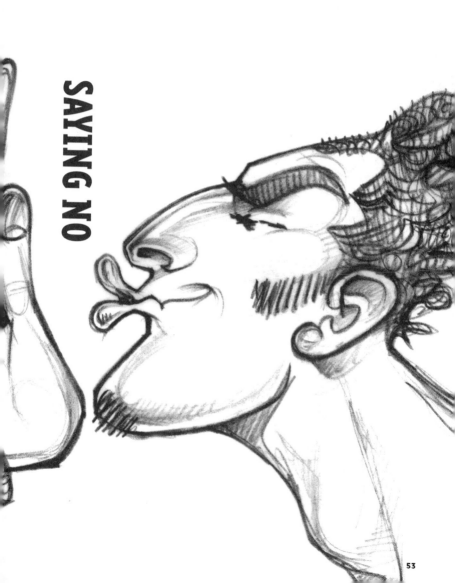

Bonus Fact
High school guys (84 percent) are less likely to report feeling comfortable refusing sex than high school girls (91 percent).

PRIY, 23: I feel like anyone who's in the position of having to say no becomes the heavy. And in reality, the guy may even want me to say no, but I sort of feel like most of the guys I have known feel like it's their obligation to take it one step further—even if they really wouldn't want to.

KIM, 20: I always used to feel guilty when I said no. I thought the guy would think I was a tease, or that I didn't want him. But it's not that I didn't want him, but that I didn't want sex. And I have every right to choose that.

RYAN P., 20: I have no problem with saying no. That's also a test I use in my relationships. I look at their facial expressions and their mannerisms right after I say no, and if it's like shock or dismay, I say, "We've got to talk."

When a partner says no or when one person is really drunk or high beyond good judgment and the other ignores these red flags and pursues intercourse anyway, then they are getting into date-rape territory. (See Chapter 12 for more on this issue.)

VIRGINIA, 20: I've never been one who's like, "I was drunk; I didn't know what I was doing." Even when I've been in situations when I'm hooking up with somebody, I'm like, "Wait, what am I doing?" I don't care how drunk you are; there's a flash of just complete soberness that lasts about three seconds. And it's that window of time where you can decide what it is that's going on. I've never been one to say that you can use being drunk as an excuse.

SEX AND MIND-ALTERING FORCES

CHARLIE, 17: I cheated on my girlfriend a couple of times when I was trashed. I was at a party—everybody knows how it is to be drunk. You just don't know what you're doing. I mean, you do know what you're doing, it's just like you don't have a conscience. It's kind of an excuse.

BRADFORD, 21: When I was on the prowl, drinking was the way to get rid of those problems of "What will she think if I say this?" Drinking relaxes me, and I thought it made me more attractive to girls. It seems like I always went to drink so I could go and find sex. At times I got past the level of being confident and was just out of control and irresponsible. I ended up going home with people I wouldn't have otherwise. My record of safe sex dropped.

GINA, 24: I had no judgment when I was drinking. Once, I saw a guy at a party and he reminded me of a guy who had just broken my heart. I told my friend, "I'm gonna have him by the end of the night." And I did. I got home at eight the next morning. I felt awful. "I can't believe I did that." That was the first of a couple of more times. It was low self-esteem. I drank so I'd be confident at parties and clubs. If that was the way I got attention, then that was fine. I don't think sex was the main point. It was about getting someone to hold you, even for a little while. Then there's the day after, and you're down—twenty feet lower.

Drugs and alcohol take away inhibitions, but fooling around wasted is like driving wasted—it puts you in danger. You might think that sex would be a blast if you could just put all your inhibitions aside, but that voice in our head that says "stop" also protects you. You need it.

The link between use of substances and risky sexual behavior is clear.

- One study found that among sexually active adolescents who drink and/or use drugs, 16 percent used condoms less often after drinking and 25 percent less often after drug use.
- A study of unplanned pregnancies and adolescents showed that almost 50 percent of the teenagers had been using alcohol or drugs before the act of intercourse that resulted in conception.
- In a study of sexually active young males admitted to a substance-abuse program, 53 percent were found to have one or more sexually transmitted diseases.

Acting like a jerk and having a hangover are experiences from which you will recover. But if substance-induced bad judgment gets you an STD or unwanted sex or a pregnancy, you'll have to live with the consequences longer—sometimes even forever. Besides, how much pleasure can you really give or receive when your senses are numbed? Abuse of alcohol and drugs may inhibit your ability to have sex (for guys, getting it up can become a difficult chore) and can mess up your immune system, making it easier to get infections of all kinds.

More important, regular use of drugs and alcohol can get in the way of your life outside the bedroom. If you find that you turn to drugs and alcohol to help deal with a problem, if drugs and alcohol affect your personal or professional relationships, if you need to consume increasing amounts to achieve the same high, if you hide the amount of drugs or alcohol you take, then you might have a serious abuse problem. You need to talk to someone you trust and maybe get outside help to stop. Whether you're a regular user or not, if you're at a party and there are substances available, it's a good idea to have a friend look out for you, and vice versa. It's too big a job to shoulder alone. (See Resources, page 310, for some places that offer support.)

And So . . .

Consent is one of the hardest things to learn to negotiate. It's not as clear-cut as putting on a condom, but it's just as important. Listen to your instincts and summon up the gumption to speak up, to ask questions when the picture is not clear and to get out when you are no longer comfortable.

iNTERVIEW →

**INTERVIEW WITH
JANEANE GAROFALO**
Actress, comic

SMART SEX: WHEN DID YOU START HAVING SEX?

Janeane: Well, I'll tell ya, I am late to the game, sexually speaking. Total late bloomer. Didn't even understand the politics of flirting until very late in life.

Didn't even lose my virginity till I was twenty-one. And that was with someone I was in love with.

I never felt bad about being a virgin late in life. There's a lot of pain that goes along with sexuality and with getting that close and being that vulnerable. So the more emotionally mature you are, I would say the better off you are. There is no crime in waiting until you think that you're ready. I think twenty-one was about right for me.

SMART SEX: WHAT WAS THE FIRST TIME LIKE?

Janeane: The first time for me was extremely physically painful. I remember thinking, "Oh, no! Is it always gonna be like this? This isn't so great. What's the big deal? I'd rather just make out. I don't wanna do this again." So I waited a long time after the first time to do it again.

SMART SEX: WHAT DO YOU ASK YOURSELF BEFORE YOU HAVE SEX WITH A NEW PARTNER? HOW DO YOU GET TO KNOW SOMEONE?

Janeane: I ask myself, "Okay, how do I really feel about this person? How do I really feel if something goes awry, if I get pregnant? How do I really feel about what I'm gonna think about this person three months from now?" Those kinda questions. I look at their reactions in certain situations. Day-to-day. What do I feel like when I hang out with someone during the day? How do they react to this movie, to this comic, to this song? You can tell a lot about a person by their musical taste and their comedy taste. I don't condemn anyone, but chances are I am not gonna be sexually attracted to a guy whose CD collection has a lot of Michael Jackson and Mariah Carey.

Janeane: Very uncomfortable with my body. Never have gotten over it. I don't think I ever will. I am not comfortable having sex in broad daylight. A lot of insecurity there. Like many women, being bombarded with impossible images from cradle to grave in every magazine, every TV show, every commercial, how can you not think, "Oh, my God, this guy's gonna see the stretch marks. He's gonna see the cellulite." He's gonna see the hairs. This is what I think: Deep down, he's repulsed by me. You know, I'm in an industry that covets **perfection,** and I fall so short of that that I can't help but take it into the bedroom with me.

Janeane: Well, it's gotta start with self-esteem at a young age. That's gotta come from the home. And I think the media has to take some responsibility, which they won't do. Unfortunately. *Seventeen* magazine has to take some responsibility. *Young Miss, Sassy.* Aaron Spelling's gotta get the **f**k** outta town, you know what I mean? He's as responsible as anyone for damaging young girls.

Janeane: Well, at the bottom of it, sex is **power.** Women have such a hard time getting respect in a lot of arenas that sometimes you mistake the hold you have over someone's d**k for power. And since it's the only thing that feels close to power, you utilize it. Or if somebody is attracted to you, leading them around a little bit on a Saturday night is intoxicating in and of itself. But you lose more in the long run. Unfortunately, the small gains that are made on a nightly basis are not really power.

Janeane: Well, a lot of times for me it's that the person is not going to stay all night. And I make that clear up front. And even if I have to put it delicately, I do say, "I gotta get up really early. I hope you don't think I'm rude, but I'm probably gonna have to kick you out of here at two." So that is kinda helpful for me. That you've set the boundaries of time, if nothing else. And then you might even say, "You know what? We're just gonna stay on the couch. I don't want you in my room, my room's a mess. We're not gonna go in the bedroom." Or something like, "No matter what else comes off, my pants stay on."

SMART SEX: Have you ever felt pressured into sex or into going further than you wanted? Janeane: Well, not necessarily pressured, but after I lost my **virginity** there were some nights where I certainly had let my guard down a little. There were nights where it was like,

"I don't feel like doing this, but it's actually almost easier to just do this than go through my rap, you know, of why I don't feel like it.

And also, I don't wanna hurt this person's feelings, I like him." And I've probably gone further sexually than I had wanted to. Not that it was a big trauma. But it was like, "You know what, Janeane? Just say it next time. This was a couple of hours you could have been reading a book."

SMART SEX: Are you ever embarrassed to buy condoms? Janeane: I used to be. Not anymore. Now I just toss 'em up there. It's no big swig.

SMART SEX: Have you ever witnessed homophobia? Janeane: Well, unfortunately there's a lot of homophobic and sexist stand-up comics. Just being on the road, you get your fair share. The further out into the hinterlands you go to perform stand-up, the more likely you're going to run into homophobia and misogyny and racism. If I can, with a crowd like that, I try and do whatever I can to dispel stereotypes, to show somebody else another way of thinking when

I'm behind the microphone. It does not always work. In fact, a lot of times it doesn't make a dent.

SMART SEX: WHAT'S THE BEST THING ABOUT SEX? Janeane: I guess if the relationship is good, it makes it

great

if there's good sex. It really establishes a kinship, if you will, a bond. If it's good sex, that is. If it's healthy, good sex, then it's something you can carry with you even if you guys are separated for a long time.

SMART SEX: WHAT'S THE WORST THING ABOUT SEX? Janeane: That it can be *emotionally devastating.*

It can take a relationship that was a good friendship and ruin it. That if you have it too soon with somebody, you may have just thrown away the relationship. It can make you oversensitive, it can make you insecure.

SMART SEX: WHAT TO YOU IS SMART SEX? Janeane: Totally retaining your sense of self.

Smart sex to me, is not being afraid at all to still be you, whether you're naked or whatever. If you don't like something someone is doing, you have to say it.

If you want something done, you have to say it. And I'm not just talking about the touchy-feely. I'm talking about emotionally. If somebody's behavior is weirding you out, making you uncomfortable, you absolutely have to retain your strength and your convictions. And that to me is smart sex.

DOING IT

So you want to do "it"—the human act that is so often the subject of song lyrics, poetry, artwork, gossip, psychotherapy sessions, cable TV shows and bumper-sticker slogans (à la TEACHERS DO IT WITH CLASS). Whether sex is brand new to you or not, you may still be wondering, What's all the hoopla about? Sex can feel great. Sex can make you live completely in the moment—it's very hard to think about the past or future or anything except what is going on right then and there. But these statements are also true of masturbation and other types of sex play. Intercourse might carry so much mystique because it's an act that can create life. And sexual intercourse is literally the closest two people can physically get. If you care deeply for another person, lovemaking is a way to communicate feelings that you can't put into words. It's a powerful gesture of mind, body and spirit. Therefore, sexual intercourse deserves respect, thought and readiness.

TODD, 22: Sex can be such a meaningful and lasting thing. I remember all of the details. It's a period of time that you're completely vulnerable to somebody else, but you also have complete trust in them.

KIM, 20: I think that sometimes, even though I'm open with my friends, I can be kind of closed off. And I think sex is a way for me to connect with someone on the purest level. It's opening up in a way that you can't with anyone else.

Smart Sex Poll

When asked how they feel about having sex for the first time with a new person: 75 percent of young adults said it is a very big step in a relationship 16 percent said it is a pretty big step 8 percent said it is not that big of a step

THE ANATOMY OF SEX

Though much of sex is mental—love, caring, fantasy—it's helpful to understand what is physically going on down there during solo or partnered sex. Note that sexual response doesn't exactly follow a blueprint, that it can be different every time. You might feel some or all of these phases. (See Glossary for diagrams and definitions of body parts.)

A kiss, a touch, a thought, a scene from a movie and so many other things can start sexual response in the body. For both sexes, this means the heart beats faster (which might make you feel warm) and extra blood heads toward the genital area and flows into the vaginal walls and special spongy tissue in the clitoris or in the penis. In guys, this tissue swells up, causing the penis to get bigger, darker and more erect. In females, the vaginal lips thicken, the vagina becomes moist inside, and the clitoris swells a bit. The vagina (which is a soft, flexible organ) gets longer inside. The outer muscles of the vagina contract. The guy's sperm factory (the testes) pulls up a bit and the scrotum tightens. Sometimes breasts swell a little in females, and both sexes can get hardened nipples. Muscle tension increases, and the whole pelvic area might feel full and turned on. It's possible to stay in this state for a long time. It's also possible to ebb in and out of this stage.

If stimulation continues (stroking, fantasizing, thrusting from sexual intercourse), you might go into the next phase of reaction. The penis gets fully erect. The outer lips of the vagina swell even more and get darker. The outer one third of the vagina narrows. The uterus rises up high inside the body. The clitoris pulls in under its hood of skin. The testicles pull even closer to the body. The male often secretes a little fluid ("precome") that can have sperm or STDs in it (which is why "pulling out" is not a reliable birth control method). Breasts swell more, nipples get harder. Many women and a few men get a red rash, known as the "sex flush" at this stage. Muscle tension around the pelvic area and butt gets stronger. If you stop sexual activity at this stage, your genitals and pelvic area might ache (this is more common for guys—"blue balls"—but can happen to women, too). The feeling will go away as the extra blood flows back to the rest of the body.

For most men and many women, the peak of sexual excitement brings orgasm. Orgasm is not a requirement for either sex. If and when it happens, an orgasm probably won't happen to both partners at the same time. But when an orgasm occurs, a few mechanisms go to work. Fluid from the guy's prostate gland and sperm from his testes (which together make up semen) flow into the male urethra (the pipeline that normally carries urine). For the guy, there's a moment right before he ejaculates (spurts semen) when he feels like there's no turning back. Then the valve between the bladder and the urethra is closed off so the semen can be released. All that buildup of muscle tension is then released through a series of contractions in the penis. The muscle spasms cause the semen to spurt out. In the female, the vagina also contracts, as does the uterus, deep inside. Orgasm releases the blood from the swollen genital parts. For both men and women, the heart beats faster and blood pressure rises. Climax generally lasts about ten seconds, but it can be longer or shorter. Many describe the feeling as waves of warmth and energy that radiate out over the whole body—but it's different for everybody, and it can be different each time.

THE ANATOMY OF SEX

In the next phase, the body returns to its normal state. The heart and breathing rates slow down. Genitals gradually return to their normal size, shape and color. The body relaxes, and partners usually feel very close. There are some interesting differences between the sexes here. Right after orgasm, the man's level of sexual excitement usually drops quickly, and there's usually no way he can get aroused again unless he waits awhile. Although some men can stay hard, immediate repeated ejaculation is rare. The woman's level of excitement drops more gradually after she comes; she could even get aroused again and have another orgasm. Whether you're solo or with a partner, you might have a healthy glow of perspiration—or at least sweaty palms.

OPTIMAL CONDITIONS—

Anticipation is a great aphrodisiac. The excitement of getting that close to someone can sometimes put you in a big hurry. But ask yourself if you think the conditions are really right, and if you are emotionally ready—you only get one first time with this person. Good sex is more likely after you get to know each other's bodies and turn-ons, after you build trust, after you talk a lot. It takes time and practice to get to that level.

Everyone's formula for readiness is different. Trust, attraction, love, time, geographic proximity and other factors all matter in varying amounts to each person.

ESTHER, 17: I don't go to bed with someone unless I'm in love.

CATHERINE, 19: I form a mental checklist: "Does the other person care about me on a fairly deep level? Is there attraction? Are there future prospects?" I don't like to have one-night stands because I think they're unfulfilling. I don't want to hook up with somebody I don't feel like I could have a future with. I want someone I know and trust and love and who loves me.

RYAN S., 19: When I can totally open up and share my feelings with that person, and they accept me for who I am, then I feel I'll be ready. When there's no holding back, it's all just out there in the open. When I can talk to her and tell her about me and we're really good friends.

HOW DO YOU KNOW?

KIM, 20: I think to myself, Would I be embarrassed if we did it with the lights on? I think about how I am going to be treated afterward. I don't think I deserve disrespect after sleeping with somebody. So if I think this person's just going to treat me like crap later, then I'm not even going to deal with it, because I don't need to feel bad about something that I think is completely natural.

THE PROPER PRELIMINARIES

Once you feel emotionally ready for sex,
there are a number of less-glamorous
practical concerns. The biggest of
these is protection from disease and
pregnancy, so even if you like the
sound of your partner's sexual history,
you should consistently use condoms.
There are many sexually transmitted
diseases out there. Your partner
could be carrying an STD and not
know it. And, creepy as it sounds,
people do lie to get what they
want—that is, you, in bed, naked.
(See Chapters 8, 9 and 10 for the
dirt on discussing sexual history,
safer sex and STDs.)

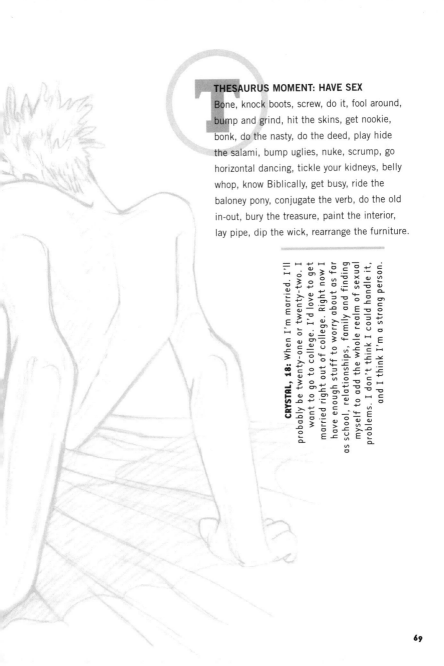

THESAURUS MOMENT: HAVE SEX

Bone, knock boots, screw, do it, fool around, bump and grind, hit the skins, get nookie, bonk, do the nasty, do the deed, play hide the salami, bump uglies, nuke, scrump, go horizontal dancing, tickle your kidneys, belly whop, know Biblically, get busy, ride the baloney pony, conjugate the verb, do the old in-out, bury the treasure, paint the interior, lay pipe, dip the wick, rearrange the furniture.

CRYSTAL, 18: When I'm married. I'll probably be twenty-one or twenty-two. I want to go to college. I'd love to get married right out of college. Right now I have enough stuff to worry about as far as school, relationships, family and finding myself to add the whole realm of sexual problems. I don't think I could handle it, and I think I'm a strong person.

If you are female and about to be sexually active—or are sexually active already—you should make a pilgrimage to a doctor or nurse-practitioner. Call your family doc, or go to a women's health center or family-planning clinic. During this visit, you should discuss your choices of birth control (see Chapter 7) and disease control (see Chapters 8, 9 and 10) and their pros and cons. The exam will more or less consist of being asked your health history (and that of your family), getting your weight and blood pressure measured, having your breasts examined, and getting a Pap smear and a pelvic exam (as in, checking inside your vagina). You may also take a blood and urine test.

The pelvic exam can seem scary or embarrassing, but remember that all women go through this. Also, it gets easier over time. You can ask your doctor to explain everything he or she is doing at each step of the way. And if you feel pain or discomfort, you can ask him or her to stop. Here's a preview:

- First, you lie on your back and put your heels in footrests ("stirrups") that are slightly out to the side of the examining table.
- The doctor inserts a speculum (a smooth metal or plastic device that looks like a long duck bill and slides into the vagina) and separates the walls of the vagina so he or she can see inside. It helps the doctor if you take deep breaths and let your muscles relax. The doctor will look around for any sign of pregnancy, infection or any other problems.
- Then he or she will use a small brush or cotton swab to gently remove some cells from your cervix (the knob on the back wall of the vagina, and the entrance to the uterus—see Glossary) for laboratory testing. This procedure is a Pap smear. A Pap smear can be painless to icky-feeling to slightly painful. But it only takes a couple of seconds.

•Then the doctor will take out the speculum and perform the bimanual exam—an exam that uses two hands. The doctor will insert one or two fingers into your vagina while the other hand rests on your belly. The doctor will feel between the two hands for your ovaries and other abdominal organs, making sure all is well.

That's it. If fear or nerves are keeping you from a needed exam, bring a girlfriend, mom, sister or boyfriend with you. It's usually fine for a dear one to be in the examining room.

CHECKUP TIME–BOYS

Guys: When you are visiting the family doctor, you can get your plumbing checked, too. The doctor will ask you about personal and family health history, maybe take blood and urine samples and check your scrotum, penis and testicles for lumps or unusual pain or sores. It's a less complicated exam for guys because, obviously, almost everything is on the outside.

When you're looking around for health care, a good place to start is your family's regular doctor. If there's someone out there who knows your health history and/or your family's health history, so much the better.

WHERE TO FIND HEALTH CARE

In some states, physicians do not have to inform parents about a child's STD or pregnancy status (see page 198, Chapter 9). If confidentiality is important to you, ask about your doctor's policy when you make the appointment. If your parents are paying for the visit, be aware that they may very well see the doctor's bill and know of any lab tests (like screening for pregnancy or STDs) unless you make other arrangements with your doctor (like paying for lab work yourself).

If you do not feel comfortable going to a family doctor or you don't have one nearby, there are other resources. You can look up your state's department of health or health services in the phone directory and ask them what is available to someone of your age and income. Some areas have STD clinics or young-adult clinics. Certain hospitals have specialized clinics for young adults that deal with sex-related health issues. If you are still in high school, you can ask the school nurse or health care person (who should also be bound by confidentiality laws) what is available in the area. Colleges usually have some kind of health care service on campus, often paid for as part of standard school costs.

Also, there are Planned Parenthood and other health clinics nationwide.

THESAURUS MOMENT : PENIS

Weenie, Ralph, third leg, centurion, soldier, cuttlefish, magic wand, junior, him, it, divining rod, Jimmy, the Little General, Willy, Pee-pee, love pump, Old Faithful, main vein, dick, Little Elvis, Little [your name here], schlong, heat-seeking missile, trouser mouse, one-eyed Jack, tool, pecker, pud, prick, johnson, roscoe, trouser trout, meat puppet, tuber, throbbing gristle, member, thumper, pleasure pole, pocket rocket, love hammer, purple-headed warrior, tower of power, unit

Bonus Fact
Most teenagers don't seek contraception until almost a year after they have started having sex.

Young people, especially ones still living at home, don't always have a private time or place to have sex and end up doing the deed in cars, outdoors and sometimes other unusual places.

PRIVACY, PEACE AND GERMS

THOMAS, 18: The time I lost it? It was really bad. I was with this girl, and we did it in an alley. It wasn't like a nasty New York alley, but you know . . . . For young people, because sex isn't accepted for us, we can't be in houses all the time, because our moms or dads will have a fit. And so we had to do weird things like that.

Nasty places can be unsanitary. Hurried sex is often not-well-thought-out sex. You might not have condoms nearby, for example. Quick, anxious, grungy sex may not be that much fun—especially when you're doing it that way because of circumstances, and not by choice. Try to plan a time and place for the two of you that is safe, private and clean.

There is much hype and folklore about the deflowering of a girl—bloodstains on the bed sheet to prove she was pure, her girlish cries of pain and ecstasy, whatever. Virginity is to be respected, but losing it (when you're good and ready) doesn't have to be a melodrama.

THE FIRST TIME

What makes a first-time-ever experience positive or negative? Lots of factors. Trust, attraction, respect, gentleness of touch, comfort level of both partners, sense of humor, feeling safe both physically and emotionally, being comfortable, ability to talk about the very personal.

Be forewarned that you can get an STD (including HIV) anytime you have unprotected sex. You can get pregnant anytime you have unprotected sex—even the very first time, even if you do it standing up, even if you douche afterward (see Glossary). Don't buy any myths that tell you otherwise. Using a condom can put your mind at ease and let your body enjoy the experience.

On a practical level, mucho lubrication is good, especially if you're female and it's your first time—it eases the way, so to speak. Score yourself a water-based lubricant like KY Jelly, Astroglide or Probe, available in most drugstores. Smooth a bit over the outside of the condom after the guy has put it on (an extra drop of lube inside the condom can increase pleasure for the guy wearing it). Don't use Vaseline, baby oil, moisturizer, oil-based sex lubes, or cooking oil— they can eat through condoms in minutes.

Most devirginizing worries are about the stretching or tearing of the girl's hymen. In real life, there is a very broad range of experience. For some people, first-time intercourse hurts a lot; for others, only a little. Tampons, fingers, even sports, could cause the hymen to be open already. Whether or not the hymen is intact, intercourse could cause some pain and take a few tries before penetration is comfortable. The main rule is: If it hurts, stop until later. Discomfort might also be due to tense muscles, so maximize foreplay.

CHARLIE, 17: Well, she knew it was gonna be painful, and she cried while we were doing it, but she said it was really good. It was more emotional than physical. I guess love ties in a lot with it.

VIRGINIA, 20: I just don't remember it being painful. I don't really remember even feeling it. I remember thinking that it felt really weird the couple times I did it after that. But the first time, no.

ANDREW, 25: We had been dating long-distance; we weren't seriously involved. I'd been out drinking a little. I said, "Let's do it, let's have sex." She said, "Really?" Afterward she was a little concerned that I wasn't jumping for joy, but I was more content. I just wanted to go to sleep and let it sink in. I wasn't disappointed, but it wasn't that big a deal. It sank in over time. Each time after that, I enjoyed it more.

PRIY, 23: The first time I had sex with my ex-girlfriend, we'd been wooing for a month. Even though I had never had sex with a woman, it was magical. Something we both wanted together for a month came true. It was the buildup, the desire, the tension that erupted. What felt magical was that it happened so naturally. It wasn't something I was supposed to know how to do. So I didn't feel pressure to perform.

ANDRE, 25: The first time I had sex with a girl, it was really sexual. I was seventeen, and I was embarrassed to be such a late bloomer. She was older. She was the seducer. We'd gone on a couple of dates and kissed, and I went to get my coat and she pounced on me in the closet. After, she said, "Was that your first time?" Not because it only took three seconds or anything, but because I wasn't exactly sure how to roll the rubber on. A year later, when I lost my virginity to a man, it was more empowering and earth-shattering. I really can be attracted to both men and women, but I find myself more emotionally connected to men.

FOR THE ALREADY SEXUALLY ACTIVE FOLK

Once you've had sex, you don't have to *keep* having it. Sex is not something to do out of habit (or pressure, or desperation). It should be a deliberate choice. Every time.

CATHERINE, 19: Sometimes it's easier to go along with sex, because as much as girls think they're women of the 90s, lots of us are also innate people-pleasers. Girls will sleep with a guy to make him happy. You hope he'll be more inclined to do what pleases you—even if it's not sex. Women crave affirmation, emotional support.

BRADFORD, 21: We'd set the precedent of having sex if we went out. If I don't have sex with her, she'll say, "What's the matter? You don't love me?" Sometimes if you don't want to have sex, it doesn't mean you're not attracted to a person.

If you are comfortable with the word *no*, then the word *yes* has much more meaning.

Among sexually active young men, one in two says he "went out with someone just for sex." Fewer than one in six women says the same.

Casual sex is hard to define. Loosely, you could say it's less emotional and more physical. Some people aren't ready to put their hearts on the line. Others might be looking to be the next Romeo or Juliet, but casual sex is all they can find. Some people are more spontaneous about it. Whatever the reason, casual sex definitely happens.

CASUAL SEX

TODD, 22: The occasional casual sex is a learning experience. If it wasn't for some casual sex in the beginning, I wouldn't know what I know. You learn from the bad experiences, too.

CATHERINE, 19: Sex should be with someone you really care about. I have had one-night stands and woke up the next morning saying, "Oh, God, what did I do?"

ANDREW, 25: Casual sex, a one-night stand, is the polar opposite of committed or married sex. There's a lot of gray area in between. You could have sex with a good friend. It's not love, but you still have a lot of feeling for them if you know them.

Sex without love does not mean sex without responsibility. If you're going to have sex just for pleasure, all the safer-sex boundaries still apply—STDs have nothing to do with feelings. In fact, if your relationship is casual, it may be a little harder to trust the other person, harder to talk intimately. If you don't know the person well, they might be less likely to tell you their sexual history, less likely to contact you later if there's an STD in the picture. Casual sex means taking extra precautions to safeguard yourself and others.

OLDER GUYS, YOUNGER WOMEN

Some young people look for validation, comfort, love, security by dating guys or girls much older. This can be iffy. Such relationships can have a really uneven power dynamic. The older partner gets to play the worldly-wise sophisticate and be the sexually knowledgeable one. If you're not feeling really good about yourself to begin with, coping with an older lover who may not really view you as an equal can make things worse. It can be hard to talk someone into practicing safer sex, using effective birth control or doing something to please you sexually when they're older, more sure of themselves, or perhaps simply paying for everything. And anyway, experience doesn't always make for sexual smarts.

What is important is having equal power in a relationship, and this is probably easier to come by with someone roughly your own age.

• More than two-thirds of all teenage mothers are impregnated by men over the age of twenty.

• Men over twenty-five cause more than 400 teenage pregnancies every day.

PRIY, 23: My first boyfriend was ten years my senior. He was my elder on many different levels. It really became a relationship of protector/protectee. What was really tragic was that I was very young—seventeen, eighteen. It was dangerous, destructive—not just with sex but power relations on all levels—cultural, intellectual. I made less of an impact on him than he did on me.

LETDOWNS AND RECOVERY

KIM, 20: I think in my past I've made some really bad choices. This one guy in particular, he dared me to have sex with him, and I did it. It was really quick, and afterward I felt so bad. I thought I could handle it, but I couldn't. I had to realize that maybe I wasn't ready and that I should think about it more before I did it again. I've learned from those mistakes. I'm a little more careful about who I sleep with, even who I flirt with. I guess I've just learned to control myself a little more.

Certainly there are emotional and physical risks that must be weighed carefully each time you have sex.

But if you're well-informed, a good listener, a sensitive soul and healthy, sex can be one of the most rewarding experiences on the planet. It can be one of the best parts of your life for years and years hereafter.

Sometimes, despite all the planning and thinking and buildup (or sometimes when there wasn't enough planning and thinking), sex can make you feel bad. Maybe it wasn't the right person or it wasn't at the right time. Maybe the mechanics of it just weren't very smooth or fun. A bad sexual experience does not make you a bad person. It doesn't mean all your sexual experiences will be crummy. It does not mean that you are locked into this kind of sex for the rest of your life. It's normal to feel down for a little while, but know that you will move on and that this moment will fade in the light of better sexual encounters in the future.

SAME SEX STUFF

6 Many people believe that sexual identity–gay or straightness–is not so clear-cut. Imagine a scale or a spectrum with TOTALLY HETEROSEXUAL on one end and TOTALLY HOMOSEXUAL on the other. Everyone, some sex researchers argue, can mark a place for themselves somewhere near one end or the other (or in the middle, for bisexuals). Those who feel desire in the middle and towards the gay end of the scale have more challenges and obstacles ahead than the hetero folk. But there are resources galore to make that road a little less rocky.

Minidictionary

BISEXUAL: A person who is sexually attracted to people of both genders.

BI-CURIOUS: Someone who's been straight, but is experimenting with same-sex experiences. Someone trying on new sexual behavior.

COMING OUT (OF THE CLOSET): The act of telling others about your homosexuality or bisexuality.

GAY: Usually means a homosexual male, but can also apply to homosexual women.

HETEROSEXUAL: Someone who has a primary romantic and erotic attraction to people of the opposite gender, and few or no erotic feelings for the same gender.

HOMOPHOBIA: Irrational fear and hatred of homosexuality in ourselves and others.

HOMOSEXUAL: Someone who has a primary romantic and erotic attraction to people of the same gender, and few or no erotic feelings for the opposite gender.

LESBIAN: A homosexual woman. *Lesbian* comes from the Greek island of Lesbos, home of woman-loving female poet Sappho. Lesbos was also reportedly a haven for women artists at a time in Western history when the arts were usually the domain of men.

QUEER: Once a derogatory term, now often used as an all-inclusive word for people who are gay, lesbian, bisexual, even transsexual. Basically everything non-mainstream-hetero.

TRANSSEXUAL: Someone who believes that the body he or she was born with does not match the gender he or she best identifies with, and who changes the sex of the body through surgery and/or hormones.

TRANSVESTITE: Someone who enjoys dressing in the clothes of the opposite sex.

(Note: Neither transsexuality nor transvestitism are matters of sexual orientation. And neither transsexuals nor transvestites are automatically homosexual—in fact, they're more likely to be hetero. But there is great confusion, since people often lump since these two groups in with gays.)

FIGURING IT OUT

PRIY, 23: I feel like everyone tries to fit the mold that was given to them in the very beginning of coming into one's sexuality. I did that. I know that a lot of my gay friends did that. And it's only when I've gained insight that the world has opened up to me. Now, if I had to hide these parts of myself, if I had to hide the fact that I was dating a woman, that would make me so tormented. It's not a very healthy way to live your life, not to admit that you desire someone.

PRIY, 23: I think I figured out I was bisexual when I was pretty young. I remember looking at soft-porn magazines when I was eleven or twelve and finding those images of women erotic. But at the same time I remember watching *Happy Days* and finding Fonzie erotic. I didn't actually feel it was okay to admit that I liked women until I came to a safe place like college. There were a lot of women around me who were experimenting and pushing their boundaries.

One of the toughest parts of being gay is figuring out who you are and who you are designed to love. In a predominantly straight culture like ours, going against the norm is, for most, no party. It's okay to experiment and avoid labeling yourself for a while. As long as you play it smart (consensual and protected sex play), you do no harm exploring. But if you deny who you really are, gay or straight, you are shortchanging yourself.

Looking back at childhood, some people can trace early feelings of homosexuality. Or at least a sense of being different without knowing why. Some people go through this at a very young age; for others, feelings arise in the early teen years or later.

RYAN P., 20: I noticed that something was weird when I was very young, like six years old. My parents used to watch *Dallas*, and I had a crush on Patrick Duffy. I used to dream about brushing his hair or tying his shoelaces. I had several little crushes on boys. I had this one friend and I just wanted to hug him. I almost asked him if I could, but somehow I knew I shouldn't. You have to think of creative ways to deal with and process those feelings. Back then I thought I wanted to be a girl.

As people get older and start to realize how the world works, these feelings can be less sweet and more scary. Overwhelming even. It may feel like there's no one to answer questions about homosexuality, and you have to get information from whatever source is available.

ESTHER, 17: I always knew I was different from my peers. The summer before seventh grade, I went away to a summer camp for gifted kids, and I experienced my first crush on a girl. Nothing happened, but it was a very intense feeling. When I came home I saw a talk show about lesbians, and I figured that's what I was. I was terrified. I thought I was going to get AIDS, right? I thought I was evil, wrong, hurting my family. I thought I was being selfish. I never denied it, though. I thought, I'm a lesbian, but what am I going to do about it?

NATASHA, 19: When I was little, I had a little boyfriend, but I knew I was attracted to women. In the seventh grade, I had a big crush on a teacher. Around then I read a book on sexuality and it said "lesbianism" and I was like, No way! Not me! I was a Jehovah's Witness, and I knew God destroyed whole cities, Sodom and Gomorrah, due to homosexuality. I just cried. I tried to commit suicide.

Hating your sexuality and hiding your sexuality is painful. It can lead to destructive behavior like substance abuse, eating disorders, unsafe sex, even suicide. If you think you're interested in a nonhetero kind of sexuality, you owe it to yourself to find support and community. There are probably friends, teachers, counselors, family members, who will support and accept you. See Resources, page 310, for suggestions of where to turn beyond friends and family.

IS THIS ME?

Many sex experts believe that almost everyone has at least some feelings of same-gender sexuality. It's not uncommon for young people—especially teenagers and preteens—to dabble in sex play with the same gender. It's a form of experimentation and it doesn't automatically mean you are gay. It's also totally common for straight people to have the occasional erotic dream about someone of the same sex or to have a crush on a same-sex friend.

ALLISON, 22: Have I had the odd latent homosexual dream? Yes, of course. I think it's totally natural. I had one about my history teacher in high school, I had one about a friend here in school. Women are taught to appreciate women's bodies. Open a *Vogue* and we're supposed to say, "Oh, she's beautiful, and I want to be like her." It's a natural response for girls to get that line blurred. When am I supposed to appreciate the body, and when am I supposed to fall in love with it?

BRADFORD, 21: If you have a dream, you can't control that. If a straight person has a fantasy, they're just curious about what goes on on the other side.

Some people just take note of these thoughts, perhaps enjoy them on a fantasy level and leave it at that. For others, the desires might be strong and consistent, but get pushed away. The important thing is to learn to be comfortable with who you are and accepting of people who are something else. It's also crucial that if you decide to experiment, you do it safely.

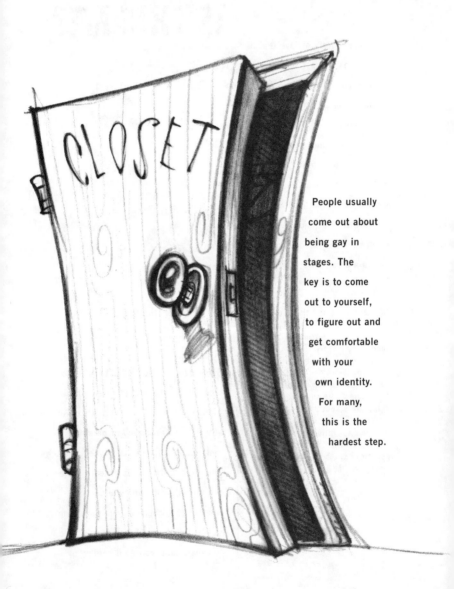

People usually come out about being gay in stages. The key is to come out to yourself, to figure out and get comfortable with your own identity. For many, this is the hardest step.

COMING OUT

RYAN P., 20: Freshman year of high school, I started hooking up with girls because I was so confused and thought, I need to find out what's going on here. It was kind of sad. In a way I used girls, but I used them to find out who I was. I mean, my environment was so antihomosexual that it was really an individual struggle. I was like, "Okay, I'm normal." Those feelings for guys are just weird. I don't like guys. I like girls. I've just got to keep getting comfortable with it. But the attraction wasn't there. I mean, it was physical to a degree, but there was no intimacy, no love. I mean, love of friendship, yeah, but no sexual love. And that went on for a while. But I realized I was stupid. I was trying to get something out of this act that wasn't giving me anything. I was really lonely. And then, my junior year, sometime in the summer, I had an experience with my close [male] friend. And that's just when I was sort of like, "Whoa, what's going on here? Could this be right for me?" And it was.

ESTHER, 17: I was in eighth grade. The first person I came out to was my guidance counselor. Actually, she kind of guessed what was up. Some gay people had spoken at my school for diversity day, and I was giving her this impassioned speech about the unfair oppression of gays. And my counselor was like, "Esther, does this have to do with you?" When she asked that, it made me so nervous that I thought I was going to faint. She was very supportive. She told me it was okay to be gay. But I construed it more like, "It's okay to have a disease." I still felt like it was such a scandal. I came out to my sister a year later. I told her when I had a relationship. Her first words were, "You better not complain about me liking boys." She's been okay about it; I'm really proud of her. I also sat my dad down and told him, because I needed a ride to a meeting. He thinks it's a phase. He thinks it's my politics.

Once you feel solid about your own sexual identity, you can come out in a variety of ways. You might start by telling a friend or family member that you trust—a person you can count on to be accepting. If you discuss your sexuality with a couple of people and they respond with support, you will probably feel even stronger. Others start coming out by telling an acquaintance instead of a close friend or relative—fewer emotions on the line that way. Be prepared for rejection though, and know that it doesn't make you less of a person if others can't deal with your sexuality. If one person lets you down, don't be afraid to try telling others. If you are still living at home and/or are financially dependent on your folks, weigh out the possibility of getting cut off or kicked out. If this is really a danger, maybe wait until you can take care of yourself. Go at whatever pace you feel comfortable. You are under no obligation to tell anyone that you're gay (or tell anyone anything about your sexuality), but you shouldn't have to hide it either.

TINO, 17: I was raised in a Rasta religion where they talk about cutting off your genitals if you're homosexual. I grew up hearing songs like "Kill the Faggot." My brother would kick my ass if I came out to him. So when I came out to my mother, I was so afraid. She's a single parent, and I admire her so much. I was so afraid of losing her respect and her love that I hid it for a long time. I had a boyfriend when I was fourteen, and once she heard us arguing and she said, "You sound like a man and a woman. Are you gay?" I said, "No, Mami!" But one day I just said, "I have something to tell you." I started to cry. "I'm gay." She said, "Why are you crying?" She hugged me. She said, "I love you, but you're going to have a hard row to hoe." But my mom, she is so cool. We went to a dance together—she came with her boyfriend and I introduced her to mine. She's very open-minded. We were close, but now we're even closer.

RYAN P., 20: First you tell people where you know you'll get support the quickest— like I told this peer youth group at school, and suddenly they were all, "Ryan, we love you!" But the people closest to you you have to live with every day, so that's harder. I'm going to tell my parents when I finish college. I know dozens of people who are dealing with the parent thing. Coming out to them. I know people who have rushed. You're ready at a point where you've discovered yourself, and you know who you really are. And continuing that role of playing the heterosexual son, it just wouldn't be you anymore. What's the point in that? When you tell your parents, there's gonna be tears, there's gonna be anguish, there might even be extreme anger. I mean, you've gotta go into it knowing that you've gotta have a box of tissue with you.

Coming out can be a time of great emotional highs and lows, when you rocket between depression and euphoria. You're looking for affection and acceptance, and your self-esteem is fragile. You might also feel like you are doing (or thinking about doing) something morally wrong. Traditional religious views saying that sex is only for procreation and that man is only made for woman (and vice versa) can send you spiraling guiltward. If you'd like to talk about these issues, and if you'd like help coming out to your family and friends, you might ask PFLAG (Parents and Friends of Lesbians and Gays; see Resources, page 312) for their suggestions. If your loved ones are supportive of who you are, it can help your sense of self and maybe make you less likely to get reckless. If your blood relatives give you a hard time, surround yourself with people who do care for you unconditionally—sometimes called a family of choice.

There is no legally recognized same-sex marriage in America (well, lots of states have legislation in the works, and Hawaii has come the closest so far). Many states do allow domestic partnership, which is described as "two adults of the same sex who have chosen to share their lives in an intimate and committed relationship, live together and share a mutual obligation of support for the basic necessities of life." Domestic partners get some (but not all) of the tax and health care benefits that married folks get.

I'D MARRY YOU, BUT...

You can check with your local city hall and see if domestic partnership is an option in your area. If so, you trot down to city hall and stand in line with the blushing brides and bridegrooms and get a certificate that's sort of like a marriage license. If your state doesn't have domestic partnership, some employers and insurance companies still let you and your true love sign up as domestic partners or "spousal equivalents." In any of these cases, you probably need to prove that:

•You live together and intend to stay that way.

•You share expenses and finances.

•You have both reached the age of consent (usually eighteen).

•You are not married to anyone else.

•You are not related by blood in a way that would prevent legal marriage.

Though many churches feel that same-sex marriage does not fit their definition of family, others do accept gay couples who wish to walk down the aisle. If it's important to you to have a religious wedding, talk to your clergy person (if you think he or she can handle the topic), or ask your local gay community center which churches in your area are gay-friendly. In any state, country or solar system, you can have your own spiritual ceremony of commitment—which might be more important to you anyway.

THE RULES OF SAME-SEX SEX

Everybody (who's not living under a rock) gets some idea of how straight sex works from movies, books, TV shows and dishy talk among friends. Gay and lesbian sex play is either blessed or cursed with a shortage of easy-access examples. So if you have just begun experimenting with gay sex, you might feel awkward because you think you don't know what you're doing.

RYAN P., 20: The first time, my heart was beating so fast. And when you're nervous, you're worried and you can't keep it up. I learned from more experienced partners. I saw what they did to me and I did it back.

But here's a not-so-big secret: Except for penis-in-vagina intercourse, same-sex couples can have all the same kinds of finger, mouth and genital involvement as hetero couples. Kissing, caressing, mutual masturbation, oral sex, anal sex—these are things that both gay and straight people do in bed.

BISEXUALITY

Some categories are clear-cut: your zip code, your shoe size, your income, your typing speed. But for some people, sexual preference isn't as simple as straight or gay. Bisexuals are people who date both men and women, people who say they choose their partners based on attraction to the individual—not on gender.

PRIY, 23: A lot of gay people don't like the idea of bisexuality because they feel that bisexuals don't need to take as many risks as gay people do, that bisexuals enjoy the privileges of straight culture but also have some fun on the side. They call us fence-sitters. But it's not about sitting on fences—it's about getting rid of fences.

DEBUNKING THE MYTHS OF BISEXUALITY

Priy responds to 5 misconceptions:

Myth #1: Bisexuals have sex with everything that moves.
Not only are gay and straight folk likely to run screaming at the thought of us, but just like everyone else, we don't necessarily want to have sex with everyone out there! Don't flatter yourself!

Myth #2: Bisexuals are indecisive.
I can make up my mind . . . to like both genders!

Myth #3: Bisexuals spread disease.
Bisexuals spread disease no more than gay and straight people do. I'm sure there are individuals out there who don't practice the safest sex, but you can't lump all of us into one group and call us disease-bearers.

Myth #4: Bisexuals love threesomes.
Some might—who knows? I don't, because it's hard enough to please one person at a time. Plus, that's like saying bisexuals can't be with one person at a time. Those of us who are into monogamy practice it. We're not biologically adulterers.

Myth #5: Bisexuality is a phase, an experiment.
I think it's cool to experiment. After all, how do you know what you want till you try it? But for me, being bisexual is not just a passing phase, it's an identity. And it's only fair for me to expect to be taken seriously the way I am.

Younger gay people seem to be more reckless about practicing safer sex than their older counterparts.

One survey found that **SAFETY FIRST**

44 percent of gay men under thirty had had unprotected anal sex in the last year, whereas only 18 percent of gay men over thirty had. Actually, young gays blow off safety for the same reasons as young straights do: You don't want to think ahead, you're caught up in the excitement, you're in denial about what you're planning to do that night so that you don't have to feel responsible for your own behavior, you're scared of what your partner will think if you bring up safer sex and/or you don't want to admit to yourself that you're actually doing this! But for gay folks, as for straight ones, denial isn't a good thing. Take the mature leap of planning ahead (see the negotiation strategies in Chapter 4 for help with this), or be ready to say no. There are exciting, desirable people out there who care about their health as much as you do about yours. You can find them if you look.

BRADFORD, 21: When I was in high school, I made typical fag jokes. Now I have friends who are gay. Love is love. People who are in love and homosexual should have all the rights that straight people have.

CATHERINE, 19: Most of the students at my school lead sheltered lives. They see gay people on TV and go "Oooh, gross." It's going to take a while to accept homosexuality.

HOMOPHOBIA: WITHIN AND WITHOUT

There's no avoiding the not-so-underlying message in society that gay and bi people are bad. Gays are often made to feel like second-class citizens (or outcasts, or sickos, or kid-snatching vultures, or diseased pariahs). When you hear a message over and over, you can't help but absorb it on some level. So gay and bi people sometimes have to fight harder to give themselves the respect they deserve, to treat themselves well. Likewise, even nongays who consider themselves tolerant need to make sure they don't succumb to homophobia. Would you hire someone gay? Invite someone gay to a party? Care if a teacher is gay? Dance with someone who is gay?

SIMON, 17: The people where I live think that if you have a gay friend, that friend's gonna try and turn you gay. But that's not true.

THOMAS, 18: I cannot stand people that just say, "Oh, you know, if you do something to another guy, then you're a faggot." I cannot stand that word. They're just so insecure about themselves. I just think they're dumb, or maybe it's taught to them.

Then there are the gay and bi haters who seriously lash out verbally, physically or any way that will intimidate.

•In 1996, there were 2,529 reported incidents of hate crimes against gay people in major American cities.

BRADFORD, 21: We have a student center, and there was a gay/lesbian banner up for gay-pride week. These guys ripped down the banner, spray-painted slurs on it and left it on the ground. Those guys also wrote into the school paper anonymously and said, "We don't like gays. Homosexuality is unnatural."

PRIY, 23: I was dating a woman for two years. The one time I remember getting affectionate with her in public, these guys were making comments. It wasn't violent, but just the fact that some people considered us objectionable was an issue for me. I do worry about safety, like what if people on my block see me taking home a woman, or constantly see me with women?

ESTHER, 17: I'm terrified of PDA [public displays of affection]. You never know what ignorant person is walking down the street.

Unfortunately, acts of homophobia can make it difficult and even dangerous for gay couples to show affection in public. Gay people and same-sex couples do not have the freedom to walk around as safely as others.

ESTHER, 17: A few weeks ago I was walking down the hall and wearing a big backpack. Somebody pushed me from behind, said, "Dyke," then ran. I fell right on my nose. I couldn't see who it was, and no one would say. I told my father. I reported it to the school. They said, "Next time, tell us."

If you are so threatened by someone else's sexuality that you feel a need to harass them, it's time for a big reality check. You live in a world with different forms of sexuality, just like there are different kinds of ethnicity, music and flavors of ice cream. Enjoy the diversity. Thanks to gay-rights activists, educators and even sometimes the media (there have never been so many gay characters on prime time), portrayals of gay men and lesbians are becoming more accepted. Some suggestions for increased tolerance?

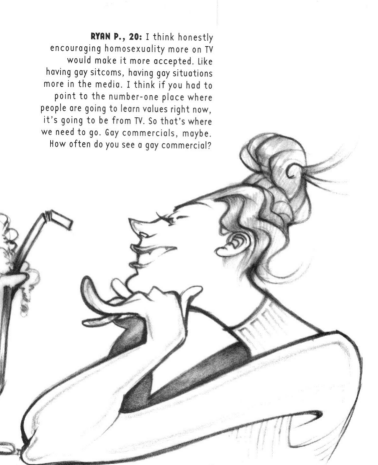

RYAN P., 20: I think honestly encouraging homosexuality more on TV would make it more accepted. Like having gay sitcoms, having gay situations more in the media. I think if you had to point to the number-one place where people are going to learn values right now, it's going to be from TV. So that's where we need to go. Gay commercials, maybe. How often do you see a gay commercial?

ESTHER, 17: Writer Emma Goldman says, "Revolution is but thought carried into action." What that means to me is that I've got to take the idea that gay people have rights and act on it. You really have to be out and educate on a one-to-one basis and on a wider scale. I enjoy the responsibility of making change.

Milestones
and Minutiae
in Gay History

3000 B.C.

The earliest-known portrayal of
gay sex: a *Mesopotamian drawing* depicts
two men discovering the joy of sex.

615–580 B.C.

Sappho, the lesbian poet, teacher and
"Tenth Muse," gains fame in ancient
Greece for her verse, but officials
eventually destroy most of her work,
because they consider the homoerotic
content sacrilegious.

1307–1327

Edward II, reputed to be gay, reigns
as king of England.

1400s

Native American berdaches sighted by
explorers of the New World. Most
commonly, male berdaches are born as
men and live as women, but there are
female berdaches also. Documented
in more than 150 societies for centuries,
berdaches were considered a third
gender by Native Americans.

1590–1609

Shakespeare writes his famous
sonnets. Sonnets 1 to 126 are
addressed to a man (leaving a
paltry 28 addressed to a woman).

1930

The *Motion Picture Production Code*
forbids sympathetic screen portrayals
of gays or lesbians. The code remains
in place for film and TV through 1968.

1933

Gertrude Stein, writer of books
and poetry, publishes the
Autobiography of Alice B. Toklas.

Gertrude and Alice consider themselves married and lived together for thirty-nine years.

1945

Psychologist *Evelyn Hooker* starts her groundbreaking research challenging the widely accepted premise that homosexuals are mentally ill.

1947

McCarthyism purges suspected homosexuals as well as suspected Communists from the federal government and other public and private agencies. Many lose jobs. Many gays in Hollywood are blacklisted.

1948, 1950

The Kinsey Reports—published results of extensive research on male and female sexuality—describe homosexuality as far more widespread than had been believed.

1954

The first magazine for gays and lesbians, *One*, is published in Los Angeles. In 1958, U.S. Supreme Court rules that *One* can be sent through the mail, which represents the first Supreme Court victory for gays.

1961

Illinois, the first state to make gay sex legal, strikes down its sodomy laws, which had outlawed anal and other kinds of sex (like oral sex) between consensual adults. In 1986, though, in *Bowers v. Hardwick*, the Supreme Court upholds Georgia's sodomy laws as constitutional. (Many states retain some kind of sodomy laws today.)

1969

Stonewall riots rage throughout New York City in response to a police raid on a gay bar in the West Village, marking the birth of the modern gay liberation movement.

1970

The Boys in the Band is the first Hollywood film in which all the main characters are gay.

1973

American Psychological Association deletes homosexuality from its list of mental disorders.

1974

First out gay people elected to public office: *Kathy Kozachenko* elected to Ann Arbor City Council. *Elaine Noble* elected to Massachusetts State Legislature.

1977–1981

Billy Crystal plays gay character, Jody, on *Soap*.

1978

The *Village People*, singers of gay-themed disco hits such as "YMCA" and "In the Navy" go gold.

1978

Harvey Milk, the openly gay member of San Francisco's Board of Supervisors, is killed along with Mayor George Moscone.

1979

First big *march on Washington* for gay rights: 200,000 people participate.

1981

A new disease, known as gay related immune disease *(GRID)*, or "the gay cancer," first reported. The disease, not exclusive to gay people, is soon renamed AIDS (short for acquired immunodeficiency syndrome).

1982

Gay Men's Health Crisis formed by six gay men. They set up AIDS hotline and newsletter. The group is now the oldest and biggest nonprofit AIDS organization.

1983

House of Representatives member *Gerry Studds* (D-MA) becomes the first congressperson to come out about his homosexuality. *Barney Frank* (D-MA) follows suit in 1987, and *Steve Gundersen* (R-WI) comes out in 1994.

1987

Larger *gay rights rally!* An estimated 650,000 march on Washington.

1988

National Education Association says that every school district should provide counseling for students struggling with sexual-orientation issues.

1991

Freddy Mercury dies of AIDS. Mercury was the gay lead singer of *Queen* and writer of such classic songs as "Bohemian Rhapsody" and "We Are the Champions."

1991

Two firsts for network TV dramas: Two women kiss on *L.A. Law*, and *thirtysomething* shows two men in bed together.

1992

Angels in America, a play about AIDS, homosexuality, religion and more, takes the *Pulitzer Prize* for its Los Angeles premiere. Angels will go on to win *four Tony Awards* for its New York City run.

Presidential candidate *Bill Clinton* promises more rights for gays. On MTV's *Face the Future*, Bill Clinton promises to lift ban on gays in the military if elected.

Actor *Doug Savant* portrays a gay character, Matt, on the new hit show *Melrose Place*.

1993

Drag queen conquers mainstream: RuPaul's album *Supermodel of the World*, with hit singles "Supermodel" and "Back to My Roots," debuts.

Even larger gay rights rally! The ever-growing AIDS crisis and the need for gays and lesbians to feel like a *force instead of a minority,* inspires March on Washington.

Rock chicks fall in love. Kate Schellenbach of *Luscious Jackson* and Josephine Wiggs of the Breeders become a couple. Both bands tour with Lollapalooza in the summer of 1994.

"Don't Ask, Don't Tell" military policy takes effect. Clinton's efforts to fully lift the ban on gays in the military is foiled by Congress, and his compromise policy gets mixed reviews.

1994
Philadelphia, directed by Jonathan Demme, wins two Oscars. Story of gay man with AIDS brings a statuette to *Tom Hanks* for Best Actor, and one to *Bruce Springsteen* for Best Song.

First gay-positive TV ad. TV spot for *IKEA* furniture features gay couple shopping for a dining room table, putting a home together.

Lesbian kiss on *Roseanne. Mariel Hemingway* guest stars as lesbian who mistakes Roseanne for a lesbian and kisses her. Not treated as fetish or joke.

Pedro Zamora dies of AIDS-related complications. The first out gay youth living with AIDS on a regular TV series, Zamora impacted everyone from President Clinton to teenage viewers through his presence on MTV's *The Real World.*

1995
Greg Louganis, a four-time Olympic gold-medalist in diving, goes public about his homosexuality and HIV-positive status.

1996
Friends episode features lesbian marriage of Ross' ex-wife. Newt Gingrich's half-sister, *Candace Gingrich,* appears as the official who performs the ceremony.

U.S. Supreme Court says gay-rights laws can't be banned. The highest court strikes down part of the Colorado constitution that undoes any civil-rights protection for homosexuals.

Melissa Etheridge and her girlfriend announce plans to become parents.

1997

The 1997 television lineup includes a *record-setting* 30 lesbian, gay and bisexual characters—up 23% from 1996.

Ellen DeGeneres comes out in April, right before a landmark Emmy Award®—winning episode of the hit series Ellen in which DeGeneres's character announces that she's a lesbian.

On November 13, Sen. *Edward M. Kennedy* introduces the Hate Crimes Prevention Act of 1998 to enhance federal enforcement of hate crimes.

If you think you are gay, lesbian or bisexual and you are having a rough go of it, take heart. You are far from alone. There are many people and groups who want to help you, because they've been through it, too. Many who come out say that it is the best thing they've ever done for themselves, and it was with coming out that their lives truly began.

RYAN P., 20: After a while, it's no big deal. People say to me, "Now that I've gotten to know you, you're not gay Ryan, you're just Ryan."

ESTHER, 17: I love being a lesbian. It's a very joyous part of my life.

INTERVIEW

INTERVIEW WITH BILL BELLAMY
Comic, MTV host

SMART SEX: WAS SEX SOMETHING YOU WERE REALLY ANXIOUS TO TRY? HOW DID IT SEEM BEFORE YOU HAD IT?

Bill: It wasn't really until high school. Maybe then it became an issue and guys started talking about it. Like, "Have you ever done it?" or **"I did it!"** I think, if anything, it was a curiosity thing.

SMART SEX: WAS REPUTATION A BIG DEAL?

Bill: I just think that, if you were a guy and involved at that point, you were cool, that was a cool thing. If you were a virgin, that was kind of like, "Woooo! You're still a virgin!" Even if they didn't know you were a virgin, they would put a rumor out.

SMART SEX: DID YOU STILL HAVE FUN WHEN YOU WERE A VIRGIN?

Bill: I think if anything in high school, heavy petting was the big deal. Petting was the best thing. I mean, it's one of those things where you get all riled up, and everything is hot and juicy. But you just don't go all the way. You know, you feel like you are because it gets really intense sometimes.

SMART SEX: WHEN YOU STARTED HAVING SEX, WHAT WAS YOUR BIGGEST WORRY?

Bill: The major thing that I thought about in high school was pregnancy. Pregnancy was the big deal. "Don't get a girl pregnant." If that happened, it would be like, not only are you having sex, but you got busted. Maybe your parents did not know that you were having sex, but they'd know now. 'Cause it wasn't like something that you wanted to come out and tell your parents: "Hey, you know what I'm doing, right?"

SMART SEX: HOW COME YOU WOULDN'T TELL YOUR PARENTS ABOUT IT?

Bill: You think your parents only want you to think about school and the importance of getting ahead in life—not getting close to some girl, or some girl getting close to some guy.

SMART SEX: WOULD YOU HAVE TURNED TO YOUR PARENTS IF YOU HAD TROUBLE, LIKE IF YOU GOT A GIRL PREGNANT OR IF YOU GOT AN STD?

Bill: Yeah. I think they would have been supportive and said, "How did this happen? And this is what we are going to do. And don't do it again."

SMART SEX: HOW IS SEX DIFFERENT WHEN YOU ARE IN LOVE?

Bill: It's enhanced because you have emotions that bring the relationship to another level, as opposed to just sleeping with someone— that's more a physical act.

SMART SEX: DO YOU THINK THAT GUYS WANT LOVE JUST AS MUCH AS GIRLS?

Bill: Oh, yeah, no doubt.

SMART SEX: WHEN MEN AND WOMEN FOOL AROUND, HOW SHOULD THEY LAY OUT THE BOUNDARIES ABOUT HOW FAR TO GO?

Bill: A guy and a girl should be full consenting adults.

When they are not communicating and just going on emotions, they can make a mistake. You talk about it. I think that a guy and a girl should talk about what they are feeling. Maybe a guy should say, "I really want to make love to you," and she says, "I want to make love to you, too." Then that's something different. As opposed to you just trying to make the moves, make love to a girl, and she's like, "No, what are you doing?" So I think you need to talk.

SMART SEX: WHAT'S THE TOUGHEST LESSON YOU'VE LEARNED ABOUT SEX?

Bill: That not all women are

orgasmic. I just think that a lot of women fake it. I think they do it because they don't want to make this man feel like less than he thinks he is. Talk to your man, girl. And maybe you won't have to fake it. Tell him what you really need. If you fake it, you are rewarding him for something that is not right.

SMART SEX: WHEN'S A GOOD TIME TO TALK TO YOUR PARTNER? BEFORE, DURING, AFTER SEX—OVER BRUNCH?

Bill: I think at all of those times. Say, "Okay, we've been there, but these are some of the things that I'd like to include in this wonderful thing that we are doing here."

And then it just gets better and better.

I think that the more you communicate, the easier it is, because you've broken that barrier once you start talking. I think that it's very hard for girls, because they are always worried about a man's

ego. "If I tell him I don't like that, he's going to think that he's a wimp."

SMART SEX: YOU WERE SAYING THAT TODAY IS A SCARY AGE. HOW DO YOU PROTECT YOURSELF AGAINST STDS?

Bill: Ah, well, first of all: condoms. Second: monogamy. That's about it. You have to educate yourself on what's out there, what you're up against. And definitely get tested. I mean, you can only do so much, but you should definitely do all that you can.

Bill: I think that they should. I know that it's hard. A lot of people are afraid, but I think that you owe it to yourself to know. And then if you are negative, you have good reason to stay that way.

SMART SEX: WHAT'S THE BEST AND WORST THING ABOUT CONDOMS?

Bill: Protection is the best thing. The worst thing is that sometimes it can be slightly awkward.

Running around, the whole "You have one?" thing. You just deal. It's a fact of life.

SMART SEX: DO YOU FIND THAT WOMEN ARE COOL ABOUT CONDOMS?

Bill: Today women are like, "Yeah, I got my own." You know, they're like, "Don't even think about coming here if you don't have one," that type of thing. Before it used to be all up to the guy, but now girls are like,

'You don't have one? I have my own.' Okay, thank you. I think that's very, very good.

SMART SEX: SO IT DOESN'T MEAN THAT THE GIRL IS EASY IF SHE HAS CONDOMS?

Bill: No, I think it shows that she's very responsible.

SMART SEX: LAST QUESTION: HOW WOULD YOU DEFINE SMART SEX?

Bill: Definitely condoms and communication.

If you don't want a kid right now, it's important to plan out your pregnancy prevention strategy. Most birth control methods do not protect you from AIDS and other STDs. Condoms are the shining exception. Used with spermicide, condoms provide both effective birth control and STD protection. The Pill and other hormonal methods provide even better birth control, but then you need to think about adding condoms for protection from disease. See Chapter 8 for safer-sex guidance. Read on to learn about your baby-prevention options.

7 | BIRTH CONTROL

ALWAYS VS. SOMETIMES

WHEN CHOOSING A METHOD OF BIRTH CONTROL, KEEP IN MIND TWO BIG CATEGORIES:

1. Hormonal birth control that stays in your or your partner's body all the time and affects that body all the time, twenty-four/seven. (This includes the Pill, Norplant, and Depo-Provera, which are all explained in this chapter.) If you have sex often and regularly, and if you find that you or your partner doesn't feel any bad side effects from the hormones, this method might be right for you.

2. Birth control that is just used during the sexual encounter (condom, diaphragm, spermicide). If you don't have sex often or regularly, or just don't want to take any of the medications listed above, then go this route.

Evaluate your needs and your lifestyle. Discuss them with your doctor. Compare notes with friends, even. Hopefully, you'll find something that's safe, effective and works for both of you. If you and your partner agree on your contraception strategy, you'll have an easier time sticking to it. Now for the lowdown on the most commonly-used methods and how well they work—or don't. The success rates you'll see will sometimes vary. This is because they are "actual use" rates, meaning they are based on typical users and must take into account human error and carelessness as well as technical failures.

ABSTINENCE

WHO CONTROLS IT: *Male and female.*

WHAT IT IS: *Refraining from vaginal intercourse.*

HOW IT WORKS: *You and your partner agree to nix or put off sex. It helps to agree with each other on boundaries, like, "Let's only do stuff above the belt for now," "No sex for at least six months," "I want to wait until I'm married" or "Protected oral sex, but no vaginal sex."*

COST: *Free, depending on level of sex play.*

WHERE TO GET IT: *No tools required.*

DISEASE PROTECTION: *100 percent, though this number can be lower depending on level of sex play. Unprotected oral and anal sex and other kinds of touching can spread STDs (see Chapter 9). So you might still need condoms or other barrier protection.*

EFFECTIVENESS AGAINST PREGNANCY: *100 percent.*

SIDE EFFECTS: *None, except maybe a buildup of sexual tension. You can relieve this through solo or mutual masturbation. Exercise helps let off steam, too.*

PROS: *No sex-related anxieties, responsibilities or expenses: no pregnancy, birth control, STDs. Also frees you from the emotional risks that can go with such an intense level of intimacy.*

CONS: *Peer pressure, sexual frustration, burning curiosity.*

Note: The oldest, simplest, most effective form of contraception.

CONDOM

WHO CONTROLS IT: *Male.*

WHAT IT IS: *Thin latex covering that fits snugly over an erect penis.*

HOW IT WORKS: *Prevents the exchange of body fluids (and STDs).*

COST: *Around $3 for box of three, $7 for box of twelve.*

WHERE TO GET IT: *Pharmacy, grocery store, convenience store.*

DISEASE PROTECTION: *Best weapon against STDs, including HIV.*

EFFECTIVENESS AGAINST PREGNANCY: *88 percent on the average,
   higher when used carefully.*

SIDE EFFECTS: *For an unlucky few, latex allergies or sensitivity to
   Nonoxynol-9 spermicide.*

PROS: *Cheap, accessible, tidy, prolongs male erection. Relieves STD anxiety.*

CONS: *Less reliable than other contraception methods when used alone.*

Some claim reduces sensation. Requires interruption of sex to put it on.

*Note: Use latex with water-based (not oil-based) lube. Some condoms have
spermicide, including Nonoxynol-9, on the outside, which adds to effectiveness.
There are condoms made from natural animal products, which are all right for
pregnancy protection, but do not prevent against STDs. Condoms are best combined
with another method of birth control. When putting on a condom, you must
leave room at the tip, with no air pocket, to catch semen. Be sure to hold the condom
at its base when removing. Condoms should be stored in a cool place; time and
heat can hurt them. (See page 154 in Chapter 8 for lots more info on condoms.)*

*(Note to guys: Since the rest of these contraceptives are female-controlled, the
"you" usually means the woman. But it behooves you to know what they are and
how they work. Unless, of course, you like to be called "Daddy.")*

SPERMICIDE

WHO CONTROLS IT: Female, unless male uses spermicide-enhanced condoms.

WHAT IT IS: Jelly, cream, foam, or thin tissuelike squares (vaginal
contraceptive film) or waxy suppository that melts with body heat.
Active ingredient is usually Nonoxynol-9.

HOW IT WORKS: Chemically kills sperm and many other organisms.

COST: $9 tube of jelly yields about twelve applications. Suppositories
go for around $7 for a box of twenty. Vaginal contraceptive film
runs about $6 for twelve applications.

WHERE TO GET IT: Over the counter at pharmacy.

DISEASE PROTECTION: Helps fight STDs, HIV and other infectious organisms.

EFFECTIVENESS AGAINST PREGNANCY: Up to twenty-one pregnancies per
hundred users when used alone. Not great.

SIDE EFFECTS: Some people are sensitive to the chemicals in spermicides,
finding them itchy and irritating.

PROS: Only birth control method besides the male and female condom that
offers some disease protection. Great combined with the condom.

CONS: Not effective contraception or disease control when used alone.
Also, can get a bit messy.

*Note: Spermicidal foams, sheets and suppositories seem to work better than creams
or jellies (which are generally designed to be used with a diaphragm). You have to
insert/apply spermicide immediately prior to sex—if you put in too early, it doesn't
work. Tastes disgusting, so if oral sex is on the menu, do so before applying.*

Bonus Fact
A healthy sperm can swim about
three to seven inches per hour.

DIAPHRAGM

WHO CONTROLS IT: Female.

WHAT IT IS: A shallow bowl made of soft rubber, looks like a miniature Frisbee.

HOW IT WORKS: Flexible disk is folded in half (sort of like a small taco shell) and inserted into vagina with spermicide cream or jelly, where it opens back up and covers the cervix. Blocks sperm from entering uterus. Must be kept in place for at least six hours after intercourse.

COST: $20 plus the cost of a clinic visit and spermicide (about $9 a tube).

WHERE TO GET IT: Through gynecologist, health services or clinic.

DISEASE PROTECTION: Minor disease protection due to spermicide.

EFFECTIVENESS AGAINST PREGNANCY: 82–94 percent.

SIDE EFFECTS: Spermicide can be an irritant. In some women, the diaphragm can press against the urinary tract and cause urinary tract infections (UTIs, which make you feel the pressure to urinate constantly and cause a burning feeling when you go; see page 300 for more info.

PROS: Can be inserted up to six hours ahead of time to avoid interruption of sex play. Provides a good alternative to hormonal methods.

CONS: It takes practice to put in a diaphragm. Can interrupt sex if you don't plan ahead. You may ooze spermicide after sex. Does not give full STD protection.

Note: You have to be examined by health care practitioner and fitted for the right sized diaphragm, like shoes. You can also change sizes over time, especially if you grow, or gain or lose weight. You must always add more spermicide (though you can leave the diaphragm in) each time you have sex.

CERVICAL CAP

WHO CONTROLS IT: Female.

WHAT IT IS: Much like diaphragm, but smaller.

Looks like an overgrown rubber thimble.

HOW IT WORKS: Fits over just the tip of the cervix. Spermicide along
with the cap's special design create a suction bond over the cervix.
Blocks sperm from entering the uterus. Cap must be kept in place
for at least six hours after intercourse.

COST: About $30, plus cost of clinic visit, plus spermicide (about $9 a tube).

WHERE TO GET IT: Not available everywhere. Ask doctor or health practitioner.

DISEASE PROTECTION: Some disease protection, thanks to spermicide.

EFFECTIVENESS AGAINST PREGNANCY: 82–94 percent.

SIDE EFFECTS: None, for most users. Spermicide can irritate.

The cap can cause an odor when left in too long. Some doctors think it
increases risk for toxic shock syndrome (see Glossary for more info on
toxic shock syndrome). For some women, there's an increased risk of
urinary tract, yeast, and other vaginal infections.

PROS: Can be worn for up to forty-eight hours at a time. Helps avoid
interruption of sex play. Less messy than diaphragm and doesn't require
additional spermicide for repeat intercourse.

CONS: Does not provide effective disease prevention. Also,
some women have trouble inserting and removing the cap.

*Note: The cap only comes in four sizes, so it doesn't fit all women. A health
practitioner needs to size you and give you a lesson in cervical cap use. Cap
should be checked after sex to make sure it's in place. To reduce odor and risk
of infection, the cap can be soaked in a cup of water plus a teaspoon of lemon
juice or cider vinegar.*

BIRTH CONTROL PILLS, THE PILL, ORAL CONTRACEPTIVES

WHO CONTROLS IT: Female.

WHAT IT IS: Hormone pills you take at the same time every day.

HOW IT WORKS: Releases a hormone that stops egg from developing in the ovary. This is what your body does naturally during pregnancy. In a way, you are tricking your body into acting like it's pregnant. Hence the pregnancy-like side effects for some women.

COST: About $20–$30 per menstrual cycle, plus price of regular doctor visits.

WHERE TO GET IT: Through a doctor or family planning clinic.

DISEASE PROTECTION: None.

EFFECTIVENESS AGAINST PREGNANCY: Used correctly, nearly 100 percent. More like 97 percent for most users. Effectiveness reduced when you skip a day or two. Effectiveness sometimes reduced when taken with antibiotics.

SIDE EFFECTS: Some women experience tender breasts, bigger breasts, bloating, nausea, mood changes, irregular bleeding, headaches, increased acne. For others, the Pill reduces headaches, makes skin clearer. Some women gain weight, but that might be due to an increased craving for carbohydrates. Many Pill users feel few or no side effects at all. The options are vast, and there are many Pill varieties out there with different levels and combinations of hormone. Your doctor might have you try a couple different brands over time until you settle on the one that works best for you. See note on the next page for long-term side effects.

PROS: The most effective contraceptive available. Makes your period short, light, regular, almost cramp-free. Great to use with condoms.

CONS: No disease protection. You need to remember to take your pills regularly. Affects your body every day, even if you are not having sex.

Note: There is an oral contraceptive called the minipill made of only one hormone instead of two, but you must take it at the same time every day for it to work. If you go off the Pill, you are immediately vulnerable to pregnancy. The whole reason you have to take it every day is that you have to beef up the new hormone levels continuously and consistently. Once you stop, hormone levels return to normal pretty quickly.

NORPLANT

WHO CONTROLS IT: *Female*

WHAT IT IS: *Six match-size capsules implanted under the skin of the upper arm. A two-rod version has been approved by the FDA, but was not yet on the market at the time of this printing.*

HOW IT WORKS: *Capsules are placed in a fan shape under anesthetized skin. Over time—up to five years—capsules slowly release a hormone into the body that prevents ovulation and impedes sperm by thickening cervical mucus.*

COST: *Norplant costs about $365, which works out to be cheaper than birth control pills over five years.*

WHERE TO GET IT: *Through a physician or family planning clinic.*

DISEASE PROTECTION: *None.*

EFFECTIVENESS AGAINST PREGNANCY: *Excellent. Only about 1 in every 1000 women will get pregnant in the first year of use.*

SIDE EFFECTS: *Discomfort around capsules for a day or two. After that, they shouldn't bother you, though some women have had problems with removal by poorly trained physicians. About 75 percent of women using Norplant have irregular menstruation the first year, and some have serious spotting between periods. Some experience headaches, weight gain, mood changes, acne. With the exception of bleeding irregularities, side effects are similar to those with other hormonal methods.*

PROS: *Extremely convenient. Great for people who have trouble taking the Pill religiously. No little packets to carry around. Studies show that teenagers are much less likely to get pregnant with Norplant than with birth control pills. Lower level of hormone than the Pill and no estrogen. Goes well with condoms.*

CONS: *No disease protection. Affects your body every day, even if you are not having sex. If it would bother you to have more bleeding or spotting days, then don't use Norplant.*

Note: Some people are concerned about women getting inappropriately coerced into using Norplant, especially teenagers and poor women.

DEPO-PROVERA

WHO CONTROLS IT: *Female.*

WHAT IT IS: *Contraceptive hormone in the form of a shot.*

HOW IT WORKS: *You get injected with synthetic progestin, which gradually seeps into your bloodstream and is effective birth control over the following three months. Prevents ovulation. Makes lining of cervix unfriendly to sperm.*

COST: *About $120 a year, making it comparatively cheap.*

WHERE TO GET IT: *Physician or family planning clinic.*

DISEASE PROTECTION: *None.*

EFFECTIVENESS AGAINST PREGNANCY: *99 percent.*

SIDE EFFECTS: *Most evidence says that Depo causes fewer health problems than the Pill, and most women who use it are happy with it. However, some women have menstrual irregularities, depression, hair loss, acne, breast tenderness and/or weight gain. There is more mention of a possible breast cancer link with this hormonal method than with others. If there is breast cancer history in your family, don't use it.*

PROS: *Extremely convenient. Great for people who have trouble taking the Pill religiously.*

CONS: *No disease protection. Affects your body every day, even if you are not having sex.*

Note: As with Norplant, Depo may sometimes be pushed too hard on teenagers, low-income women and women of color. Unlike other hormonal methods, once you get the shot, you can't change your mind and reverse it. It will still serve as birth control for at least three months. And if you feel side effects, you might keep feeling them for up to eight months.

Contraception Misconceptions

Just to clear up wrong ideas about hormonal birth control . . .

•If you are on the Pill or another hormonal method over a long period of time, you do not need to "take a hormone break" to clear out your system. You can use the method long-term and take a break when you want a baby.

•Hormonal methods do not hurt your odds of having a baby later.

THE PILL, NORPLANT, AND DEPO-PROVERA IN THE LONG TERM

If your mom took the Pill in the 70s, it was a much different, more hormone-heavy prescription than what's out now. No one really knows all the effects of using daily hormones for a long time, but improvements have been made and more are in the works. Hormonal methods, which include the Pill, Norplant and Depo-Provera, have been linked to strokes and blood clots, but mostly in users over 35. You should not use a hormonal method if you have high blood pressure. If you're a smoker under age 35, you should try to cut down or quit the habit—and tell your doctor so he or she can keep it in mind when choosing your prescription. There are controversial and conflicting studies linking hormonal birth control to various cancers. Some say you run an increased risk of breast cancer, but there is no clear evidence either way. Other studies say the Pill may protect you against ovarian cancer.

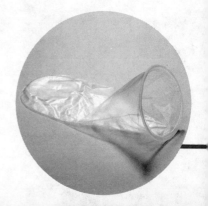

FEMALE CONDOM (A.K.A. Reality IN THE U.S., Femidom IN OTHER COUNTRIES)

WHO CONTROLS IT: *Female.*

WHAT IT IS: *Thin loose polyurethane sleeve, closed on one end and with a ring at each end.*

HOW IT WORKS: *The closed end goes inside the vagina, covering the cervix, and the other rests outside, creating a little plastic tunnel. Blocks semen (and germs, viruses) from touching vagina.*

COST: *About $2.50 each.*

WHERE TO GET IT: *Over the counter at pharmacy.*

DISEASE PROTECTION: *Great for preventing STDs, including HIV.*

EFFECTIVENESS AGAINST PREGNANCY: *82–94 percent.*

SIDE EFFECTS: *None.*

PROS: *Only birth control method besides the male condom that offers effective disease protection. Good alternative for women whose lovers refuse to wear a condom or have trouble functioning while wearing a condom.*

CONS: *Not cheap. Some people find it visually strange.*

Note: Available since 1992, a relative newcomer to the birth control game.

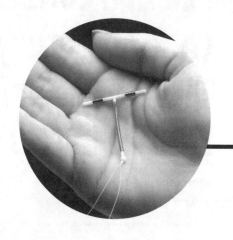

EMERGENCY CONTRACEPTION

If you're female and have had
unprotected sex within the past
seventy-two hours and definitely
do not want to become pregnant,
you can ask your doctor about the
morning-after pill. (See Chapter 11
for more information on this option.)

ALSO OUT THERE

IUD

The IUD (intrauterine device) is a small device placed in the uterus and attached to a string that comes out the cervix. There are two IUD models available in the U.S.: ParaGard (plastic with copper) and Progestasert (plastic with progesterone). The ParaGard is FDA-approved for 10 years, while the Progestasert must be replaced annually. An IUD works by interfering with the movement and union of the sperm and egg, and by creating an inflammation in the uterus that prevents implantation. The IUD was very popular in the 60s and 70s as an alternative to the Pill. But the models used at the time were suspected of causing many cases of pelvic inflammatory disease (PID—a serious infection in the inner reproductive organs that can cause infertility). Now there are only two kinds of IUDs available, both FDA approved. IUDs are the most widely used reversible method of birth control in the world, but they pose a relatively high risk of PID in the presence of other infection, like chlamydia or gonorrhea. In other words, if you are at risk of being exposed to STDs, the IUD is not the best method for you. The IUD is popular with women in long-term mutually monogamous relationships and with ones who have completed their families. Ask your doctor for more information.

SURGERY

There are also surgical procedures for both men and women that can make you permanently sterile and baby-free. These are expensive. And you'll still need to worry about STD protection. If you go the surgical route, then change your mind and want kids later, you're in for a rough ride. Reversing these procedures means more surgery and no guarantee of success. Surgical sterilization is more common among older, monogamous people who have already had all the children they want.

PULLING OUT (A.K.A. COITUS INTERRUPTUS)

This is one of the oldest and most common methods of birth control, probably because it requires no special tools or preparation. It's almost like using nothing—and is almost as ineffective. Pulling out offers no protection against disease and has a very high failure rate. Guys may say they won't come inside a girl, but that's a big promise. Though most guys have the best intentions, in the heat of the moment they may be unable or unwilling to pull out before they shoot the sperm-filled (and possibly STD-carrying) load.

But even if men do manage to pull out before firing the rocket, *a woman can still get pregnant.* Soon after the penis becomes hard, a few drops of fluid (precome) drip out—usually unnoticed. Sperm (as well as STDs) can be in that little droplet. Look at the period at the end of this sentence. Know how many sperm can fit in there? 278. If just a decimal-point-sized amount of come or precome touches a girl's vagina, the sperm can swim all the way to the fallopian tubes and start a baby. That's the main reason pulling out is risky, and why you shouldn't get in even a few strokes before putting on a condom.

THOMAS, 18: I've tried pulling out, and I hate it. Just when I'm about to come, I pull it out. It doesn't feel as good. So, a lot of times when I've said I was going to pull out, I just wouldn't. I was just too worked up, so I just didn't. Then she'd ask, "Did you come in me?" and I was like, "No."

The other reason why coitus interruptus is not a great method is the enormous anxiety it causes. The guy has to concentrate and get ready to go against all his instincts. The girl has to worry if and when he's going to make his exit. The guy might also have to pull out before she climaxes, which can be extremely frustrating.

VIRGINIA, 20: Pulling out, that's what we did before I went on the Pill. I felt sorry for him. But a couple of times I would freak out while we were having sex and literally just spaz, because all of a sudden I'd have this flash of me getting pregnant. And I'd be like, "Stop, stop, stop, stop." He'd be like, "Okay."

RHYTHM METHOD, ETC.

What else doesn't work? Following the woman's cycle and trying to predict "safe times." This is called the rhythm method. Actually, there are no true "safe times." Pregnancy can occur if you have sex a few days before or after ovulation (see explanation of menstrual cycle in the Glossary). Women, especially young women, don't always ovulate smack in the middle of cycles and right between periods— ovulation could happen very early or late in your menstrual cycle. An egg can live in the woman for a day or two after ovulation and the sperm can live for up to three days, waiting for an egg to come along. So it's hard to know when you're definitely not at risk. Fertility awareness has superseded the calendar-watching of the old rhythm method and is a little more successful at helping you monitor and predict the menstrual cycle (ask your doctor), but you have to be superdiligent, it's never a sure thing and if offers no protection at all against STDs.

A Little History of Birth Control

Almost 3,500 years ago, ancient Egyptian men wore condoms as attractive penis covers. The ancient Egyptians also reportedly inserted honey, crocodile dung and acacia leaves into the vagina as a method of birth control. By the eighteenth century, condoms were being made from sheep intestines. In Victorian England, sexual stimulation was believed to shorten one's life (and oral sex was thought to cause mouth cancer), so a once-a-month bonk was considered more than enough. On long desert journeys, Arabs used to put pebbles in camels' uteruses to prevent them from getting pregnant when they hooked up with the boy camels. Today, the IUD (intrauterine device) is based on the same theory. Women in ancient Sumatra used to mold opium into cuplike shapes and insert them to block the cervix. Casanova wrote of a similar trick—a contraceptive diaphragm made with half a lemon. The citric acid served as a bonus spermicide.

Don't try these at home.

CREEPY-MAN ALERT

Some men absolutely refuse to wear a condom. If you're a woman and that's your man's scenario, you need contraception you can control without his cooperation. Some protection (from pregnancy, if not from STDs) is better than none at all. But in such cases, perhaps you ought to rethink the relationship.

There are definitely guys out there who care about their own health and yours.

CREEPY-WOMAN ALERT

Since most forms of birth control are female-controlled, it's easy to just assume the gal is taking care of business. If for some reason you are a guy who is not using condoms, you should ask her what protection she is using. Not to promote mistrust or anything, but if she says, "Oh, don't worry, I'm on the Pill," or, "My diaphragm is in," ask a few more questions to make sure ("What kind of pill are you on?" "When did you put your diaphragm in?"). Sometimes a woman lies and evades responsibility for the same reason a guy might resist condoms—she's turned on, she doesn't want to think about the consequences at the moment. A girl might even want to get pregnant—but that is a decision you two should make together and after much thought.

KARLEY, 17: I have a friend who tried to get pregnant, and now she's pregnant and has ruined the guy's life. Just fully ruined it. On purpose. I think they used birth control once in a while, but they weren't really consistent. Then she said she was pregnant when she wasn't. So they just kept having sex, and he was thinking, Okay, she's pregnant. Then she got pregnant for real. They went to the doctor and it was true. They're not sure whether they're going to give the baby up for adoption or keep it. It depends on how their relationship goes.

We live in an age with plenty of pregnancy prevention options that are pretty easy to get and easy to use. It's called "birth control" because you can take control. So please do.

The only completely safe sex is abstinence or solo sex, but many people still choose to have sex despite the risk of contracting sexually transmitted diseases. Safer sex allows you to keep these risks to a minimum. Safer sex goes beyond condoms. It means talking. It means keeping your eyes wide open—for STD symptoms, for honesty from your partner. It means getting regular tests and checkups. It means thinking about the future even when you're getting hot, bothered and sweaty with someone right now. And of course, it means being handy with the love glove. (For detailed information about the diseases you are trying to avoid, see Chapters 9 and 10.)

SAFER SEX

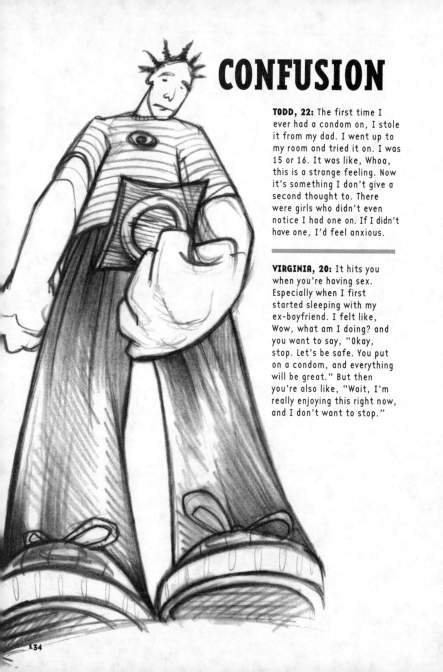

CONFUSION

TODD, 22: The first time I ever had a condom on, I stole it from my dad. I went up to my room and tried it on. I was 15 or 16. It was like, Whoa, this is a strange feeling. Now it's something I don't give a second thought to. There were girls who didn't even notice I had one on. If I didn't have one, I'd feel anxious.

VIRGINIA, 20: It hits you when you're having sex. Especially when I first started sleeping with my ex-boyfriend. I felt like, Wow, what am I doing? and you want to say, "Okay, stop. Let's be safe. You put on a condom, and everything will be great." But then you're also like, "Wait, I'm really enjoying this right now, and I don't want to stop."

Technically speaking, safer sex means encasing and draping various bits of your anatomy in latex during sex play so as not to get an STD. Using a condom anytime a penis penetrates a lover's mouth, vagina or anus is the basic starting point.

But beyond that, there are many questions you need to ask yourself: What sexual activities am I comfortable with? How much barrier protection do I think I need? How much contact with body fluids is okay? Then you put your game plan into action.

Smart Sex Poll

When asked to define *safer sex*, these 16- to 24-year-olds had the right idea: 54 percent said, "Protecting yourself and your partner from STDs." 32 percent said, "Always wearing a condom." 14 percent said, "Abstinence." But others came up with answers like, "Use birth control," "Know your partner, know your partner's history," "Love your partner," "The opposite of what I do," and the plain but honest, "I don't know."

If you are using birth control other than a condom, you are *not* practicing safer sex, you are merely reducing the chances of pregnancy. Most forms of birth control don't protect against HIV or other STDs, so if you're using the Pill, Norplant, Depo-Provera or a diaphragm, you should also be using condoms. (For more on birth control, see Chapter 7.)

OVER SAFER SEX

The Safety Equations

PLASTIC WRAP

FINGER COT

DENTAL DAM

SURGICAL GLOVE

BARRIER PROTECTION FROM DISEASE ONLY

PILL

DIAPHRAGM

NORPLANT

**PROTECTION FROM PREGNANCY,
NOT PROTECTION FROM DISEASE**

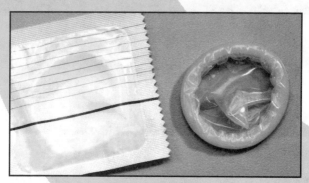

MALE CONDOMS

FEMALE CONDOMS

PROTECTION FROM DISEASE AND PREGNANCY

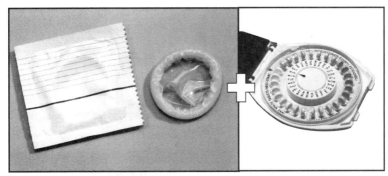

MALE CONDOM **PILL**

MALE CONDOM

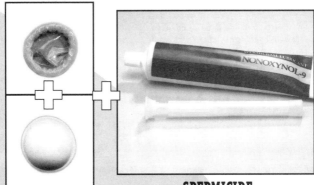

DIAPHRAGM **SPERMICIDE**

**EXTRA PROTECTION FROM PREGNANCY
AND DISEASE PROTECTION**

PRIY, 23: Yeah, safer sex is very important, but realistically, it's hard to know what safe sex is. It just seems so complicated. I mean, what is that fine line between what is safe, what is safer, what is safest? And sometimes I feel it is all a compromise and inevitably you're gonna do something that you're gonna question yourself on afterward.

MELISSA, 23: I think that people are always looking to other people to figure out what's safe and what's not. And it's not black and white. There's nobody who has the rules 100 percent right. I never talk about what I practice as safer or not because then I'm afraid somebody will take that to heart and will do exactly what I do. And that's bad. You need to come to your own conclusions about what you believe to be safer and safest.

Clearly the condom is the main tool of the safer-sex trade. But there are also latex products to cover fingers, hands, the vagina. And check out the risk chart below. Different forms of sex play have different risks. You need to decide not only which activities you're willing to do, but also how much you're going to cover up with barrier protection. There's no single perfect definition for *safer sex*. It's called *safer* sex, as opposed to *safe* sex, because most forms of sex play carry at least some risk.

VARIATIONS ON SAFER SEX

If you're a woman sleeping with a woman or a man sleeping with a man, or if you're anyone having only anal sex or oral sex, you don't have to worry about pregnancy, but you still need barrier protection from disease. Finding out about your partner's history is a good first step toward protecting yourself. But if you are not using condoms and latex products, you are not practicing safer sex. One of you might be carrying an STD and not know it. And as crummy as it sounds, one of you might be lying about the number of lovers (past or present), the nature of past contact ("Oh, we made out, but we never had sex . . . ") or other risky behavior, past or present. Why not just use the proper gear and play it safer?

RISK: A RELATIVE ISSUE

Most forms of sexual contact carry a certain amount of risk, some more than others (Chapters 9 and 10 outline the major sexually transmitted diseases and the ways they are transmitted). When assessing risk, past or future, first think about the following:

1) *Which body fluids you might encounter.* Saliva is a low-risk body fluid. Vaginal fluid carries some STD risk, blood and semen are more dangerous.

2) *What amount of body fluid you might encounter.* Deep kissing passes on more saliva than a little peck. Unprotected oral sex on a man to orgasm will mean a lot of semen in your mouth. Oral sex that stops before orgasm means a little semen (the "precome" that is released), but there's no way to be absolutely sure that he won't come in your mouth, even if he promises and tries not to.

3) *Where the body fluid is going.* Anal sex is particularly risky—either because the rectum is more vulnerable to little tears or because it has a higher concentration of blood vessels. Unprotected vaginal sex is more risky than unprotected oral sex. Blood or semen on the skin should be safe, but if there are open cuts or sores, skin is more vulnerable. Shared needles can obviously transmit fluids right into the bloodstream.

4) *Amount of genital contact.* Herpes, genital warts (HPV), syphilis and crabs can all be passed on through skin contact, even if you don't have sex. Symptoms or genital sores that might indicate these STDs sometimes go unnoticed, even by the person who has them.

Some people like to look at STD risk as a continuum or a series of steps that climb from least risky to most risky. You need to think hard about how much risk you want to take and where you choose to draw your lines. For some people, creating an all-or-nothing situation sets them up for failure. It's essential that you set your limits and be prepared to keep to them. And you definitely shouldn't be considering these questions for the first time in the heat of the moment.

ASSESSING STD RISK

EXTREMELY LOW OR NO RISK

- abstinence
- fantasy, talking dirty
- hugging, caressing
- masturbation
- dry kissing
- massaging
- petting (above the waistline)

MINIMAL RISK

- French kissing
- coming on unbroken skin

LOW RISK

- mutual masturbation
  (if there are no cuts on
  hands, or ulcers or lesions on
  genitals, of either partner)
  oral sex on a woman,
  using latex or plastic wrap
- oral sex on a man
  wearing a condom
- vaginal intercourse with
  a condom
- anal intercourse
  with a condom

RISKY

- unprotected oral sex
  on a woman
- unprotected oral sex
  on a man

HIGH RISK

- unprotected vaginal sex
- unprotected anal sex

STDs infect people of every sexual
orientation, income bracket, race,
zodiac sign. STDs don't care
who you are; they only care what
you do. And sexual behavior
and history do not show up on
someone's face. Many people with
STDs look and feel perfectly fine.
Your lover may not even know he
or she has an infection or virus.
Do not make life-or-death choices
based on appearances. This
doesn't mean you should become
paranoid and run screaming from
the bedroom. It means you should
(as doctors do) treat every person
as if they have HIV or another
STD. Then decide how you
want to protect each other.

THE HE-OR-SHE-LOOKS-CLEAN-TO-ME TRAP

BRADFORD, 21: When we talked, we kept running into the subject of sex, and we also covered the not-so-good things. I think it was in the back of both our minds to cover that stuff before we had sex.

DISCUSSING THE PAST

CATHERINE, 19: With any future partners, I want to know their sexual history. It's so awkward in the college scene. In the past, I just didn't ask, but that left me wondering. I regret not knowing.

Do you know the unedited, NC-17 version of your partner's sexual history? Do you know all of his/her partners' histories? And all *their* lovers' histories? Did anyone in that sexual-history tree practice unsafe sex? Did anyone in there shoot up? You know the saying: You're sleeping with everyone your lover has slept with.

MELISSA, 23: You know, I think the history thing is such a load of s**t, because people lie. I don't think it's important to ask somebody about their history. I think it's important to be comfortable with where you are, and if you're going to have sex, to be ready to practice safer sex. I mean, if some swinging guy has got some really cute girl at home and she says, "So, what is your history or sexuality?" he's going to think about the easiest way to get it over with as quickly as possibly with as little pain as possible and get her into bed. You know? So it's ridiculous. Your best bet is to take care of yourself.

Others take a more cynical but practical approach to this topic.

People do lie. People engage in high-risk behavior and forget it on purpose because they don't want to remember. People do stuff they regret and neglect to tell you the full story because they want you to like them. People edit the number of folks they've slept with and the drugs they or their ex-lovers have done. Sometimes people *believe* they are telling the truth but don't know what that is, because *they* have been lied to in the past. The point is, there are too many unknowns in the mix to not practice safer sex. Make condoms a habit. Here's how.

Scientists used to say it would take 3 years
for symptoms of HIV infection to surface.
Then they said it would take 5 years.
Then up to 12 years. Now they won't say.

Last night,
Sara and Miguel
slept together.

Tiny footnote: This didn't really happen.
The people in these pictures don't know each other. We don't know who slept with who.
We are saying this here because our lawyers made us.

Los científicos solían decir que podían pasar
hasta 3 años para que se manifestaran
los síntomas de la infección del VIH. Luego
dijeron que podían ser 5. Luego hasta
12 años. Ahora ya no quieren decir nada.

Anoche, Sara y Miguel dumieron juntos.

Pequeña nota: en realidad esto no sucedió.
Las personas de estas fotos no se conocen. No sabemos quién se acostó con quién.
Estamos diciendo esto aquí porque nuestros abogados nos obligaron a hacerlo.

**Last year;
they each slept
with three
other people.**

El año pasado, cada uno se acostó con otras 3 personas.

**Each year before that,
those people each
slept with
three other people.**

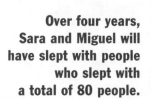

**Over four years,
Sara and Miguel will
have slept with people
who slept with
a total of 80 people.**

Cada año antes de esto,
cada una de esas
personas se acostó con
otras tres personas.

En 4 años, Sara y Miguel
se habrán acostado
con personas que se han
acostado con otras
80 personas en total.

Over 7 years, those people will have slept with 1,460 people.

And over 12 years, those people will have slept with 531,441 people. (It would take another 728 pages to show you all their pictures.)

By the way, in Paris, where Sara and Miguel live, one in 100 people is HIV positive.

You might want to use a condom.

En 7 años, esas personas se habrán acostado con 1.460 personas.

En 12 años, todo ésto implica un total de 531.441 personas. (Necesitaríamos 728 páginas más para mostrar las fotos de todas esas personas).

A propósito, en París, donde viven Sara y Miguel, una persona sobre 100 es seropositiva.

Quizás convendría usar un preservativo.

1 Use a new condom every time you have sex—anal, oral or vaginal. Latex, please. The animal-skin kind only prevents pregnancy, not STDs. When opening a condom package, slide the condom away from where you're tearing the wrapper—this helps prevent damage. If the condom is brittle, sticky (like rubber left out in the sun) or discolored, toss it and find a fresher one.

THE SEVEN STEPS TO CONDOM NIRVANA

2 Put the condom on *after* the penis is erect and *before* the penis even touches any part of the partner's mouth, anus or vagina. If the penis is uncircumcised, pull the foreskin back before putting on the condom.

3 To put the condom on, first pinch the tip to squeeze out all the air. This will be easier if your condom has a convenient "reservoir tip"—a little space built in at the tip to trap the flow of liquid love. If there's no reservoir tip, then create one by pinching the end of the rubber and leaving a little extra space at the top. Air trapped in the tip (no matter what kind of tip) can cause a condom to break. Doing this will also help you figure out which way to put the condom on so it rolls. Place the ring-shape on the head of the penis. Unroll the condom all the way down the penis.

4 The condom is less likely to break if it's well lubricated, so you may want to apply extra lubricant. Some lubes even have spermicide—that goo that helps kill sperm and STD-causing organisms. Just make sure your lubricant is water-based (it'll say so on the label).

5 If you feel a condom break or slip off during sex, stop and put on a new condom.

(CLIP 'N' SAVE!)

6 After ejaculation, and *while the penis is still erect,* hold the base of the condom and carefully withdraw, making sure no semen is spilled (this is one of the most-often flubbed steps). Throw used condom in trash.

7 Store your condoms in a drawer or closet—somewhere cool, dry and out of direct sunlight. Bathrooms, glove compartments and wallets are not great for condoms due to temperature changes. Variance in temperature and rough handling can make latex brittle or gummy, so be nice to your condoms. Most kinds have an expiration date printed on the box. Skip the vintage condoms.

When a condom breaks, it's usually because you or your partner tore it with teeth or fingernails while opening the package or putting it on, or because you flubbed one of steps one through seven. Usually the condom is blameless.

WHICH CONDOMS ARE THE BEST?

The government, as represented by the CDC (Centers for Disease Control), says that all condoms made in this country have to pass stringent tests by the manufacturer. In addition, both imported and domestic condoms are randomly tested by the government to be sure they meet quality-assurance requirements. Therefore, says the CDC, there's no need to worry that you're buying an inferior brand of condom. There is an incredible variety of condoms out there. Start your own personal consumer test with a loved one. Ask friends which brands they like.

SPECIAL FEATURES

CONTOURED: the body of the condom forms a special shape—not just a plain cylinder. Most commonly, contoured condoms get narrower just below the head for a tighter hold and better feel. Or else they get bigger at the head, flaring out a bit.

RIBBED: concentric rings, sort of 3-D, all the way up the shaft. The texture is there "for her pleasure," but most women say they can't tell much of a difference. Ditto for little nubs all over.

RESERVOIR TIP: just what it sounds like, and a good feature to look for. As mentioned before, it's an extension at the top of the condom (looks like a nipple), provided to catch the semen.

Bonus Fact
Testing condoms and getting rid of faulty ones represents a third of condom manufacturing costs.

SPECIAL CONDOMS

Certain condom complaints have inspired alternatives. If any of these sound like what you need, look for them at your drugstore. If you don't see them there, ask the pharmacist if he or she can order some.

POLYURETHANE CONDOMS

A few people are sensitive to latex *(itch, itch)*, so polyurethane can be a nice alternative. There's a fairly new polyurethane *boy* condom called Avanti. It's promoted as being twice as thin as latex, so you can feel more. And it's impervious to oil-based lubricants. Testing showed a higher rate of breakage compared with latex, but the company claims that improvements are in the works. So use at your own risk if latex drives you batty.

THE FEMALE CONDOM

The female condom, called Reality, is also made from polyurethane, and protects against AIDS and other STDs, just like her brother, the guy condom. The female condom looks like an oversized male condom with a ring at each end. One ring goes inside the vagina and holds the thing in place, the other ring remains outside, protecting the vagina from direct contact. A good option for guys who lose their hard-on with regular condoms. A good option for women who want more control of safer sex. However, some users complain that the female condom doesn't stay in place, and the product may require more testing before it is perfected. (See page 125 for more info.)

TESTICLE-COVER CONDOMS

These stay on much better, for even safer safer-sex, and provide better protection from skin-contact STDs like herpes and HPV.

BLACK CONDOMS

Dark-skinned guys might not always feel sexy putting on an ordinary condom, which results in a beige-pink penis. Black (actually very dark brown) condoms are more realistic, less noticeable. Also may be difficult to find. Ask at the drugstore.

EXTRA LARGE

For men who say that regular condoms feel too tight and pinchy. Will also work on the average penis. There's also a condom that's got a large, pouchy top third, meant to allow more friction.

NOVELTY

From glow-in-the-dark to flavored to American-flag-decorated to nub-covered—you can't imagine all the wild mutations. These can really perk up a dull weekday evening. But watch for labels that say NOT FOR USE AS A BIRTH CONTROL DEVICE, which also means not reliable for STD protection.

The Stretch Factor

If a guy ever says he's too well-endowed to wear a condom, let him know that any regular condom can stretch big enough to fit over your whole head. Don't try at home, since you need to breathe. *Do* blow up a condom like a balloon and see how big it gets.

Additional spermicide (suppository, foam, gel, small dissolvable sheets) in the receiver's body (though not in the mouth!) will make sex even safer—the wearer has a better chance of killing sperm and STD-causing organisms. The most common spermicide is Nonoxynol-9, which is

CONDOM CONDIMENTS

also the most highly regarded spermicide for the possible prevention of STDs. Many condoms are treated with Nonoxynol-9 directly (read the box). It lubricates, too. However, it does make some people itch or get a rash. If this is you, try condoms with a different kind of spermicide (look for boxes that don't specify Nonoxynol-9). Or if it's just lubrication you're looking for, buy untreated condoms and use a side of lube (Probe, Astroglide, KY Jelly). As mentioned earlier, spread the lube on the outside of the condom after you put it on. And if you wish, put one pleasure-increasing droplet on the inside before you put it on—not too much, or the condom could slip off.

Enemies of Latex

Do not use any of the following on, around, near or in conjunction with condoms: petroleum jelly (like Vaseline), hand lotion, mineral oil, baby oil, vegetable oil, olive oil, butter, animal fats, whipping cream, chocolate, peanut butter, liqueurs, massage oil, oil-based lubricants, oil-based perfumes, suntan lotion.

Safer sex can be hot, fun and creative. It can bring you and your lover closer together. The hottest way to actually put on a condom is to be really good at it; skill is sexy. Practice on veggies. A guy can put on his own condom, or his partner can put it on for him, staring seductively into his eyes. If you or your partner slips it on really fast, you don't lose any momentum. Or you can ease it on really slowly, saying enticing things as you go.

BRADFORD, 21: If I knew I was going to have sex, to be kind of funny, I'd put a condom on before I'd go anywhere. I got pretty creative. I would perform oral sex while I was putting it on.

Smart Sex Poll

Younger and Wiser
56 percent of sexually active 16- to 18-year-olds play it safe every time, while only 32 percent of 22- to 24-year-olds are as consistent in having safer sex.

MAINTAINING THE THRILL

EDDIE, 22: I'm only just starting to get it down. Even when the person is my best friend, and we've been having sex for six months, it's still embarrassing. It has to be really playful and fun. No one who is nervous is going to put on a condom right. If nothing else, the struggle can make the guy lose his excitement. It really comes down to the issue of insecurity about ourselves. People need to poke and prod themselves to get familiar, they need to take a mirror and examine places they couldn't otherwise see. If they did that, I doubt wrapping themselves and using condoms and other protection would be as traumatizing.

DAVID, 20: I've found it's best to stop and say, "Hey, put this on for me."

KIM, 20: I know how disruptive it can be to halt all the action and just watch the guy put it on. So I've started trying to take a little more control and be more involved in it, because it's for both of us. The guys think it's just for me. You know, "Well, she doesn't want to get pregnant." But it's really for both of us. So if they let me—which most guys do—I put it on them. And that makes it more of an intimate thing. It's also a huge turn-on for some guys.

SEALS IN THE JUICES!

In addition to condoms, there are dental dams—six-inch sheets of latex to place over a woman's vagina when you perform oral sex on her. You can get them at health clinics, AIDS organizations and some drugstores. Some people find they're too thick, or that they slip around. If this is the case for you, try cutting a condom open and laying it flat. A better bet is nonmicrowave plastic wrap. You can even put a little jam on the licker's side and a little lube on the lickee's side for more fun all around.

PRIY, 23: Most of the women I know of who sleep with women don't practice safer sex. There have been a couple of people that I've fooled around with who have, but that's probably because they're in safer sex communities. That's not to say that women don't have a certain concern for their health. I just think that there hasn't really been concrete advice targeted to women who sleep with women. I mean, when was the last time you ever saw an ad like that? So I feel like there's a lack of knowledge about what specifically you need to do to protect yourself.

THE ORAL SEX ISSUE

LENA, 21: I usually don't use a condom for oral sex. I really have to know and like a guy to go down on him.

BRADFORD, 21: I don't think expecting people to use condoms for oral sex is realistic. People don't think they can get STDs from that. I'd hasten to say that most girls won't buy mint condoms.

Unprotected oral sex is unsafe sex. Semen can carry the HIV virus, gonorrhea and other STDs. Vaginal juices can, too, though in lesser amounts. Men and women can spread STDs like herpes and genital warts through skin contact made during oral sex. Some people reduce their STD risk by performing oral sex with condoms (on guys), or with dental dams or nonmicrowave plastic wrap (on women). More (if not most) people rationalize that unprotected oral sex is okay, or they decide that the risk is low enough to take a gamble. In fact, more than three fourths of female college students report never using condoms for oral sex.

But if you are performing oral sex on a guy, you really should use a condom. If you're using condoms for vaginal sex, you are, to some degree, undermining that protection when you perform or receive unprotected oral sex. If using a condom is not realistic for you, the next best thing is to perform oral sex up to a point, and then use your hand instead of your mouth to make him climax. Or switch partway through to regular sex with a condom. But these alternatives are risky (though less so), because even before the guy ejaculates, a little bit of semen comes out—maybe carrying sperm and STDs. Also, it's difficult to predict and control exactly when a guy comes. If you ingest semen, your stomach acids will most likely kill any virus. The danger is that virus-carrying semen could get into any cuts or sores in your mouth. Even brushing your teeth causes lots of tiny cuts in your mouth, so don't brush your teeth right before you head down south on your partner.

WHO'S NOT USING CONDOMS? AND WHY?

Smart Sex Poll

Sexually active young adults who don't use condoms give the following explanations:

39 percent
Faithful to each other, monogamous relationship

18 percent
Using other birth control

13 percent
Doesn't feel good, ruins the mood

1 percent
Inconvenient, a hassle

8 percent
Other

4 percent
Trying to have baby

THESAURUS MOMENT: CONDOM

Jimmy hat, party hat, bush hat, latex, raincoat, joybag, rubber, helmet, balloon, shield, wrapper, sleeve, parachute, scuba gear, diving suit, phallic thimble, bag, love glove, envelope, overcoat, bulletproof vest, umbrella, supergalactic prophylactic.

THOMAS, 18: Once I was with a girl and we were inside my friend's house. She said "Yeah, well, whatever, go and get a condom." I was a real d**k, and I'm not happy about this, but I faked: I went out, and I said that I had a condom, but I didn't. Yeah, and she didn't check it or anything. I shouldn't have lied, but I was real horny, and I didn't want to ask my friend for it or anything. I don't think he even had one. I just wanted to do it. Later I was kind of upset with myself. That was a real d**k move.

CATHERINE, 19: One guy I slept with refused to wear a condom; he had trouble climaxing with one. I felt like all the responsibility was on me. I felt like if I had to ask him to use one, I was being a bitch. He was persistent—he'd give me a little-boy act, like, "Do I have to?"

CHARLIE, 17: I don't really use them at all. It's kinda stupid. I don't know, they kinda just get in the way of the intercourse itself. Oh, my girlfriend and I always talk about using them, and I'm always telling myself that I should definitely start, but when it comes down to it, I never do. That kind of upsets her, too. Once you get into it, you just don't feel like stopping, but I worry about it a lot. She worries, too.

KIM, 20: I didn't even ponder the whole idea that if a guy's so easy that he won't use a condom with me, how many people has he not used them with?

DAVID, 20: Fifty percent of women don't say anything and would let you have sex without a condom. The other 50 percent have one, help you with it, talk about it.

SIMON, 17: A lot of my friends use a condom the first couple of times, then they stop. If the girl's a virgin, I don't really have much to worry about, so I wouldn't use a condom. If a girl's not a virgin, I'll take more precautions.

STDs are a two-way street, and Simon's girl (even if she's a virgin) needs latex protection from any diseases that *he* might be carrying—especially since he's an admitted condom-avoider. And a virgin could have an STD from sex play other than intercourse. All sex involving any males should involve rubber sheaths. Yet this is not the reality.

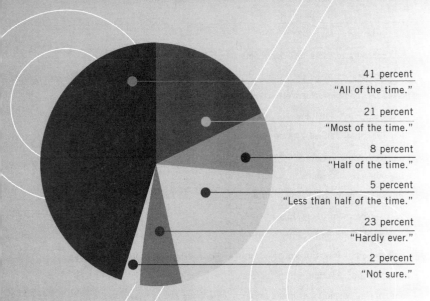

41 percent
"All of the time."

21 percent
"Most of the time."

8 percent
"Half of the time."

5 percent
"Less than half of the time."

23 percent
"Hardly ever."

2 percent
"Not sure."

Smart Sex Poll

Sexually active young adults between the ages of 16 and 24 say they use condoms:

Those who are in the "faithful, monogamous" category, were hopefully tested for STDs at the start of their romance, used condoms for 6 months, then got tested again for HIV.

CHAD, 20: A lot of people say they don't use condoms because it doesn't feel good. But there's more to sex than physical sensation in your genitals.

For all people who complain that condoms don't feel good, try to remember two things:
1. The relief you'll feel from practicing safer sex should give you a mental comfort that outweighs the physical annoyance;
2. For many people, *condoms make sex last longer.* The slight dulling helps the guy keep his erection longer before coming.

BRADFORD, 21: Sex with a condom doesn't feel as good. Any condom company that tells you it does is lying. The feeling is not as intense. But I'd say it makes me last longer. Twenty minutes without a condom equals forty minutes with a condom.

According to some men, condoms sometimes make their erections disappear. The performance pressure, the self-consciousness, the loss of momentum caused by stopping to deal, can all send the flag down the pole. This happens to almost all guys at some point. If you're drunk, it's even more likely. Just use the moment as an opportunity to enjoy all the other forms of sex play. You may find your erection returns before long. You may find it returns another night. If this is happening to your partner, be patient and don't make too big a deal of it (avoid saying "That's okay" 1,000 times in a row). If you're a gal and this keeps happening to your male partner, try the female condom (see above), so the pressure will no longer be on him.

For those people who find condoms to be "inconvenient" and "a hassle": It's also a hassle to get an STD—what with all the antibiotics, the awkward phone calls to ex-partners, the doctor's bills, the potential infertility. It's so much easier to prevent STDs than it is to deal with them. If you have to renegotiate safer sex every single time you sleep with a person, you really should reconsider the relationship.

LENA, 21: Now it's, "Put it on or don't get none." I don't feel the difference. It's psychological. If you concentrate on your lover and not your condom, you'll enjoy sex just as much. And you don't have to worry about the consequences.

GETTING LAZY

Smart Sex Poll

Who's Got the Condoms?
56 percent of sexually active
young adults think that
"safer sex is the responsibility
of both partners equally."
18 percent say that "the
man takes responsibility."
11 percent say that "the
woman takes responsibility."
5 percent say that "neither
takes responsibility."

Many couples are diligent about condom use when they first start having sex. Great. Then, as they fall in love or as sex becomes more routine, the condoms fall by the wayside. It's not like STDs magically go away because of love or monogamy. If you want to switch from condoms to another form of protection, discuss your sexual history with your doctor or a counselor at your STD test-site to assess what tests you should get. (An HIV test is always a good idea.) If your tests are negative, then stick with the condoms consistently until you can take another HIV test in six months. (The virus may be undetectable in your system for up to six months after you acquire it). If that test is also negative, and you have both been monogamous, you can safely switch methods of protection, but stay monogamous and vow to use a condom and to tell each other about it if you ever stray. (See page 214, Chapter 10 to find out more about getting tested.)

Whether or not you worked it out in advance, it's always smart to have some latex in your pocket, bag or briefcase. Not having safer sex just because no one made the essential purchase is a pretty weak excuse—condoms are so widely available. It's probably the only birth control you can get at the local convenience store. Sometimes the options are overwhelming. Sometimes you're just plain embarrassed. Why do so many pharmacies keep condoms back behind the counter, where you have to ask for them? They should be front and center. More places, especially the big chains, are putting condoms out in the aisles, where you can pick and choose, and read the labels at your leisure (spermicides are usually there, too—so you can buy both).

But if condoms are hanging over the cashier's shoulder, then step up proudly, point and say, "Gimme a box of those."

GINA, 24: Who cares what anyone else thinks? This is your life. What's important to you here? What the checkout person thinks?

ANDREW, 25: For men, it's like, "Hey, man, I'm getting some." It's kinda fun.

Remember that Mr./Ms. Behind-the-Counter:

1) sells tons of these things all the time and is way over the giggle factor;

2) will probably never see you again, or if so, will probably not remember you;

3) is happy just to make a sale;

4) hopefully has his/her own stash of condoms at home.

KIM, 20: I used to be embarrassed about it, but now I'm pretty cool with it. I don't really care anymore about buying condoms. I'll just go buy them. The person selling them doesn't really care what I'm doing, and it's not like I'm telling them what I do with the condoms or anything. So I figure, if you're too embarrassed to buy condoms, maybe you're not ready to be having sex.

Women, especially young ones, sometimes have a harder time buying condoms or showing up on a date with condoms because they feel like it makes them seem slutty. Gone are the days where women are supposed to be coy and passive. A lady protects her own health. A guy should be impressed by a woman who takes care of herself (the same way he respects a girl who jogs three times a week). If not, he's living in the caveman days. And by the way, just because a girl has a condom doesn't mean that she's promising to have sex. It's sort of like carrying an umbrella in case of rain.

PUT IT ON

Once you've got a condom, you need
to wear it. Or even tougher, get your
partner to wear it. If he is being
ornery, try these lines.

1 If he says, "I hate condoms; I can't
feel anything," then say, "Sorry, sweetie,
but in my experience, when a man
comes too quickly I don't have a good
time. Condoms make sex last longer."

2 If he says, "Why should I wear a
condom? I'm clean!" then say, "Honey,
how do you know where I've been?"
Then laugh huskily and roll it on him
yourself before he knows what hit him.

3 If your same-sex bedmate says, "We
don't need to worry about that stuff,"
tell him/her that "that stuff" is going
to keep us healthy and happy so we
can do this for years on end.

4 If your partner is of the opposite sex,
you can use fear of pregnancy as your
all-purpose condom-use excuse. Say, "I
just don't want to be a parent right now."

5 If your partner says "You have
condoms? I thought you were a nice
boy/girl," then you can respond, "I
use these because I like to be careful,
and it's nice to be careful."

6 If your partner says nothing (because
he or she doesn't want to make waves
or worries what you'll think), then
bring the subject up yourself. No
need for a big production, just say, "I
believe in safer sex" or "I'd be more
comfortable if we used one of these."

Top Ten Possible National Condom Week Slogans

10. Cover your stump before you hump.
9. Don't be silly, protect your willy.
8. When in doubt, shroud your spout.
7. Don't be a loner, cover your boner.
6. You can't go wrong if you shield your dong.
5. If you're not going to sack it, go home and whack it.
4. If you think she's spunky, cover your monkey.
3. It will be sweeter if you wrap your peter.
2. Wrap it in foil before checking her oil.
1. If you go into heat, package your meat.

Bonus Fact
Although 74 percent of state HIV/AIDS education programs in schools mention condoms, only 9 percent include information on how to use them.

SEX WITHOUT LATEX

If you or your partner has tested negative for HIV and other STDs, use barrier protection for six months thereafter, then get tested for HIV again. If you both come up negative a second time, you can skip the condoms and choose another form of birth control *if* you are truly monogamous. This takes a lot of trust, so talk about it with each other and with your doctors.

INTERVIEW

Smart Sex: Did you talk to your parents about sex when you were growing up?

Idalis: My mom, she was pretty open. I mean, it wasn't like it was taboo. We could talk about it if we wanted to. My mom set me and my sister up in terms of like, "If you're gonna do anything, let me know, and when you come of age, we're gonna go to the gynecologist. And if you want birth control pills, let me know." But I kept to myself about sex.

I was a virgin until I was twenty, so I didn't ask much.

All of my friends had already had sex when I was, like, sixteen; I really didn't get influenced by them.

Smart Sex: No kidding. Did your friends give you a tough time about that?

Idalis: No, but they would talk about it around me and they wouldn't include me in their conversations.

So I felt left out, but in the back of my head, I knew I was doing the right thing.

Like, I was with my sister one time (she had already had sex), and we went to her boyfriend's house and he had a roommate who was a babe—so fine! They'd been dying to hook us up. And he took me in another room. I'm, like, sixteen and he's, like, nineteen, twenty, and he has a water bed. I remember we were laying on the bed and we were kind of laying up, looking up at the ceiling, talking. And my sister was in her boyfriend's room hanging out, talking. And her boyfriend was saying,

"Oh, he is like a Casanova, they're probably doing it right now."

My sister said, "Nope, my sister's a virgin." She knew that I would stick to my guns. And he said, "No way." At that point, everybody had already done it, and he was like, "No way, she is not." And she was like,

'Yup, she's a virgin and she will not do it, trust me.'

So I kissed and hugged and petted and made out and stuff, but we never did it.

SMART SEX: DIDN'T YOU FEEL PRESSURED?

Idalis: You'd be surprised; guys really will follow your lead. I mean, they do push a little bit sometimes. But you really just say, "No, let's not." There was no way—I wasn't going anywhere near that. They knew that, they felt it.

If you don't intend on being sexually active that evening, it's important to communicate your feelings through body language or just saying, "No, I don't want to go upstairs." Make sure that if being alone with some sexy music on in his apartment is very sexually enticing to you or him, that you just don't put yourself in that position. Just don't put yourself in positions where you feel like you can't turn around and go, where it feels really uncomfortable to say no. Or keep it in a public place.

SMART SEX: THAT'S GOOD ADVICE. HOW ABOUT THE BIG MOMENT WHEN YOU FINALLY DID LOSE YOUR VIRGINITY? HOW'D THAT COME ABOUT?

Idalis: It was so nerve-racking. I really don't know if it counts, because, well . . . I guess it counts. It was this guy who was, like, three years older— I was twenty and he was twenty-three. He was a dancer. A beautiful, beautiful man. And this guy had his own apartment, and I was like, "wow!" He really was an adult. Took care of himself, cooked, did everything himself, so I was totally impressed. I didn't tell him I was a virgin;

I was too scared. And one night, he put on a Stevie Wonder album.

Oh, it was so good!

He dimmed the lights and we were sitting on his couch and he kissed me and hugged me, and we got into it and I was so scared. I was nervous, I was so nervous. I was so sexually attracted to him. I had decided, "I think I want to do this." And my mother had had those conversations with us as far as protection. I had recently gone to the gynecologist and everything. So anyway, he pulled out a condom, which, in that day, in that time, was really rare. He was so nice, he was a sweetheart. He totally had it together, but we couldn't do it all the way because he was too big or I was too small. At that point he must have known that I was a virgin, but we never spoke about it.

SMART SEX: SO THE GUY WHO ENDED UP BEING YOUR BOYFRIEND, WAS HE PATIENT WITH YOU ABOUT LEARNING ABOUT SEX?

Idalis: Oh, the best. He fit perfect, and I was like, "Wow!" I was hooked. It was amazing, especially since I loved him.

SMART SEX: HOW DID YOU FEEL ABOUT HOW LONG YOU WAITED?

Idalis: I was happy I waited that long. I was pretty mature, you know, by then. That's why it's better to wait. There's other things you have to learn, and there are so many things you have to conquer in the world. And you've got to discover yourself in order to share that with someone. Your head's gotta be straight, because sex is such an intense experience.

It can really rock your world, you know, so you really need to have your head on straight first or it can totally make you crazy.

Smart Sex: Now, when you meet someone new, how do you get to trust him before you'll fool around with him?

Idalis: Well, I ask about the family, what he thinks about his mom, his sister—women that are in those primary roles and how he treats them. Ask him about his first kiss and see how he describes it. You can also learn a lot about a guy from how he treated his girlfriend in the past. Whether he's friends with her or not, or if they don't talk at all.

Smart Sex: What, to you, is the best thing about sex?

Idalis: The bond that can't be created any other way. To me, sex is like dancing—a spiritual, kind of uplifting expression of feeling.

It's more than just physical; it's emotional as well.

It's really hard for me to separate the two. I've tried, and to me it's empty. Nothing beats having a relationship, you know, having that special relationship with someone and then having great sex with them.

Smart Sex: Last question. What, to you, is smart sex?

Idalis: Smart sex is always being mentally, emotionally and physically prepared. Mentally ready for the consequences of whatever comes out of that sexual experience—whether you're gonna be with someone for a commitment or if it was just a casual experience. To be mentally prepared for the day after. To be emotionally prepared for the day after, and the day after that, and the month after.

And definitely a condom. That's smart sex, that is the only sex that should be.

9 | SEXUALLY TRANSMITTED DISEASES

STD is shorthand for "sexually transmitted disease." AIDS, since it's deadly and there is currently no cure, gets the most attention. But many more people get genital warts, herpes or chlamydia. These diseases are spreading in epidemic proportions. If you've read Chapter 8, you already know that condoms and other kinds of barrier protection help prevent all STDs, and that condoms plus spermicide are even better.

JULIA, 25: Two years ago, I was in this really intense relationship. This guy looked like a rock star—one of the things I loved about him was his style. He was so tragic and cynical and talented, and he'd bring out your most intense feelings. But I was a sucker. He was very arrogant, and he just wouldn't wear a condom. It was an insult to his manhood. It was like I was questioning his love for me. We broke up and got back together a lot, and during one of our breakups, he had a one-night stand and disappeared for a while. Then he came back. Over the next few weeks, I knew something was wrong. I had discharges, I got sore during sex really easily, I would get this sharp pain in my cervix. Soon it hurt too much to have sex. Any excuse I could use to get out of having sex, I'd use. He wasn't sympathetic. Finally, I went to the doctor. I didn't have insurance, but I didn't know what else to do. The doctor did a chlamydia test and it turned out positive. He put me and my boyfriend on antibiotics.

DEFINING MOMENT: STD
Sexually transmitted disease. A malady or infection that gets passed through sexual contact. Hepatitis B can spread from kissing. Crabs and herpes spread through skin contact. And the whole bunch can spread through unprotected sexual intercourse.

KIM, 20: When my ex-boyfriend and I first slept together, we used a condom. But it came off. He said that he was too big for them, and we didn't make any effort to look for others. I went away to school for a semester, and I came back home over spring break. We hooked up again, and he said I was the last person he had slept with. I said, "Okay, I believe you." I was on the Pill so I just said, "Hey, don't worry about it. If you haven't been with anybody, you don't have anything. I don't have anything." We didn't use protection again. Like, two days later, I had very painful sores. I was so afraid of what it could be.

THESAURUS MOMENT: SEXUALLY TRANSMITTED DISEASE

Venereal disease, VD, the gift that keeps on giving, the love bug, social disease, pox, biological chastity belt, mood killer. For gonorrhea: the clap, dose, drip, hot piss, morning dew. For syphilis: siff, Old Joe, haircut. For pubic lice: crabs, ants in your pants.

STDs AND YOU

If you're familiar with these villains, it will be easier for you to prevent them, or at least spot them early and get treatment. The symptoms can be painful, especially if you let the problem go for too long. Even scarier, anyone who has had unsafe sex play could have an STD and feel no symptoms. And untreated STDs can lead to infertility. So use barrier protection, and get regular STD screening from your doctor if you're sexually active—twice a year or with each new partner is a good idea. If you or your partner feels any symptoms, a doctor can best diagnose and ease the pain, so see one the moment you get suspicious. And remember, doctors are not out there to judge or berate you; they want to help you. This is not the time to be shy.

THE
EIGHT
MOST
COMMON
STDs

CHLAMYDIA

WHAT: *Chlamydia is an infection caused by a bacteria called* Chlamydia trachomatis.

HOW COMMON: *Every year in the U.S., there are about 4 million new cases with symptoms (this number does not include the estimated millions more who have asymptomatic chlamydia). Up to 30 percent of sexually active teenagers have it. Chlamydia is highly transmissible, and it is the most common STD among adolescents and young adults.*

HOW SPREAD: *Through vaginal, anal and oral sex.*

SYMPTOMS: *Half or more of the women and 25 percent or more of the men who get it have no symptoms. If there are symptoms, they'll appear in one to three weeks and may include discharge, burning pee, mild abdominal pain, itchy genitals, rectal pain, or discharge—and for guys, scrotal pain or tenderness.*

CONSEQUENCES: *If left untreated, chlamydia can move further into the reproductive organs and/or urinary tract and cause very serious damage. Chlamydia can lead to pelvic inflammatory disease (PID) in women—a severe infection in the uterus, fallopian tubes and/or ovaries that may put you in the hospital. In men, it can lead to epididymitis (an inflammation of the tubes in the testicles) and damage to the urethra (urine tube). This spells potential pain and possible infertility for either sex.*

TREATMENT: *Luckily, if diagnosed early, chlamydia is easily treated with antibiotics. If one person is diagnosed and treated, their partner(s) should automatically undergo treatment, too. Since so many people are asymptomatic, since the disease is so widespread and since tests for guys aren't always conclusive (see note below), the treat-your-partner-too policy is wise.*

Note: Chlamydia cultures are becoming a routine part of a pelvic exam for women. The test for men who are asymptomatic is unpleasant and not always reliable—it involves putting a very thin swab into the urethral opening and dipping in a little bit to get a specimen for the lab. But if the chlamydia lurks deeper inside the penis, it won't show up. In addition to testing, men should pay close attention to symptoms and get treatment if a partner tests positive for chlamydia.

CRABS

Bonus Fact
In a recent study, 37 percent of people with crabs had other, co-existing STDs.

WHAT: *Pubic lice, Pthirus pubis, also called crabs, are actually parasites—little yellow-gray wingless bugs about the size of a pinhead that feed on blood (sort of like something out of a cheap '50s monster movie). Without a live host, the insects die in about twenty-four hours. With a host, the bugs can survive for up to a month. They like to live anywhere moist and hairy, including the pubic region, armpits, belly, thighs, chest, anal area, the area between the anus and genitals—and sometimes even in beards, eyebrows or eyelashes. Females lay eggs (called nits) each day, and attach the eggs to hair shafts.*

HOW COMMON: *Fairly common. Not tracked very well, since it's not an official STD. And cases of head lice and pubic lice are often lumped together.*

HOW SPREAD: *Through close contact with someone who has them. Can also spread via pets, bedding, upholstery, shared clothing, towels and bed linens.*

SYMPTOMS: *Though some people just carry them without feeling them, crabs usually cause mild to superintense itching. Little dots of blood in your underwear might be a tip-off. And red bumps, marks caused by the crabs biting into the skin, or scratches in the pubic (or other) area can also be signs of crabs. You don't need a microscope to see the little pests—so you can often diagnose them for yourself.*

CONSEQUENCES: *Highly contagious and sometimes hard to get rid of.*

Can bring about scabby, infected skin from all the scratching. Can carry disease such as typhus.

TREATMENT: *Go to the doctor to confirm your suspicions. Then get some special debugging shampoo (look for Nix, Rid or A-200, a generic anti–body-lice shampoo; or your doctor may prescribe another medication). Regular soap and water won't kill them on your body. Apply medicated shampoo to the affected area(s), let it sit there per instructions on the bottle, then rinse. Use a fine comb (often included with shampoo) to remove any leftover bugs or nits from the hair. If the nits are stubborn, vinegar and water should loosen them. After a week, have a doctor check to make sure the crabs and any eggs are all gone. Sometimes retreatment is necessary. As for treatment of your surroundings, wash every sheet, towel and item of clothing you've used in the last forty-eight hours in detergent and really hot water. Dry cleaning works, too. At the very least, store clothes and linens in sealed plastic garbage bags for seventy-two hours, and the bugs will die. There are special insecticide sprays for upholstery, but staying off the couch or chairs for a few days should suffice. And you don't have to fumigate. Roommates should wash their stuff, too, and look out for symptoms. Anyone you've slept with in the last month should go ahead and get treatment.*

Note: *Similar to crabs are scabies (caused by the mite* scarcoptes scabiei var hominis*), except that these tiny beasts burrow under the skin and lay eggs— pretty nice, huh? While crabs love hair, scabies love warm, moist folds of skin, like under the female breast, around the penis, in the webs of fingers. They are also found in the bends of the wrists or ankles. They cause intense itching and red sores. They are tiny and hard to diagnose. If you think you might have them, don't scratch. Check with a doctor who might look at a skin scraping to confirm diagnosis. You beat them with a medicated cream. Retreatment is often necessary. Scabies are spread through skin-to-skin contact or through shared clothing or linen. Wash clothes and linen as you would for crabs.*

GINA, 24: About a year ago I went in for a Pap smear. My results came back abnormal. After two irregular Pap smears, the doctor sent me to get a biopsy [taking a tissue sample, in this case from her cervix—the entrance to the uterus, deep inside the vagina]. My mom had cervical cancer. I was freaked out. "Will I ever have children?" I go get the biopsy. A few days later he says, "You have HPV"—warts. Of all places, on my cervix. Because I work at a bookstore, I read every book on women's health. I went to the library. I took every brochure, because I've always been intimidated by doctors. I never knew the right questions to ask. So I said to myself, "You're an adult. It's the rest of your life." I went for the treatment with two pages of questions that I made the doctor answer. Even while he was treating me, I kept asking questions. He basically burned off the warts. He showed me the tissue. It looked like little warts you'd get on your finger. Now I have Pap smears every three months. Then it'll be every six months for the rest of my life.

TODD, 22: It was a bad scene. This girl I was dating, it was the second time we'd fooled around. I ended up with little bugs. I itched really bad. I got my friend to take me to the store and get shampoo for body lice. I had to wash everything, use that little comb that comes with the shampoo. It was embarrassing. I was angry. I didn't talk to the girl after that. She had to have gotten them from somewhere. I could have handled it better—if it happened to me now, I'd go talk to her about it, ask her if there's anything else going on.

GENITAL WARTS (HPV)

WHAT: *Genital warts are brought on by the human papilloma virus (HPV), a very close cousin of the virus that causes warts on hands and feet. Genital warts come in different forms, depending where on the penis or vagina they appear (see symptoms).*

HOW COMMON: *A close contender for the most common STD, and definitely the number-one sexually transmitted virus. Very common among college students—one estimate says 30 percent are affected. There are one million new cases a year, and there may be forty million people who now have it. HPV is most common with people who started having sex early and people who have had many partners.*

HOW SPREAD: *Vaginal, oral or anal sex with someone who has warts or is carrying the virus.*

SYMPTOMS: *It takes anywhere from three weeks to eight months from time of exposure for warts to appear (though some people are asymptomatic). Warts can have different form or color depending on location. In dry areas near the genitals they can appear as grayish-white, hard bumps. In moist places, like inside the vagina, they can be soft and pinkish. They can appear as one or two pinhead-size bumps or sometimes in cauliflowerlike clusters. Any unusual growth(s) on, in or around the penis, anus, vagina, urethra, or perineum (area between anus and genitals) should be checked by a doctor as soon as possible. HPV-induced warts are usually painless, though they can itch. Warts on the cervix can be diagnosed through regular Pap smears. Anywhere else, a doctor might be able to diagnose them by sight.*

CONSEQUENCES: *Untreated warts can also grow bigger and grosser. They can even start to bleed when traumatized (during sex or when you wipe). If they form in the urethra, you risk trouble with urinary tract infections and basic urinary functioning. Certain strains of HPV are associated with precancerous cells on the cervix. The five-year survival rate for women with advanced cervical cancer is only about 40 percent, whereas it is 90 percent for women with localized cancer—so there's good reason to get that Pap smear. There might also be a connection between some strains of HPV and other cancers.*

TREATMENT: *Possibilities include laser surgery, electric-current surgery, surgical excision (cutting out). Doctors can freeze off warts with liquid nitrogen, or burn off warts with a special acid. Unfortunately, it's difficult for doctors to know if they've gotten all the warts, and if any are missed, they can multiply. These treatments don't necessarily rid you of the virus; they are ways to treat the growths and abnormal cells that are symptoms of the virus. People with HPV can carry the bug around for months and even years. So safer sex is important. The good news is that the virus often goes into remission for long periods or even indefinitely.*

GENITAL HERPES

WHAT: *A virus called herpes simplex, which has two strains—types 1 and 2. Herpes simplex virus type 1 usually appears as a cold sore on the mouth (many people develop this at some point in life, and it goes away without much notice or consequence). Herpes simplex virus type 2 usually appears as one or many painful, blisterlike sores in the genital area. Type 2 is the one with the nasty reputation. Most genital herpes infections are caused by type 2.*

HERE'S THE CATCH: *You can have outbreaks of type 1 on your genitals. And it can be as awful as type 2. This is a true illustration of the risk of unprotected oral sex—the no-big-deal cold sore on your lip can become a serious genital malady in your partner. Some genital herpes infections are caused by herpes simplex virus type 1. Either type of herpes virus may also cause sores on the fingers, groin, buttocks, inside of the mouth and eyes. If you think you have a herpes infection of the eyes, go to your doctor immediately.*

HOW COMMON: *One in four sexually active adults has herpes. There are 500,000 new cases a year, and over 30 million Americans are affected. Adolescents may account for 25 to 50 percent of all patients with genital herpes.*

HOW SPREAD: *It's primarily spread through genital, anal and/or oral contact with a herpes sore. There should be no sexual contact during herpes outbreaks. And you should plan on barrier protection the rest of the time (unless you're trying to get pregnant), because it's possible to pass on the virus even in outbreak-free periods. Doctors recently discovered an unfortunate phenomenon called "asymptomatic viral shedding," which means you're never totally sure if and when there's a safe time. A friendly kiss on the mouth when someone has a cold sore can give you herpes simplex type 1. You can also spread it by touching a herpes sore of either type, then touching a warm, moist place like*

the eyes, mouth or genitals on your own or another's body
(this is the only time masturbation is not safer sex).

SYMPTOMS: *Sometimes no symptoms at all—especially in women. For those who feel their herpes, early symptoms are itching or tingling around the genitals. Then a genital aching, even a whole-body achiness—especially at the first outbreak. Herpes can even make it impossible to pee, even though you feel the urge—if this happens, get to the doctor pronto. There might also be flulike fever, headaches and swollen glands. Next come painful, blisterlike sores around the genitals and/or anus. These sores usually appear within a month of the first sexual contact, but they can also delay their debut for several months or even a year. The blisters break, leaving weepy, ulcer-type sores that are very contagious. Be sure to wash your hands often during this time. Eventually, the sores will dry up and heal. The initial outbreak can last two or three weeks; after that, outbreaks are usually shorter and milder. When a herpes outbreak is over, the virus camps out in one or more nerve centers and stays dormant for a while (sometimes forever). Often, when someone with herpes is under stress—illness, anxiety, lack of sleep, overwork, or too much sun—the virus can act up and sores reappear. Other times, sores appear for no obvious reason. Some people mistake the discomfort of an outbreak (especially a mild one) for yeast infection or jock itch, and they never realize they have the virus. Such folks are more likely to spread herpes unknowingly.*

CONSEQUENCES: *Herpes really requires lifelong management and care. It's believed that plenty of sleep and a healthy diet will help reduce outbreaks. If you are a woman who has herpes and you're thinking of having kids, be sure to tell your doctor: In rare instances, herpes can seriously hurt or kill a baby delivered vaginally, so the baby may need to be delivered by cesarean section.*

TREATMENT: *Unfortunately there's no cure, but there are antiviral drugs that help prevent outbreaks and make living with the disease quite manageable.*

When sores do appear, keep them clean and dry. Take an over-the-counter painkiller and have a sitz (shallow) bath in lukewarm water or Burows Solution (an antiseptic) to make life more comfortable. Try applying ice. Your doctor can also prescribe an anesthetic cream.

Note: You can only truly diagnose herpes by letting your doctor examine you. So if you have an uncomfortable outbreak of some kind, get it checked out. If you know you have herpes, there is a national organization called HELP, designed to help those with herpes get information and support (see Resources, page 310).

KIM, 20: I told a friend of mine who had been a health educator about my sores, and she said, "You know, it sounds like herpes." And even I knew that herpes couldn't be cured. I was like, "Great." So I went to the gynecologist, and she took a culture from the sore. It was herpes. I had to wear really loose pants. Anything that touched it made it hurt.

GONORRHEA

WHAT: *An infection brought on by the* Niesseria gonorrhoeae *bacteria. Survives only in moist places in the body. In the open air, dies quickly.*

HOW COMMON: *Over one million new cases last year. 60 percent of gonorrhea cases occur in young adults ages 15 to 24.*

HOW SPREAD: *Through vaginal, anal and/or oral sex with an infected partner.*

SYMPTOMS: *The majority of women with gonorrhea show no symptoms— especially at the early stages of infection. More men feel symptoms, and they are not pleasant. For men, two to six days after contact there is usually pain, burning and/or difficulty with urination. Also a discharge from the urethra, often first thing in the morning, before you pee. Discharge can show up as spots on the underwear. For women, if there are symptoms, the most common is a grayish-white discharge (coming out of the cervix—but you need a doctor to confirm that). The labia can feel irritated or tender. A sore throat, especially* a severe sore throat that appears soon after performing unprotected oral sex on a man, might mean a gonorrhea infection. Gonorrhea from anal sex might cause anal discharge as well as swelling and tenderness just inside the anal opening (rectum).

CONSEQUENCES: Untreated gonorrhea will not go away. In either sex, the bacteria can move deeper into the reproductive system and cause infertility. Gonorrhea can lead to pelvic inflammatory disease (PID) in women—a severe infection in the uterus, fallopian tubes and/or ovaries that may put you in the hospital. For men, it can cause inflammation of the epididymis (the tube that carries semen out of the testes). And gonorrhea can even cause arthritis in either sex.

TREATMENT: It's curable with antibiotics, though there are more drug-resistant strains now than before. It's smart for sexual partners to go ahead with treatment even if they are asymptomatic.

Note: Resembles and often coexists with chlamydia.

HEPATITIS B

WHAT: A virus that causes liver infection. The virus lives in all the body fluids of infected persons (including saliva).

HOW COMMON: Fourteen people a day die from hepatitis-B–related illnesses like cirrhosis and liver cancer. There are 300,000 new cases a year. Hep B has increased 77 percent among young people in the last decade; 75 percent of those infected every year are 15 to 39 years old.

HOW SPREAD: The virus can travel through contact between any body openings—mouth to mouth, mouth to genital and vaginal and anal sex. Heterosexual intercourse is the most common mode of transmission. Hepatitis B can also be passed through shared needles. About 50 percent of those infected are asymptomatic and may pass on the disease without knowing it.

SYMPTOMS: *May include fatigue, nausea, vomiting, loss of appetite, abdominal pain, jaundice (yellow skin), skin rashes, darkening of the urine and arthritis.*

CONSEQUENCES: *Hepatitis B can lead to liver cancer and cirrhosis, even death.*

TREATMENT: *Postexposure vaccine and immune globulin can help, if caught early. Since hepatitis is a virus, there is no cure. It has to run its course under medical supervision, and the body's immune system will most likely beat it over time. Good diet, zero alcohol (to ease the strain on the liver), and maximum rest will help recovery—which usually takes two to three months. An unlucky few are chronic sufferers.*

Note: This is the only STD for which there's a vaccine. A series of three shots should protect you for a long time (you'll need a booster after ten years or so). If you are sexually active (or someday plan to be), you should ask your doctor for the shots. The American College Health Association recommends the vaccine for all college students. The vaccine takes a while to kick in, so if you've been exposed to hep B, you need to go to your doctor to get a shot of immune globulin, which will help protect you right away.

SYPHILIS

WHAT: *An STD caused by a tiny spiral bacteria that gets into your bloodstream. A very old STD, syphilis has been mentioned in history for centuries.*

HOW COMMON: *On the rise. Right now there are more than 136,000 cases in the U.S.*

HOW SPREAD: *It's usually transmitted sexually (kissing included), through open syphilis sores or an open syphilis-related rash.*

SYMPTOMS: *Syphilis has four major stages, but you definitely want to stop it before it runs the whole course. The first stage (primary syphilis) usually starts about twenty-one days after contact—but can appear anywhere from nine to ninety days after contact with the bacteria. A painless sore (or sores) called a chancre (pronounced SHANK-er) appears where initial contact was made, most often on or around the genitals. Sores can also be on the mouth, anal area, hands, breasts or cervix (where they're harder to spot). When the sore is ulcerous or oozy, that wet stuff is very contagious. The initial chancre scabs over and heals. Although you may not feel any symptoms after the chancre disappears, the bacteria can still be in the bloodstream. Usually about three weeks after the onset of the chancre, symptoms of secondary syphilis occur—a rash on the body and possibly fever, nausea, headaches. There might be more moist sores around the anus or genitals. This phase can pass, too, leaving the infected person a healthy-looking carrier (that's the third, or latent stage).*

CONSEQUENCES: *Infected people in any stage of syphilis can spread the bacteria to others. If it goes untreated, and gets to the fourth stage (neurosyphilis), the bacteria can attack your inner organs, which can lead to brain damage, blindness and death. The bacteria can also seriously hurt the fetus of a pregnant women.*

TREATMENT: *If it's caught early, syphilis is treatable with antibiotics. Sexual partners should go ahead and get treatment, too. It's important to follow up with return visits to the doctor over the next year to make sure the syphilis is gone.*

Bonus Fact
An estimated 100,000 to 150,000 women in the U.S. become infertile each year because of STDs and the complications they can cause.

TRICHOMONIASIS (A.K.A. TRICH)

WHAT: *An infection caused by a one-celled parasite,* Trichomonas vaginalis. *Under normal circumstances, this tiny beast is usually harmless.*

HOW COMMON: *There are 3 million new cases a year.*

HOW SPREAD: *Through manual and genital contact with the vagina. Can also be carried in the male urethra (urine tract). Trich can live outside the body for more than an hour, so it's possible to catch trich from wearing someone else's bathing suit or using someone else's towel. And your mom's fear of catching something from a toilet seat is technically valid (though it's unlikely to happen).*

SYMPTOMS: *There are often no symptoms, especially in men. If there are symptoms, they'll appear in four days to four weeks. For men: discharge, a minor tickling in the penis. For women: itching, tender vaginal lips; burning pee; stinky discharge; discomfort during sex.*

CONSEQUENCES: *Females can get an inflamed urinary tract or cervix. Men can get infections in their urethra, bladder, testicles, prostate gland.*

TREATMENT: *Metronidazole, a trich killer. You need a prescription from your doctor for it, and partners should undergo treatment, too.*

Note: At the risk of sounding like a sixth-grade health teacher, remember good hygiene.

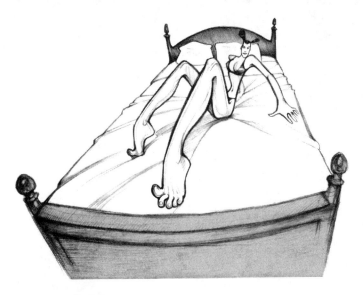

SEXUALLY TRANSMITTABLE, BUT NOT ALWAYS

The following entries describe infections that you can get from sex, but that you can also get from organisms that are naturally present or were introduced into your system another way, causing your chemical balance to get out of whack. The organisms that cause yeast and gardenerella infections might be unleashed by pregnancy; illness; stress; the Pill; douching; failure to wipe; supertight pants, leggings, stockings or nylon underpants that don't allow air circulation; dye in colored toilet paper; bath oil; bubble bath; vaginal deodorant; antibiotics, even hanging out in a wet bathing suit.

YEAST INFECTION

WHAT: *An overgrowth of an organism called* candida albicans, *which is always present in the vagina and anus.*

HOW COMMON: *An estimated 75 percent of women get one at some point in their lives. Guys can be affected (though it's pretty rare).*

HOW SPREAD: *Usually not acquired through sexual activity (see list of causes below), but can spread or be aggravated through sex and sex play.*

SYMPTOMS: *White lumpy discharge (like cottage cheese), genital itchiness, pain or tenderness around the vagina or opening of the penis. There is usually no odor. Can give men an itchy rash on the penis and scrotum.*

CONSEQUENCES: *Will return if not treated effectively.*

TREATMENT: *For men and women, your first yeast infection should be treated by a doctor. Women can be treated with medicated creams or suppositories (medicine that is inserted in the vagina) that work over a three- to seven-day stretch. Thereafter, women can buy the topical medicines over the counter. Guys get a topical cream.*

GARDENERELLA (A.K.A. BACTERIAL VAGINOSIS, OR BV FOR SHORT)

WHAT: *An infection caused by overgrowth of the bacteria* gardenerella vaginalis.

HOW COMMON: *Forty percent of sexually active single females have the* *gardenerella bacteria living in their vaginal mucus—usually in harmless amounts. Though health departments are not required to track numbers on BV, it is one of the most common infections in women. One STD clinic reported gardenerella infections in 32 to 64 percent of its female patients.*

HOW SPREAD: *BV can be sexually transmitted—it rarely affects people who aren't sexually active. But it can develop from other causes, too (see list below).*

SYMPTOMS: *Half of the ladies with gardenerella bacteria don't show symptoms. But there can be grayish-white discharge with an unusually strong fishy odor. Sometimes there's a burning discomfort. Abdominal pain or irregular or long periods might also trouble you.*

CONSEQUENCES: *Symptoms don't go away and get worse.*

TREATMENT: *A medicine called Flagyl, or other antibiotics, for a week.*

To keep the bacterias that cause yeast infections and gardenerella at bay:

• *Wear cotton underwear.*

• *Use undyed, unscented toilet paper.*

• *Wipe yourself front-to-back after relieving yourself (you don't want to spread organisms from your anus to your vagina or urethra).*

• *Don't let hands wander from anus to vagina during sex play.*

• *Wash your genitals before and after sex.*

• *Pee before and after sex (especially after; this flushes out foreign germs and bacteria).*

THE SEXISM OF STDs

In general, during your garden-variety hetero sex, the woman is far more at risk than a guy. It's a matter of anatomy. The vagina has a much bigger vulnerable surface area than the penis does. Also, STDs are more concentrated in semen than in vaginal fluid or, for that matter, in saliva. Sex is also more likely to cause tiny cuts or abrasions in the soft, mucus-covered skin of the vagina than on the dry skin of the penis. If you are not using a condom, semen (and any STDs it carries) squirts directly into the vagina. The transfer of vaginal fluid (and any STDs it carries) into the penis through the skin or through the urethra is less intense. It only takes one unprotected episode to give either sex an STD, but women take on a higher risk when they do the deed without latex.

TESTING, TESTING

In case you haven't gotten the message, if you suspect any symptoms described above, it is unwise to have sex until you know that you and your partner are healthy. You should both get checked out by a doctor or health care practitioner.

SIMON, 17: I really don't think I have any STDs, but I do try to give, like, a visual test before I do anything with a new girl.

It's good to keep your eyes open for physical signs of disease, but there's a lot you can't see. Even if you don't have any symptoms, you should still get a checkup and tests a couple of times a year or with each new partner if possible. So many STDs leave people symptomless! A routine round of testing usually means taking cultures for chlamydia, gonorrhea and (in women) a Pap smear, which can indicate HPV.

It's harder to test accurately for STDs in asymptomatic men—biological sexism again. When the doctor takes a culture from the inside of the man's urethra, he can only get samples of what's near the end of the penis. If there are microorganisms farther in, they might not show up. Men should still get tested, but they should note that there's a chance of getting a false-negative result. Guys should pay close attention to their partner's STD test results and assume that they are infected with anything that their partner has.

CONFIDENTIALITY

A quick word to minors out there about confidentiality: All fifty states allow the testing and treatment of minors for STDs without parental consent. (Note that the definition of minor varies by state.) Keep in mind that *without parental* consent doesn't mean that your parents won't be notified later, and there are some doctors who ignore the laws. And one last hitch: There are some states that allow the doctor to notify parents if it seems appropriate. So when you make an appointment, find out what the current laws are in your state and quiz the nurse-practitioner or doctor about whether they respect their patients' privacy and under what circumstances they'd feel a need to, say, call someone's parents. (See page 72 in Chapter 5 for suggestions of places and ways to get confidential health care, including STD testing.)

COPING WITH STDS

Hearing "You tested positive for gonorrhea," or, "Yes, those are definitely warts" may make you feel like tainted merchandise, a total loser. Or at least embarrassed.

KIM, 20: After being diagnosed with herpes, I thought I would never be able to have sex again. I thought that any person who knew about this would be scared of me and not want to touch me. It's like a tag of dirtiness.

News flash: If you get an STD, you're not alone, and this doesn't make you a bad person. But sometimes people's thoughtlessness and preconceived notions can make things worse instead of better.

KIM: You can be watching TV with friends, and they see some really raunchy looking person who just doesn't look like they take care of themselves. And they just say, "She probably has herpes and this and that." People will say stuff all the time, and they don't know I have it. To me, it's really hurtful when I hear that. That's exactly what I'm afraid of when I tell somebody I have it. You know, that they're going to think I'm dirty, that I can't take care of myself. And it's so far from the truth. People tend to think that people who get it are the ones who are just out doing everybody. I think there's a whole feeling that it's just quantity of sex that will get you an STD, when it only takes one time.

Eventually, Kim came to terms with her virus.

KIM: It took me a while to get beyond just being upset about the herpes. I don't have that many outbreaks. I have maybe four a year. It's okay. It definitely made me more aware of sex and its implications, and of my behavior. I changed my behavior completely. Before, I didn't put a lot of judgment into it. Now I think, Do I want to have sex with this person enough to do this? It just makes sex a little more mental for me than physical. I know my own mind. And I know what I want more. And I know now I have the strength to do what I need to do for myself.

Another thing to remember is that your medical file is your own business. Friends can be great to lean on if you're feeling bad, but you are under no obligation to tell them about your STD if you don't feel like it. It's none of their business unless you make it so. Parents can be a great resource, too—especially when it comes to help in getting health care—but telling them is your choice. However, in the case of past and present sex partners, you should feel obligated to tell them if you have an STD, because you might be endangering other people's health if you don't.

BREAKING THE CYCLE—

If you discover that you have an STD, you need to figure out all the past and present partners who might be affected and get in touch with them pronto—they might need medical care, they might unknowingly spread the STD further. This might not be your most graceful social moment, but it's an important one. Wouldn't you want the news if your ex had an STD? A quick phone call to say something like, "I'm calling because I want to make sure you're okay. I just found out I have [fill in the blank], and I think you should get a test just to make sure you don't have it." Short and to-the-point. Don't spend time focusing on who gave it to whom and who had it first.

TELLING YOUR PARTNER(S) ABOUT AN STD

The goal is to make sure you and your lovers and their lovers and everyone's future lovers all stay healthy. Ask the health care provider how far back you could have gotten the disease, so you know which old partners you should ring up.

There are some cases where contacting an ex is just not possible—they won't talk to you, you don't have the money or privacy for long-distance calls, the ex might get physical when angered. In these cases, it's sometimes possible to have the public health system break the bad news for you. Ask your doctor how to arrange contact tracing, or call your local public health office. It's certainly better than not telling an at-risk ex at all.

If you're on good terms with an ex or if you have a present-day bedmate, you'd be a sport to accompany him or her to get tested and examined (this will also ensure that it happens). If you're emotionally involved, you can be bummed together and comfort each other, as well as put up with treatment together.

IMPORTANT: No sexual contact with affected body parts while you and/or your partner are being treated for an STD. It is very easy to reinfect each other and start the whole unpleasant process all over again. No one wants that. Talk to your health care provider to find out whether there is any type of sex that would be safe while you are taking your medicine, or just hold off until the treatment is over. You (and your partner) must take all of your medication until it is finished—even if all symptoms are gone.

Jonah could still be passing on chlamydia, even if he has no symptoms at all. So many STDs don't show up for a long time, if ever—especially for guys. Telling potential new lovers is not only a duty, but it shows them you respect them and that you care about their health enough to be honest about something awkward.

JONAH, 24: I supposedly got chlamydia from my college girlfriend, but I only knew about it because she called me after we broke up and told me to go to the health service. I don't remember if I took any medicine for it. Honestly, it's never been a problem. I don't tell my current partners unless they ask directly, because it never bothered me.

ESTHER, 17: I had a partner who had herpes. We were having coffee in this restaurant. We were talking about a sex documentary that we'd seen. We asked each other, "How do you feel about safe sex?" and we agreed. Then she got a funny grin on her face and gave me this sheepish look and said, "I have herpes." We both laughed, and then we talked and planned for that situation. If there's an outbreak, we wouldn't do anything. If there's no outbreak, I'd take precautions—barrier stuff. It really made me feel secure that we both had this commitment to each other's health. You cannot sit around and mope about something like herpes. You have to incorporate it into your life.

KIM, 20: When I found out for sure that I had herpes, I called the guy I had slept with and told him. I was hysterically crying, "You gave me herpes." He said, "I don't know who's been with you, but my s**t is clean." I was just like, "I can't believe you're saying this to me. I know it was you." And he was like, "No, it wasn't me. It wasn't me." He didn't even ask, "Why do you think it's me?" He didn't get into anything. He just was in complete denial. The fact that he really didn't care how upset it made me upset me even more. I haven't talked to him since. I don't even know if he's gotten tested. Other guys have been better. This guy and I didn't even have sex, but we almost had sex. I told him about my herpes. I said, "You know, I don't want you to think I would put you in danger." And he said, "No, it's okay. I'm glad you told me. I'm glad you feel you can tell me this." And he gave me a hug. Later on he told me that from then on—you know, with me—it wouldn't have been casual sex, because I had opened up to him and placed a certain amount of trust in him that he knew isn't easy to give. That was great for me.

Lives of the Rich and Infected: Historical Figures Who Had STDs

PIONEERS IN STD PREVENTION

Wolfgang Amadeus Mozart claimed he was faithful to his wife because of the risk of catching a disease from other women. Though this would not count as safer sex these days, Catherine the Great required all her lovers to undergo physical examination by the royal physician, and then to be bedded by one of her ladies-in-waiting before they made it into the royal bedchamber.

(SORT OF)

If you think you are now STD-free, try to stay that way. It's your right to know if you're putting your body at risk. Ask what STDs your partner has had. Ask what unusual symptoms he or she has ever felt, and whether he or she sought testing or treatment. It's also perfectly legit (even wise) to hold off sex until you've both been tested for STDs. If you'd wait for an AIDS test, why not wait for a chlamydia test? In fact, why not take both tests at the same time?

THE BOTTOM LINE

When you are ready to have sex, condoms (especially condoms plus spermicide) are very effective in preventing diseases spread by body fluids—AIDS, gonorrhea, chlamydia, syphilis, hepatitis B—but not as effective in preventing STDs spread by skin-on-skin contact, like genital warts (HPV), herpes and crabs. Even when practicing safer sex, on rare occasion you can still get an STD. And don't forget that unprotected oral sex is not safer sex (see Chapter 8). Abstinence is the only guaranteed way to prevent STDs. So if you're sexually active, pay close attention to your body and your partner's body. Stop all sexual contact if you suspect any symptoms. Be sure to go to the doctor at least twice a year and tell him or her that you are having sex these days, so that you can get tests and cultures. A clean bill of health will help you relax and enjoy sex with less anxiety.

AND AIDS | 10

- One million people in the U.S. are believed to be infected with HIV.
- HIV infection/AIDS is the second leading cause of
  death among adults ages 25 to 44.
- Approximately 42 percent of adults living with HIV/AIDS
  are women, and this proportion is growing.
- In a nationwide sex poll, one in four young adults said
  they know someone with HIV or AIDS.
- AIDS has killed six times more Americans than died in Vietnam.
- The World Health Organization estimates that 29.4 million
  people worldwide had been infected with HIV through 1996,
  resulting in about 8.4 million AIDS cases worldwide.

Though there are a lot of frightening stats about AIDS, there are really only three facts that you need to know:

- AIDS is preventable.
- AIDS is hard to get.
- A few simple precautions will keep you protected.

The thought of living in a time of plague is so extreme and frightening that sometimes it's easier to block it out and pretend it's not there. Like, if you stopped to really think about all the nuclear bombs in the world and their destructive powers, you'd go nuts. But there's one big difference: You don't have much say about a nuclear bomb going off, but you are fully capable of preventing AIDS. All the tools and information are right in front of you.

VIRGINIA, 20: See, everyone I know is really worried about AIDS, but no one wants to talk about it. It's just something that people don't do—talk about their fears. When you talk about AIDS, you talk about, "I don't want to get it," but you never talk about how you personally put yourself at risk.

THOMAS, 18: I don't think about AIDS. I see it every day in the city, but I don't think about it for me. Oh, I know I'm at risk. My friend thinks I'm really dumb, and he swears that a lot of people have it. I don't think that anybody I know has it. I guess I just don't believe it yet. I think of it more as an older thing, like for people in their twenties.

Just because you are young does not mean you are immune from AIDS. If you've never had an STD, if you don't know someone with HIV yet, if you've never been seriously sick or hurt, if you do other risky things (like drink, take drugs) and nothing has gone wrong so far, then you might feel like life is a long, long road stretched out in front of you without any visible roadblocks. Hopefully, that will be the case. But you live a long and healthy life by assessing risks along the way and making the best choices. It's an active, not a passive, process. Often, a personally scary moment will serve as a wake-up call.

LENA, 21: I lost a friend to AIDS. For the last three years, I've been as careful as it gets. AIDS scares me to death.

PRIY, 23: I think about AIDS more than any other STD. Especially when I'm having sex. It adds a lot of anxiety to sex, especially with new partners when you don't know their history. It's hard to enjoy the heat of the moment if you're worried, if you think you're going to die from this encounter.

GINA, 24: I used to think about AIDS a lot after I found out my boyfriend of eight-and-a-half years had been cheating on me. Then my world came crashing down on me. I consider myself very lucky for only acquiring HPV [genital warts].

HIV AND AIDS—HOW THEY DO
AND DON'T GET AROUND

Acquired immunodeficiency syndrome
(AIDS) is caused by a slow-acting virus,
the human immunodeficiency virus (HIV),
which must penetrate your body to infect
you. You get HIV through sharing body
fluids with someone who has it.

HIV CAN BE TRANSMITTED
THROUGH THE FOLLOWING
BODY FLUIDS:

· semen
· vaginal fluid
· breast milk
· blood

YOU CAN GET HIV FROM
THE FOLLOWING ACTIVITIES:

· vaginal sex
· anal sex
· oral sex on a man or a woman
· sharing of needles for drugs,
  steroids, tattoos or piercing
· manual sex play
(if there are cuts on the hands)

It is extremely unlikely that you
could get AIDS from the following:
· vomit (unless blood is present)
· kissing (unless there are cuts
  in the mouth and the kissing
  is extremely vigorous—but
  it's almost impossible to
  spread the virus this way)

YOU CANNOT GET HIV
FROM THE FOLLOWING:

· sweat
· tears
· mosquitoes
· food
  (even if someone with
  AIDS prepared it)
· handshakes
· massaging
· sneezing
· coughing
· swimming pools
· toilet seats
· casual, everyday
  social contact

Many people have contracted AIDS
through blood transfusions—mostly
transfusions that occurred in the
early '80s. But America's blood
supply is now very safe.

After HIV goes into the bloodstream, it invades the white blood cells—especially a kind of white blood cell called a T-cell, which helps the body fight infection. The HIV takes over the T-cells and instructs them to produce more of the virus, which then attacks other T-cells.

Though this process is harmful and seemingly irreversible, it is also slow. Someone with HIV can remain in this phase and remain healthy and asymptomatic for years.

Eventually the body's T-cells become overwhelmed by HIV, and the immune system stops working properly. Then opportunistic infections move in. Opportunistic infections are diseases from tiny organisms that are normally around us, and can normally be fought off pretty easily. But in the weakened system, these infections can take hold. When a person infected with HIV contracts one or more of these infectious diseases, he or she has AIDS. Almost everyone with AIDS dies from a complication of AIDS, such as cancer, pneumonia or other infections.

Bonus Fact
A review of 23 school-based programs found that kids who get specific AIDS education are less likely to have sex. Those educated kids who do have sex tend to do it less often and more safely.

HOW THE VIRUS WORKS

Remember, AIDS is *preventable*. A recent study of 123 couples, in which one partner had HIV and the other didn't, found that among the couples who consistently and correctly used condoms, *none* of the uninfected partners became infected. (Check out Chapters 8 and 9 to see more about safer sex and not-so-difficult ways to prevent AIDS and other STDs.)

This book is about sex, but it would be irresponsible not to mention the role of drugs in spreading AIDS. If you are sleeping with someone who might have a drug habit, safer sex is crucial. No sex is even better.

DRUG USE

If you are addicted to drugs, be aware that snorting and smoking are safer than injecting. Then you are endangering your life on only one level instead of two. Sharing needles to inject steroids is high-risk, too. If you are self-destructive enough to use, reuse and share needles, you need to disinfect them with bleach every time you use them. Clean your works thoroughly several times with bleach and then rinse well with water. Keep in mind that cleaning does not guarantee that the virus has been killed; the safest practice is to use a new, sterile needle and syringe. Better yet, let the risk of AIDS be another incentive to kick your drug habit. Call 1-800-662-HELP (and look for more info in Resources, page 310) to get some serious help. You'll need support and medical attention to take such a step.

TESTING,

If you're concerned about your own history or that of your lover, you should really get tested for HIV. If your test comes back negative, you can heave a huge sigh of relief—and keep practicing safer sex. If you test positive, you can start treatment and make health care changes that could extend your life by decades. Knowledge is power.

VIRGINIA, 20: I asked my boyfriend to get an AIDS test, and he got really offended by that. He went through this whole rigmarole: "This girl was a virgin and this girl, well, she only slept with one other guy, and I know him." That kind of explanation. And he was like, "I can't believe that you would think that I haven't been careful or blah, blah, blah." At this point we had been discussing sleeping together for so long and I felt like it was something that I wanted. So I was like, "Okay, that's fine." And I let the issue go even though we were having sex.

Keep in mind that it takes up to six months from initial sexual contact for the HIV antibody to show up in your bloodstream. If you've had a new partner within the last six months and have had unprotected encounters, then go ahead and get tested—but plan on another test at the six-month mark after the last risky encounter, just to be safe. If you get the test with a present or future mate, you can support each other through the experience, and you will be showing respect for each other's health.

TESTING

LENA, 21: On the second or third date, if I like a guy, I ask him to take an HIV test with me. I'm usually straight out about it.

CHAD, 20: I'd like to know so I wouldn't spread it.

If this is a concern, and you go to your regular doctor to get tested, ask him or her who can and can't get access to the test results. Also keep in mind that if you or the doctor files a claim with your insurance company, they will know about a positive result.

If you decide to go ahead and get a test, keep in mind how to best safeguard your privacy. Some people worry that their medical records might be seen by other health care providers, insurers and courts, and that an HIV-positive result might mean denied insurance, prejudice or improper care for other health problems.

KINDS OF TESTS

Your other options include confidential testing and anonymous testing. Confidential testing means that you give your name but that it doesn't go on your medical records and the results aren't released to anyone without your permission—except under certain circumstances, which vary by state.

For the truly Big Brother–wary, there's anonymous testing, in which you get a code number and no one ever finds out your name. Anonymous tests are becoming harder and harder to get. There are private clinics that offer confidential and anonymous testing with quick results—sometimes just a few days, or even overnight. But quicker results mean a higher price tag—around $80 to $100. There should also be some kind of free or cheap testing in a public health clinic or test site in your area, but you might have to wait two to four weeks for your results. Call your local department of public health or an AIDS hotline (see Resources, page 310) to find test sites near you.

WHAT HAPPENS WHEN YOU GO FOR AN AIDS TEST?

This is an example of how a trip to a test site might work. Counselor training, level of questioning and sensitivity can vary from clinic to clinic, state to state. If you take the test in your doctor's office, there will probably be a simpler procedure, as there may not be counselors around, the doctor may already know your history, and so on.

STEP 1 CONSULTATION

You will fill out a form that requires some medical information and confirms your consent for the test. A trained health care worker will ask you a lot of questions about your history. How many partners? How much unprotected vaginal sex, anal sex, oral sex? Intravenous drug use? Visits to prostitutes? Gay sex? Pregnancy and abortion history? Try not to be embarrassed (though it is a bit intense), and keep in mind that there is no point in being dishonest. The counselor is there to help you, not to be judgmental. The more they know, the more accurately they can interpret the results. It gives the doctors a context in which they can frame the blood test. They will ask you some scary stuff, like, "What will you do if the test is positive? Who will you tell? Who will you lean on?" Such questions are a very good reality check, and you should think about these things. The counselor will probably talk to you about the HIV virus and how it can be transmitted—

making sure you have your facts straight for future sexual encounters.

STEP 2 BLOOD SAMPLE TAKEN

It's not fun, but it goes by quickly. Sometimes the person who counseled you takes the blood, sometimes another person does it. He or she will show you that all the instruments are sterile and sealed. The person will probably tie a big rubber band above your elbow and ask you to make a tight fist—this brings the blood right where it's needed. The person will disinfect the inside of your elbow, insert the needle (which is pretty small) into one of the visible veins and let the test tube fill up with blood. If you are truly squeamish, don't look. Then the needle comes out and the bandage goes on.

STEP 3 IDENTIFICATION INFORMATION

If this is anonymous testing, you will be assigned a number and told when to return for results. You and the health care person should check to make sure that the code number on the vial of blood matches the code number on your papers and on the little card you get for future reference. The card will say something like "Patient identifier #1234567." They will tell you when your results are expected back. You might want to call first to make sure your results are in.

STEP 4 SECOND CONSULTATION

Test results usually don't go out over the phone. If you go with a friend or lover, you are usually not allowed to hear the results together, so that each person can get the proper, individual attention. This is your chance to ask any other questions about HIV and sex that may have haunted you while you were waiting for your results.

STEP 5 RESULTS

Pretty self-explanatory. The doctor or counselor makes sure you have the knowledge and resources to handle the news. If you need further help—especially if you test positive— they should tell you where to go.

HOME TESTS

You can now take an AIDS test at your own address. There are two home-test kits on the market, and there may be more to come. Confide is available over the counter, and Home Access Health is a mail-order AIDS test (1-800-HIV-TEST). To take the home test, you prick your fingertip and put several drops of blood on a little card that you must mail within twenty-four hours. Then you call in for your (anonymous) results three days later. The home test companies use the same HIV test as the rest of the medical industry, and the results are reportedly accurate. The advantages? Obviously, there's the privacy factor, convenience, no waiting rooms. Results come back quickly, too. The disadvantages? It's a definite minus to miss all the counseling and information that you can get from a test site or doctor. It's expensive (about $50).

This can be tough. All kinds of anxieties might run through your head during this time. Think of it as inspiration to practice safer sex later. You are anxious because it is now hitting home that AIDS is a real risk that is part of your world.

KARLEY, 17: I about died waiting. For about two weeks you have to wait. I was thinking, like, What if I'm gonna die? And maybe I'll never be able to have a child, and stuff like that. The counseling helped. It let me know that, whatever happened, somebody was going to be there for me. When I got the results, I was really relieved. There was a lot of tension built up. When they told me, it was like I wanted to cry, 'cause I didn't have it.

LENA, 21: I was sitting in my office, waiting for my results. I could only think, In a minute, I'm going to find out if my life is going to change, or if it will continue the way it used to be.

WAITING

IF YOU TEST NEGATIVE

This is not a license to engage in risky behavior! If you have a clean bill of health, you want to keep it that way. Continue to be vigilant about safer sex. If you do slip up after testing negative, don't beat yourself up about it; but do remember that, for the future, you cannot slack off. Don't hesitate to get the test again if you're at all worried or if your partner requests it. Remember, if it's been less than six months since unprotected activity, you need another test when you pass the six-month mark.

Remind yourself that knowledge is power. You can start making the health changes that will prolong your life. You can start dealing instead of wondering. Call a local AIDS agency to find a group for people with HIV, so you can have a community of folks dealing with the same issues you are (look under "AIDS" in your phone book, call 1-800-342-AIDS for a referral or see Resources, page 310). You will feel less powerless if you take a proactive approach. Learn as much as you can about HIV and AIDS. And remember, you can live with this. You can be asymptomatic for years. Medicines are improving all the time—people are living with HIV a lot longer now, and early treatment is an important factor.

IF YOU TEST

POSITIVE

MELISSA, 23: I was living with my boyfriend. We were in love and planned to be together for a long time. I went on the Pill. We got a call one day from one of his ex-girlfriends. She told us to get an AIDS test. He and I tested positive together. I was lucky in the fact—or unlucky in the fact—that I knew who had infected me, and I was sitting next to that person. When I told my parents, there was just dead silence on the phone. I was just like, Oh, man, I probably just ruined any chance that they will ever love me again. I screwed up. I did the most horrible thing. My mom started to cry. She said, "Melissa, I love you. We're okay. We can deal with this as a family. We're gonna give you all the support you need."

TOM, 25: I'm negative, Chris is positive. We've been together five years. When we met, I was twenty. He's amazing; he's a great guy. Funny and witty, with a heart of gold. After two years, we got serious and moved in together. Throughout the move, he was throwing up and having fevers. We didn't guess. He came home from the clinic and said, "Tom, I'm positive" and started to cry. We both cried. Then we got a drink and cried some more. Leaving him never entered my mind. Our bond is really strong. We've been through a lot. I've never loved anyone like him. He's my soulmate.

If you test positive, your life will change, but your life is far from over. It's a good time to take the best care possible of your body, make sure you have health care and look into drugs that can prolong your life and help keep you healthy.

And testing positive does not mean the end of your sex life. You must inform and protect others regarding your HIV status. You must also protect yourself from getting other STDs that your body will have a harder time fighting.

MELISSA: Now I'm just this woman who lives in San Francisco and goes to school. I don't think about my HIV as much. People do assume that I would have a problem with sex, like, "I can't believe you'd have sex with somebody, knowing you have HIV." I don't think that's fair. I think people are dehumanizing me and making me into an animal or something.

Melissa lives with another man now, her fiancé, who is HIV-negative.

LIVING WITH HIV

TOM: At first, sex was weird. Every little zit, I was paranoid—what if his come lands on that? Then I thought, This is silly. Fear doesn't make it any easier. We have sex, but he wears a condom with spermicide and doesn't come inside me. We don't get too rough. Our sex life is pretty tame. We have a whole different set of problems in our relationship now. I feel like my issues count less, because he has this death thing going on. There's a lot of stuff we don't talk about. He jokes about how he's going to have dementia and be a burden on me. It's his way of dealing with it—it really fuels his humor. But we have plans. He doesn't feel like he has a death sentence like he used to. He takes Chinese herbs and acupuncture once a week. I can't think, Oh, he probably has eight years left. We just deal with it one day at a time.

The disease has definitely made its way into the straight world. Look at Magic Johnson, the boxer Tommy Morrison, the rapper Eazy-E. Their public struggles with HIV and AIDS have sent the world the message that no one, no matter how successful, powerful or loved, can eschew safer sex. In Morrison's words, "I could tell you what safe sex is, but I never practiced it. I associated the virus with people that subjected themselves to certain types of lifestyles—IV drug users or people that practiced homosexual lifestyles. Never did I associate it with people like myself, a normal guy, a good ol' boy who likes to do normal things with normal people. I don't live in Los Angeles. I live in Oklahoma— little Jay, Oklahoma. It's not supposed to happen here."

AIDS: A HETEROSEXUAL ISSUE

MELISSA: My fiancé and I talk about safe sex a lot. Neither of us has a problem with condoms, which makes the sexual part of it just fine. I mean, sometimes I ask, "So what are you after? You're going to have to use a condom with me for the rest of your life." He's like, "Fine." He's pretty positive about my life. He wants to spend as much time as he can with me and make that whole thing happen. He's not willing to give up the idea that we're going to spend the rest of our lives together.

If you think AIDS is just a gay concern, wake up and smell the statistics.

· Heterosexual intercourse is the source of more than 75 percent of all adult HIV infections worldwide.
· Since 1994, the number of AIDS cases has declined among gay men, but increased among hetero folk of both sexes.
· The incidence of AIDS in the U.S. is increasing more rapidly for women than for men.

h

INTERVIEW →

SMART SEX: HOW DID YOU LEARN ABOUT SEX?

Billie Joe: I remember me and my brother were over at my older brother's house. I must have been about eleven. We were sitting there and then my brother popped in this videotape. And that was the first time I'd ever seen sex. I was like, "Oh, my God." It completely freaked me out. We turned it off really fast. And then we turned it back on again. And then we were like,

"We better not watch this, because someone might catch us."

Also, my brother owned a body shop for a little while. I remember going in there because he had me clean up. I'd make ten bucks a week or something. I opened up this desk there, and it had all these *Hustler* magazines in it. And there's women spread-eagled right there. And I just go, "That's what it looks like?" I thought it was ugly at first. I mean, I didn't know about anything, you know, I thought two people laid on top of each other and just sort of moved around and out came the baby.

SMART SEX: WHEN DID YOU LOSE YOUR VIRGINITY?

Billie Joe: When I was thirteen years old, I mean, I probably turned into the horniest creature on the planet. I mean, it wasn't pretty.

SMART SEX: DO YOU THINK YOU STARTED HAVING SEX TOO SOON?

Billie Joe: Oh, definitely. I don't really want to turn my past around or anything like that. But, you know, if I knew then what I know now, of course I would have waited.

But I was super-superhorny. And I wanted to know what it was like. I used to always think, God, I just can't wait till the day that someone will say yes. That was about it.

Billie Joe: I was only thirteen, which is a pretty lame excuse. *But we were just really young and neither one of us knew what we were doing.*

SMART SEX: WHAT WERE THE CIRCUMSTANCES?

Billie Joe: I had this friend, Jason. He was a year younger than me. He always told me, "Yeah, I do it all the time." And I was like, "No way. Wow. Right on." (We wrote a song called "Jar." It's about this guy. I think he was all talk.) The girl lived behind Jason, and we'd go to her house every day, sneaking drinks out of her parents' liquor cabinet and stuff. And we just kind of watched movies, and just hung out. And then I came back one day, and then we did it.

SMART SEX: WAS SEX ALL YOU EXPECTED?

Billie Joe: Well, my back hurt a little. I remember that. I really didn't know what I was doing at all. And after, I felt really creepy. All I wanted to do is leave, to tell you the truth.

It was a long gap in between that before I ever really did it again.

SMART SEX: BY CHOICE, OR BY CIRCUMSTANCE?

Billie Joe: By circumstance. I just never had a girlfriend for a long time after that— I had a lot of zits and stuff like that. So I wasn't really attractive. [Laughs] I don't even think I kissed a girl for four years after that, to tell you the truth.

SMART SEX: YOU DIDN'T HAVE CONFIDENCE? OR WHAT WAS IT?

Billie Joe: I was just a real sappy kind of kid. I really fell in love with different people a lot. I would try to win their hearts over. I think sex was totally secondary to me after that. I think I had the [sex] experience and I think I'd rather— *I wanted to fall in love with someone.*

Because a lot of my friends had these relationships at a really young age. Fifteen-, sixteen-year-olds having sex. And they're totally in love with each other. You know, walking around school with their tongues down each other's throats constantly. And it was obvious that they were completely goo-goo over each other.

SMART SEX: DO GUYS TALK AND TELL? DO GUYS KISS ABOUT WHAT THEY DO?

Billie Joe: Oh, yeah. Yeah. I mean, me and my friends—you know, we do. I'm married now, but back then my friends would come to me and tell me, "Wow, I got to this point when we were, you know, having sex," or whatever. Just openly talking about their sexual experiences, which I think is a really healthy thing for people to do. I've also talked to a few women, and they've been pretty graphic. But I know that guys definitely get pretty graphic, no matter what.

SMART SEX: DOES THAT HELP EACH OTHER?

Billie Joe: Yeah. I think so. I mean, sometimes there's a competitive thing that happens, too, which is kind of ugly. Actually, it's really ugly. But I just sort of learned from

people's experiences. Especially when I was getting into punk rock and stuff, I just sort of became an observer of people. I was introduced to different sorts of lifestyles. And my friends would tell me about their sex lives. I was totally envious. But I thought it was great.

SMART SEX: HOW DOES SEX ON THE BIG AND LITTLE SCREENS COMPARE TO THE REAL THING?

Billie Joe: I hate these images of the young pretty girl and pretty boy with the milk-commercial smiles. You think it's gonna be perfect. I think that messed me up when I was younger.

You think it's gonna be like a smooth ride in a Ferrari, but it's more like a ride in a Volkswagen—with a lot of bumps along the way.

SMART SEX: DO YOU THINK MASTURBATION IS IMPORTANT?

Billie Joe: Yeah. I think having a sexual experience by yourself is very healthy. It keeps you sort of content. I mean, you can get these mental pictures. Like if someone does something that is attractive to you, or you might see something in a magazine (I've never been the type to keep a bunch of dirty magazines under my mattress or anything like that), you kind of create this mental picture, and then you kind of go **rraghaww!**

SMART SEX: DO GUYS ALWAYS FEEL LIKE IT'S THEIR JOB TO ALWAYS GO FOR IT, PUSH THINGS FURTHER WHEN THEY'RE FOOLING AROUND?

Billie Joe: Well, I think there's a healthy way of going about it. I mean, there's nothing wrong with experimenting with boundaries.

But there's that cutoff time, when it's no, and that means no. And that's where you stop every time. You don't push it. A lot of people push me.

SMART SEX: REALLY? HOW DOES THAT FEEL?

Billie Joe: It's kind of invading. Whether it's a sexual circumstance or just social— a drug thing or something. You're doing something that you don't want to do.

SMART SEX: HAVE YOU EVER WITNESSED ANY ACTS OF HOMOPHOBIA?

Billie Joe: Yeah. This band Pansy Division [an out-of-the-closet gay band] came and opened for us. People were throwing quarters, the drummer had a cut on his head. But when we got offstage, the band said,

'That was great. Those kids are always gonna remember that experience, the night that Pansy Division opened for Green Day.'

SMART SEX: SOME PEOPLE SAY THAT WE'RE ALL BISEXUAL TO SOME DEGREE. DO YOU AGREE?

Billie Joe: I wrote a song about someone dealing with bisexuality, trisexuality or whatever. I wouldn't call myself bisexual, I wouldn't call myself anything. I think it's okay to be attracted to someone of the same sex. I've looked at guys.

I think you're kind of taught one way. We all grow up and see Mommy kissing Daddy, not Daddy kissing Daddy.

SMART SEX: WHAT TO YOU IS SMARTER SEX? TO YOU YOU PERSONALLY?

Billie Joe: Me? I use a condom. I mean, well, you know me. I have a baby. And obviously, that was a very pleasant surprise. He wasn't planned. We weren't going to Planned Parenthood on a regular basis. We were mauling each other.

SMART SEX: HOW DID YOU HANDLE THAT WHEN YOU FOUND OUT ABOUT THE PREGNANCY?

Billie Joe: I thought it was really exciting. But then there was this other side of me—and I hope this doesn't sound evil or anything—this other side of me saying, "Thank God I can afford this right now." And that plays a big fat role in it, you know? After that, we talked about having the kid, and the things that we have to get for this child that's going to come into our lives—his own bedroom, food and clothes. And creating some sort of atmosphere and surroundings where there's some sense of stability.

There's so many things to think about, you know. It's endless.

SMART SEX: WHAT WOULD YOU SAY TO KIDS THINKING OF BECOMING A PARENT?

Billie Joe: I say, work on yourself first before anything, you know. I was fairly young, twenty-two. And I just jumped into a relationship, got married and had a kid. I'm still adjusting to it.

It's a twenty-four-hour-a-day job.

SMART SEX: HOW DIFFERENT IS YOUR LIFE NOW WITH A KID? Billie Joe: Oh, completely different. Your world revolves around this child. I was so used to living in a punk house and getting up every day at my leisure around one o'clock and just doing what I wanted. But that's not the case anymore. At first, you wake up two to three times a night. Get up around six A.M. It's the hardest job.

No matter what kind of gig or what kind of job you've got, nothing is as hard as being a parent—or being a mother, in specific.

SMART SEX: TELL ME A LITTLE BIT ABOUT CONDOM USE. HOW HAVE YOU LEARNED TO DEAL WITH THEM? Billie Joe: You just do it. You don't have a choice. My peer group, we've grown up in the shadow of AIDS. I mean, I just buried an uncle about a week ago.

It's a life-or-death situation.

SMART SEX: WHAT WAS THE WAKE-UP CALL FOR YOU, THAT YOU GOT SERIOUS ABOUT IT? Billie Joe: Just common sense. I have a lot of pressure from my peer group. The people I hung out with between the ages of say sixteen and now—it was always taken as a very big deal. And that you were a very cool person for using condoms. I still carry a condom when I'm hanging out with my wife, because we don't know if we—you know, "Wow, that tree looks pretty cool up there."

SMART SEX: YOU'RE PREPARED, JUST LIKE THE BOY SCOUTS. **Billie Joe: Yeah. I'm like a condom scout. There you go.**

11 | PREGNANCY

Pregnancy is an emotionally charged topic. It's about the creation of life itself. For some, religion factors in big-time. A pregnancy scare can be the wake-up call that makes you realize that you're an adult. Whether preventing pregnancy, coping with an unintended pregnancy or planning a pregnancy, you are trying to choose the best future for everyone. And it's not easy. These are big decisions. The worst thing you can do is sit there and do nothing.

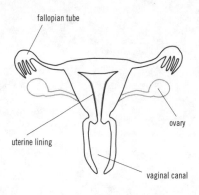

fallopian tube

ovary

uterine lining

vaginal canal

Uterine lining thickens, preparing
to receive a fertilized egg.

At the beginning of a woman's menstrual cycle, the lining of the uterus (endometrium) is not very thick. Signals that come via hormones tell an egg to ripen in one of the ovaries (the ovaries hold hundreds of thousands of undeveloped eggs, but nevertheless, women are born with a finite number; men manufacture sperm throughout their lives). The lining of the uterus starts to thicken in case it needs to hold and nourish

THE CYCLE OF LIFE—
WHAT HAPPENS INSIDE

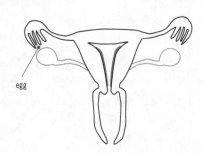

egg

Around mid-cycle, ovulation occurs.

an embryo. When an egg (ovum) is mature, it breaks out of its ovary. This part of the cycle is called ovulation. The egg is then swept up into the trumpetlike opening of the nearest fallopian tube. The egg spends the next three or four days journeying through the fallopian tube toward the uterus. If a man and woman have unprotected sex during this phase, the sperm travels into the woman's

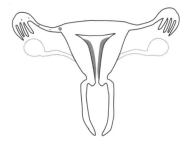

Three or four days after ovulation
the egg approaches the uterus.

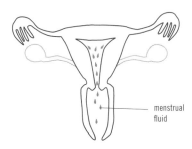

menstrual
fluid

The unfertilized egg disintegrates
and the uterine lining is shed as menstrual fluid.

body through the vaginal opening, through the cervical opening, through the uterus and into the fallopian tube, where it hopes to meet and fertilize the awaiting egg. If the egg gets fertilized, it travels the rest of the way through the fallopian tube and implants itself in the uterine lining that has been thickening and producing nutrients all the while. There, it can grow into an embryo. If the egg does not meet its mate, it disintegrates. As the thickened endometrium is no longer needed, it breaks down and sheds—exiting through the cervix, and out through the vagina. That's called getting your period. Though women are only fertile a few days a month, around ovulation time it's difficult to predict when that is. Unless you've got a physician doing fancy tests and measurements to tell you when you are and aren't ovulating, there are no real "safe" times of the month, when pregnancy is not a risk.

CATHERINE, 19:
I probably got pregnant
late May or early June
after my senior year in
high school. My cycle
was irregular. I went
two months without
my period. In late
July, I really started
to suspect. One night
my boyfriend said,
"You haven't had your
period." But then
he dismissed it
because I dismissed it.

THESAURUS MOMENT: PREGNANT

Knocked up, preggers,
expecting, bun in the
oven, pea in the pod,
with child, eating for two,
made an appointment with
the stork, flunked sex ed,
in a family way, starting a
college fund, gestational,
large with child, knitting
booties, playing
human incubator

KARLEY, 17: I don't think
my boyfriend thought that
I'd get pregnant like I did. I
had condoms right there, but
we just didn't use them. Heat
of the moment. Didn't do it.
I mean, we had talked
about having children if our
relationship had really gone
to the fullest. I remember
one time we were sitting
on the elementary school
playground and I had
been walking my dog.
And he was like, "Oh,
baby, don't worry about
it. If you're pregnant,
we'll get married, we'll
do it right." This and
that. It made me feel some
sort of security, that if I was
pregnant it would work out. Well,
obviously it didn't turn out that way.

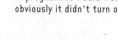

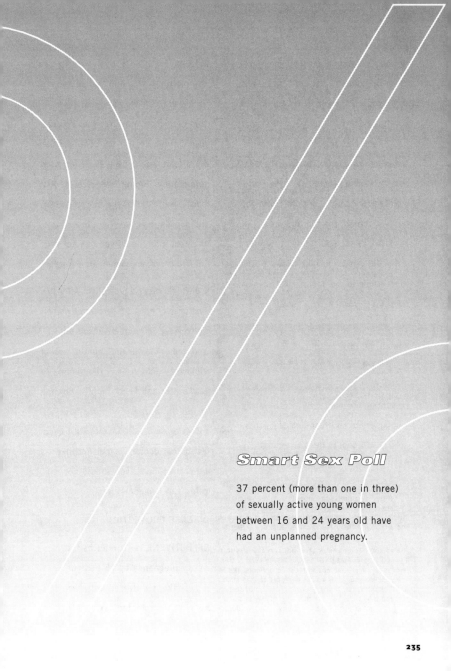

Smart Sex Poll

37 percent (more than one in three) of sexually active young women between 16 and 24 years old have had an unplanned pregnancy.

If you're female and all goes wrong—for example, the condom breaks, you and your partner completely flake and have unprotected sex or you had sex against your will—*and you're absolutely sure you don't want a pregnancy,* an option is emergency contraception, commonly called the morning-after pill.

WHAT IT IS: Four to eight hormone pills that you take in two doses, according to the doctor's instructions.

HOW IT WORKS: The morning-after pill works by preventing an egg from implanting in the lining of the womb. Technically you are intervening before pregnancy and are still preventing pregnancy. But, occasionally implantation, and therefore pregnancy, still occurs despite emergency contraception efforts.

COST: About $100.

Note: If you miss the seventy-two-hour window of opportunity, emergency contraception won't work, and/or it could hurt an implanted egg that is growing into a fetus. In this case you need to wait another two weeks, and then take a pregnancy test.

Also note: The morning-after pill is not a substitute for well-thought-out birth control. Many doctors think of it as a one-time option for their patients. It's for emergencies; your body wasn't designed to take such a big hit of hormones. If you get emergency contraception, you might want to use this opportunity to discuss other birth control options with your doctor.

EMERGENCY CONTRACEPTION

WHERE TO GET IT: If you want to take the morning-after pill, you should call your doctor to assess whether this is a smart move for you. You can also call the Emergency Contraception Hotline at 1-800-584-9911 for more information. Timing is everything. Just because it's called the morning-after pill doesn't mean you have to wait until the next morning. If you can get it into your system sooner, that's better.

CONS: No disease protection. After the first dose of pills, 50 percent of women get queasy, 20 percent throw up. You can take over-the-counter motion sickness medicine like Dramamine to feel better and keep the pills down. If you throw up within three hours of either dosage, you have to start over. Keep your doctor posted. And like other medicines, you should not offer it to someone else.

DISEASE PROTECTION: None.

EFFECTIVENESS: It reduces the risk of pregnancy by 75 percent if you take it within seventy-two hours of unprotected sex.

If you or your partner missed a period and feels any of the other symptoms, pregnancy is very likely. Take a test ASAP—either at home or at the doctor's. The sooner you know, the more options you have. Many women, especially young women, deny their pregnancy for so long that their choices are narrowed.

THE SIGNS OF PREGNANCY

Reality check: If you've been having sex, you or your partner could be pregnant. Even if you've been militant about birth control, all methods can fail. The only 100 percent effective means of contraception is abstinence.

Even a sexual encounter where sperm landed anywhere near the vagina can on rare occasion bring pregnancy. If you think you might be pregnant, watch for these early symptoms:

•missed period(s)
•tender and/or slightly enlarged breasts
•need to pee often
•feeling sick to the stomach in the morning, afternoon or nearly always
•unusual fatigue, even dizziness
•tighter clothes

LEETA, 20: This was gonna be my year, my junior year. I was getting all R's, I made it on the cheerleading team, guys were sweatin' me in the halls, I'm like, All right! But then I started feeling sick. I'm not the healthiest person out there—I'm kind of weak and I have anemia. I always used to throw up anyway. But I knew that I should've gotten my period and didn't. Every morning, I'd wake up and look and think, Okay, it'll come tomorrow. But the days went by. I put it off longer than I should have.

TAKING A PREGNANCY TEST

If you're concerned that you're pregnant, and it's been two weeks since the sex act in question, you can take a home pregnancy test. Home pregnancy tests make the we-might-be-pregnant crises more bearable. The privacy they offer is key when you have so much on your mind. You can buy a test at any pharmacy for as little as $7 and as much as $16. Find some quiet time at home to take it.

If you're the potential father, you can help by buying the test and by staying by your girl's side while she takes it (helps eliminate mistakes, too). Read the instructions carefully. Some involve catching a clean stream of urine to mix with a premeasured, premixed chemical. These days, more and more tests use the wand method, which takes only one step to use. For this kind of pregnancy test, you pee right into the end of the uncapped wand. The wand tip absorbs the urine and registers whether the pregnancy hormone (HCG) is in your system. For all methods, you should start peeing without the wand or cup in place, then take the sample from the middle of the urine stream. The first urine of the morning will give you better results, since it's more concentrated. Most tests make you wait about three minutes for the results. Then a color or a symbol will appear in the results window (or wherever the instructions tell you to look).

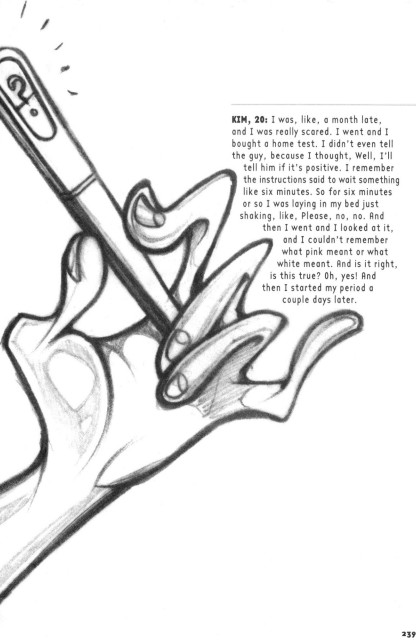

KIM, 20: I was, like, a month late, and I was really scared. I went and I bought a home test. I didn't even tell the guy, because I thought, Well, I'll tell him if it's positive. I remember the instructions said to wait something like six minutes. So for six minutes or so I was laying in my bed just shaking, like, Please, no, no. And then I went and I looked at it, and I couldn't remember what pink meant or what white meant. And is it right, is this true? Oh, yes! And then I started my period a couple days later.

If the test says you're pregnant, you probably are. You should go to a doctor for a pelvic exam and backup pregnancy test as soon as you can. False-positives on home tests are rare. If it says you're not pregnant, but your period still doesn't come, take a test again two weeks later. You may have taken it too soon so that there wasn't enough pregnancy-related hormone in your urine yet. If it's still negative, you probably just missed a period; nerves will do that. (It's also possible—though unlikely— to have two false-negative tests, so take a third test a little later if you want to be extra sure.) Stress, excessive dieting or exercise or severe illness can also make you miss a period. And some women just have irregular periods now and then. If you don't menstruate for a few months, though, make a doctor's appointment. It may be a nutritional or hormonal problem.

CATHERINE, 19: I thought I might be pregnant. So I finally got up the nerve to go to the drugstore and get a test. I went to my boyfriend's house, picked him up, and went to my house, where I did the test in the bathroom. It came out positive and I was hysterical. We went back to his house and tried to lay low. We weren't talking about it anymore. We were up on his bed curled up together. An hour later, my mom called. She called to say, "I made a three o'clock appointment for a pregnancy test." She knew I was sexually active, and she knew my period was late. Next thing, we're sitting in my doctor's office, my mother's in tears. I'm sitting there shaking in my shorts. The doctor took me into the bathroom, and I said, "I already know the answer and I don't want my mom to know." And she said okay, because of doctor-patient confidentiality. So we did the test. The doctor came back into the room and said, "The test is negative," and we talked about birth control options. Then she asked my mom to leave the room, and she was like, "What are you gonna do?" and I said, "I think I'm gonna get an abortion." We talked about the local abortion clinic, and she reassured me that it would be okay. So my mom and I took the car home. I'm thinking, Thank God she doesn't know.

IF THERE'S A PREGNANCY

A pregnancy means it's definitely time to think—and act. If you're pregnant and your partner doesn't know, you should tell him. He might be able to give you some comfort and insight that you can't get elsewhere. It might help him grow up and become more responsible if he hasn't been so far.

Next you have to weigh all your options. Sometimes a parent, close relative, friend or health care pro can help you look at the possibilities and figure out what's best for everyone. (See Resources, page 310, for places to get outside advice.) If you think you don't want the baby, the sooner you act, the better and safer the results.

A FATHER'S RIGHTS

Pregnancy is definitely not just a female issue. It takes two to tango. Sometimes guys, and consideration for guys' feelings, get lost in the scramble. It would be cool if we encouraged young men—especially ones still in school—to talk about sex issues, responsibility, birth control and being a good father. If a guy is supportive of his girlfriend's choice to use contraception, she's much more likely to use it. If a guy is hostile, the girl is more likely to let birth control slide. All guys, younger and older, should be discussing birth control when they discuss STD protection.

This is a tough issue. If you're the father, the baby is genetically half yours. But the girl carries the baby—and that is a much larger commitment in terms of health risk, energy, time and discomfort. You cannot force her to have an abortion, nor can you force her to have the baby. It's her uterus. But you can certainly express your feelings about keeping the baby or not. You can also be there for emotional and financial support. You two will have a lot to talk about.

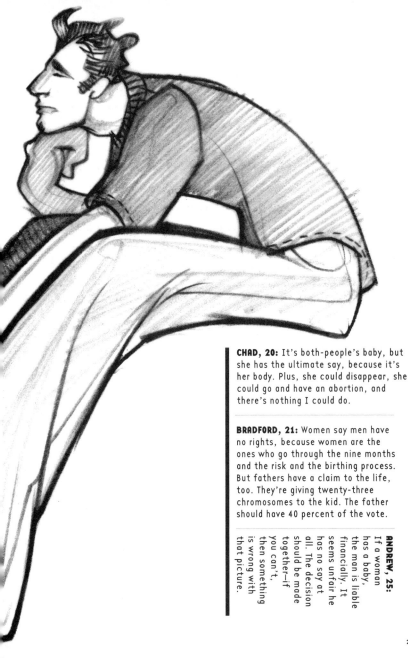

CHAD, 20: It's both-people's baby, but she has the ultimate say, because it's her body. Plus, she could disappear, she could go and have an abortion, and there's nothing I could do.

BRADFORD, 21: Women say men have no rights, because women are the ones who go through the nine months and the risk and the birthing process. But fathers have a claim to the life, too. They're giving twenty-three chromosomes to the kid. The father should have 40 percent of the vote.

ANDREW, 25: If a woman has a baby, the man is liable financially. It seems unfair he has no say at all. The decision should be made together—if you can't, then something is wrong with that picture.

If you two decide to have the baby, you should discuss what your role will be *before* she gives birth, and you should stand by that decision. Remember that there is a big difference between being a father and being a daddy. Anyone can become a father, but to be a daddy takes real caring, commitment and responsibility. There are certainly many guys out there who would make wonderful parents. Real men know they have a financial as well as a moral responsibility toward their baby (and the baby's mother).

DAVID, 20: I never knew my dad, so I promised I'd always be a father to my child. I'd collect aluminum cans in the street to make a living if I had to. My children will be told every day that they are loved, and they'll know who their dad is.

If you two decide to have an abortion, you need to give her support. Go with her and be with her during the procedure if she wants that. Pay for it or pay for half if you can. You may be taken aback at the conflicting emotions you feel. When people talk about unwed motherhood and abortion, guys' feelings get very little airtime, yet this experience can be really hard. Even if you two disagree about what to do, try to stick around and give her respect.

TODD, 22: If it was possible for her to carry the baby for nine months and give it up for adoption, I'd prefer that over being a father—there's no way. I can barely take care of myself.

CHAD, 20: I'd want to have the baby and raise it. I'd get a job. I'd get some money. You have to face the consequences of what you do. You have to live up to your responsibilities. If you're responsible enough to have sex, you should be responsible enough to take care of the girl.

ANDREW, 25: I think abortion is a viable choice. It's something I'd support. If a woman I was involved with wanted to have a child, I'd support that, but I would not marry a woman just because I got her pregnant. You should marry someone for reasons other than mistakes in the bedroom.

Though women have obviously been having children since humankind began, it is still a serious medical procedure. Before you decide to do this, evaluate your health, your eating habits, your vices (drugs, alcohol, smoking). Discuss the risks with your doctor. If you want to have the child, you should start prenatal care right away.

CARRYING THE PREGNANCY TO TERM

THE OPTIONS EXPLAINED

Deciding to raise a baby will certainly change your life. If this is your choice, be sure you have help with child support and childcare. You may have to drop out of school. You may have to take maternity leave from work. You may be stunned at how expensive a baby is. If you are out of school, if you are working at a flexible workplace, if you are married or very committed to someone, if you are on your own but financially comfortable, becoming a parent will be easier.

(Note: Since these are medically female issues, the "you" usually means the woman, though guys should definitely keep reading, because this could affect you someday.)

If you are much younger or your life is still very unstable, you will have a much harder go of it, and so will your child—though you can do it. Not to knock young parents, but the odds are heavily stacked against them. Children of adolescent parents are more likely to suffer poor health, to have low birth-weights, to lag in school, to experience behavior problems and to suffer child abuse and neglect. More than a quarter of the girls who drop out of high school give pregnancy as the reason. Only 8 percent of male dropouts say they left school because they became fathers.

Sometimes teenage pregnancies aren't an accident. In communities where young people don't have many options for the future because of poverty, or they don't have a full range of opportunities, sometimes a pregnancy seems to be a way into a future that otherwise looks bleak. But sex is no way to bolster low self-esteem, and neither is a baby.

KARLEY, 17: I knew I was pregnant because I know my body. My breasts were tender, and I just felt weird inside. I could feel my body changing. I went down to the pregnancy center and got my test. I remember seeing the pink line—*bam*, right there it was. When I told the father, he was like, "That baby isn't mine." I couldn't believe it. I was just screaming and crying. Because just a couple days before he was telling me that he loved me and that he was gonna marry me. I was fourteen years old. When I first started seeing him, I thought he was seventeen. I found out he was twenty-one after I was pregnant and I just couldn't believe it. But I thought that maybe since he was older he would stand by me and take care of his child.

Karley has these words for other pregnant teenagers:

The father of Karley's baby did not stick around, so she faced the options with the help and support of her parents. She ruled out abortion and then adoption. ▬▬▬▬

KARLEY: I just figured, Why carry a child for nine months, get stretch marks, get fat and give it away? And have that scar in my heart forever that I would not know my child and that she would be with somebody else? I couldn't handle that thought. When she was born, I was crying. I couldn't believe that something like that could grow inside me. Now I live with my mom and she watches my girl during the day. I don't get welfare. I don't get anything like that. Everybody says the best thing I can do for myself is go to school, and that's what I need to do right now. I'd love to get a job, but I wouldn't have any time to spend with my daughter.

KARLEY: Really, really think about your choices. Because the choice that you make is gonna be with you for life. A baby changes everything. You don't get to go out anymore. You can't just get up and leave and go to a party or go to the mall or go see a movie. You have to think about your child. I breast-fed for fourteen months, so I always had to be there for her. It's just hard. Trying to do school and the child and the normal teenage thing. I feel very old, like an old lady, 'cause I have arthritis. For a long time I didn't even shower by myself because I couldn't leave her alone. It's a lifetime commitment that you're making if you're gonna have that child. You have to give that child your all. You have to read to them, you have to bathe them, you have to play with them, change their diapers, feed them, do everything else. And every last penny that you get goes to your child. I miss being carefree and not really worrying about anything except school and grades and what I want to do.

It's hard to carry a baby in your body for so long and then let it go. You might feel guilty. You might feel torn and sad or depressed. But keep in mind that there are many other couples and individuals who can give your child a good home. If you don't want to have an abortion, and you can't emotionally or financially afford to keep your child, adoption is a good option.

You are probably giving your baby and yourself greater opportunities for success. If you know people who are adopted, talk to them about their experience, how they feel about their adoptive families.

MELISSA, 23: I've always known I was adopted—and it was a special thing. My parents waited a really long time to have kids, so they adopted me. They're really proud of me. I remember being a kid on the playground, saying, "Well, I'm adopted." I thought it made me cooler. I could have wild fantasies about who my parents were. When I was fourteen, I wanted to find out about my parents. My mom brought me to the adoption agency. She said, "If this is what you want to do, we'll do it." I wasn't allowed to see my [birth] mom's name or address, but I could look through the rest of my files. There was a picture of my [birth] dad in there. He was thirty-three and my [birth] mom was twenty-two. She didn't want to get married, so she had me and put me up for adoption. She picked my parents over other couples—so there were pictures of my [adoptive] parents in there, too. That's kinda cool that she played an active role. I wrote a letter to my [birth] mom and left it in the files in case she ever contacts the adoption agency.

CHOOSING ADOPTION

•About 20 percent of 15- to 18-year-old mothers choose adoption.

•It is estimated that more than 50,000 adoptions of U.S.–born children take place every year in America.

•Unmarried women who choose adoption for their children are more likely to advance in education, delay marriage, and have a job and a higher income, and they are less likely to have another pregnancy out of wedlock.

•There are an estimated one to two million couples and individuals who would like to adopt children.

KINDS OF

CLOSED ADOPTION
Traditional
Confidential

1 = Complete anonymity between birth parents and adoptive parents.

2 = Some knowledge about birth parents and adoptive parents (like what area they live in, their professions or income levels, their nationality).

3 = Birth parents have some involvement in picking the kind of parents they'd like their child to go to.

4 = Birth and adoptive parents exchange letters and photos through the adoption agency, using first names only.

5 = Birth and adoptive parents meet once, just using first names, but they don't give out full identities.

6 = Knowledge of identities, but no contact between adoptive and birth parents.

7 = Ongoing contact between adoptive and birth parents.

OPEN ADOPTION
Experimental
Not Confidential

The adoption process can allow for different levels of contact between the birth parents and the adoptive parents—depending on what you're comfortable with and what the adoption agency and lawyers are comfortable with. People who favor traditional adoption (the kind where birth and adoptive parents know little about each other) say that this approach allows for more closure. The birth mom and dad can move on with their lives, get their education, maybe start a family of their own when the time is right. The baby can fully bond with the adoptive parents as if they all were family from the start. Fans of open adoption (where birth parents keep some contact with the adoptive parents) say it's good for the biological parents to know how their kid is faring in the adoptive home. And the child doesn't have to wonder about his or her original roots. It's also easier for the adoptive parents to get answers about the medical history of the birth families. But open adoption is still relatively new and makes for some complicated relationships ("Honey, should we invite Jasmine's biological parents to her birthday party?"). So think hard about your decision. Talk to others whose lives have been touched by adoption.

To start the adoption process, your best bet is to go through a state-authorized adoption agency (see Resources, page 310). You can also arrange an adoption privately through a lawyer—like if you know a family who wants to raise your baby. All adoptions will require a state judge's approval. Beware of doctors or lawyers or others who offer large sums of money to take your baby. These are sometimes illegal adoptions where money and not the baby's welfare is the priority. Contact the department of child welfare in your state if you are suspicious. The National Council for Adoption (also in Resources) publishes a booklet of suggestions and guidelines that will help you set up an adoption in the best way possible. Hold on to all records and consent forms. It's really tough to go through this process alone. It can help to seek a friend, partner, parent, clergyperson or counselor to lean on.

GINA, 24: Abortion is about privacy. It doesn't matter to me what anyone else is going to do. I believe totally in choice.

ENDING PREGNANCY: ABORTION

BRADFORD, 21: I made the ethical decision that life itself is the most important thing. The only time I think abortion is necessary is when the life of the baby is threatening the life of the mother. That's life versus life. For victims of rape and incest, the birth of the baby will destroy the life of the mother. But in cases where the women don't want the baby because they would have to quit their careers or they don't want the responsibility, that doesn't outweigh the right the baby has to be born.

CATHERINE, 19: It really angers me to see people who think that they have the right to make a decision for you when they don't know your circumstances. I definitely think I screwed up, but I definitely think it's better for me and the child to have had an abortion. I had smoked pot, drank, done nitrous. The kid would have had so many problems. Others might think it's taking the easy way out.

CRYSTAL, 18: I think it's *ironic* that people are like, "Save the whales," protect endangered species," but they also say, "Now I'm pregnant, let's take care of it." A baby is a baby no matter how a baby was conceived. I look at it from the child's perspective. I see abortion as murder. Pro-choice? Sure, you have a choice. The choice starts with whether you have sex or not. Because pregnancy is a consequence of sex.

Smart Sex Poll

A group of sexually active young adults were asked,
"If you or your partner were to become pregnant, how
seriously would you consider abortion as an option?"
These were their answers:

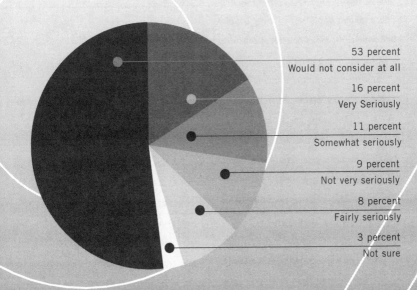

53 percent
Would not consider at all

16 percent
Very Seriously

11 percent
Somewhat seriously

9 percent
Not very seriously

8 percent
Fairly seriously

3 percent
Not sure

Actual outcomes of
teenage pregnancies:
35 percent of pregnant
girls get an abortion.
37 percent give birth even though
the pregnancy was unplanned.
14 percent give birth
to a planned baby.
14 percent miscarry.

Deciding whether or not to have an abortion can be emotionally tough. Some women feel uncomfortable or torn because they want to be mothers one day. Since the pregnancy has already begun, they feel they are bailing on a golden opportunity. Many people believe, for religious or ethical reasons, that human life begins with conception and that abortion is murder. This is not a simple, black-and-white issue, and there is great political and emotional debate, with passionate feelings on both sides. You might want to consider the quality of life you might have with and without the child. Who would be there to help you raise a child? Who would help you get through an abortion? You certainly would benefit from talking to your partner, a parent or another adult you trust. For now, abortion is a legal option and is considered a private medical procedure.

Though abortion is legal, abortion services can be hard to get. Note that about half the states have parental notification or consent laws—mostly addressing females under eighteen. If you live in a state with such a law and you're a minor, you have to talk to your parent or parents or get permission from a judge before you can have the procedure done. Sometimes getting the judge's permission is just a formality; sometimes it's harder. Many girls prefer to travel out of state instead.

Sometimes there are no legal obstacles, but there are no clinics nearby that perform this service. If this is the case, call the National Abortion Federation or your local Planned Parenthood (see Resources, page 310) for advice on where to find a safe and reliable clinic in your area. If you're sure you want an abortion and are looking for clinics in the Yellow Pages, look under Abortion Services, Family Planning, Health Agencies or Birth Control—not Abortion Alternatives. Places called "alternative" are often pro-life organizations set up to talk you out of an abortion.

DO NOT TRY TO GIVE YOURSELF AN ABORTION

(or have a friend or a friend of a friend do it to you). Abortion is a surgical procedure that requires a trained physician. Performed by anyone else, an abortion might leave you in extreme pain, infertile, mutilated or even dead.

VIRGINIA, 20: When I first started having sex and I thought I was pregnant, I used to get terrified about it. I used to do things like try and abuse my body as much as I could, so that if I was pregnant, I would have a miscarriage. I would punch myself in the stomach, drink myself into oblivion, just not eat right, run miles and miles thinking that if I ran, I'd get a cramp, and if I was pregnant, I would have a miscarriage. Just anything that I could think of. I never did anything like toss myself down a flight of stairs, but I used to think about it.

None of the things that you can think of doing to yourself is likely to induce miscarriage, and some are likely to hurt you really badly, or even kill you. Please handle your pregnancy through a health care practitioner.

GETTING PREPARED

If you decide that abortion is for you, there are some questions you should ask when you make your appointment:

1. "What do the services cost? Does the price include a postabortion checkup?"

2. (If you're underage) "Will I need parental consent? Will you tell my parents about the abortion even if I choose not to involve them?"

3. "What kind of counseling is available before (and after) the procedure?"

4. "Can I bring a friend? Can he/she be in the room with me during the abortion?"

5. "What kind of pain medication and anesthesia do you offer?" Some places only offer local anesthesia, in which case they numb the cervix (opening to the uterus) and you stay awake. General anesthesia means you are asleep for the whole thing.

6. "Is the person performing the abortion legally certified to do this procedure?" Most states require a doctor to perform the procedure. A handful of states—as of August 1996, Arizona, Kansas, Kentucky, New Hampshire, Oregon, Vermont, and West Virginia—allow a trained health practitioner to perform abortions in the first trimester.

7. "What are the emergency back-up options?" There should be an established hospital where they can send you if there are complications.

8. "Might there be protesters outside the facility? If so, how do you handle the situation?" Sometimes clinics have helpers outside to escort patients in with the minimum of harassment.

Forewarned is forearmed. The experience will be less scary if it's less of a mystery. Beware of abortion clinics that are more concerned with financial profit than your physical and emotional health. If you don't like the answers or attitude you are getting over the phone, try to shop around. But you might need to travel a bit to find a place where you feel comfortable.

Bonus Fact
Abortion performed in the early stages of pregnancy by a trained, licensed professional is less traumatic for the body than childbirth.

THE PROCEDURE

It helps to bring your boyfriend or a trusted friend or family member with you to the clinic, and to go early in the day if you can, so you have time to recover. Abortions are much safer and easier during the first twelve weeks (first trimester) of pregnancy. First-trimester abortions usually cost about $300, but some places charge as much as $500 or more. Cost also goes up if you want general, rather than local, anesthesia—that is, if the clinic offers you a range of anesthesia options. Sometimes the clinic will decide on a painkiller plan for you based on where you are in the pregnancy. The advantage of staying conscious for the procedure is that you can communicate with the doctor and nurses to let them know how you're feeling, and they can tell you how everything is going. If you want to sleep through the whole thing, general anesthesia can be given intravenously (injected into your arm). General anesthesia can cause more complications than local and it takes longer for your body to shake it off. You will probably wake up from general anesthesia feeling spacey and nauseated. If you choose general anesthesia, you must be sure not to eat or drink anything after midnight the day before the procedure (so that you don't throw up while you are asleep).

The most common kind of abortion, vacuum-suction abortion, can only be performed in the first trimester. This procedure takes about five to seven minutes. It involves dilating (widening the opening of) the cervix and inserting a tool that vacuums out the tissue. If you are further along in your pregnancy (second trimester), you might have to go to a hospital instead of a clinic, and you have a different procedure that requires wider dilation of the cervix and more tools to remove the tissue in your uterus. Third-trimester abortions are very risky and traumatic. You would definitely have to go to the hospital and the procedure is more elaborate (something akin to childbirth or a cesarean section). Doctors usually avoid this operation unless the fetus is threatening the mother's health. All the more reason to make your decision early, so that if you decide to have an abortion, you can do it as soon as possible.

AFTERCARE

You may need help getting home, and you'll probably want someone to lean on during the next few hours, when you'll feel cramps and maybe mixed emotions. You should take it easy and rest as much as possible for a day or two. Wear a sanitary pad and expect some bleeding. Excessive bleeding (more than a menstrual period), severe pain and/or fever are reasons to call the doctor. Avoid sexual activity, tampons, douches and even baths (stick to showers) for two weeks to prevent infection. A checkup after a couple of weeks will also ensure that everything is fine. Emotionally, some women feel more relief than regret; others have a harder time. There's no blueprint, no "correct" response to an abortion. Just be sure you have someone to talk to afterward.

ELLEN, 21: Last year I was in a relationship, and we used condoms almost all the time. But there were one or two times we didn't. When I missed a period, I started to worry. My boyfriend pressed me to take a test, and it was positive. I went through a few agonizing talks with him and with my mother, and we decided in the end that my boyfriend and I were too young to keep it. Even though I knew I couldn't support a child at 20, I really regret having the abortion. I cried for a week and still cry when I think about it—one of those haunting things. I cry all the time. A few months ago, I was lying in bed with someone else on what would have been my due date. And I just started shaking in his arms, just thinking that I could have been holding a baby then.

CATHERINE, 19: When I found out I was pregnant, it was assumed I'd have an abortion. We called the clinic, we made the appointment and I cried, because it was the day before I was supposed to leave for school. My freshman year in college—I was supposed to be so excited. My boyfriend was supposed to leave for school even sooner. He said he would stay, but I told him not to because it would look suspicious to our families. When he told his two best friends that I was pregnant and planning to have an abortion, he was crying—I wish he had expressed that to me.

I didn't tell my parents. And I knew that if I didn't go through with it I would have killed one of them with a heart attack and the other would disown me. They're traditional Catholics. The day of the operation, I had one of my boyfriend's friends take me. I made sure I got there good and early—first in, first out. Fifteen minutes later, protesters showed up. I was just completely numb. The clinic gives you a consent form to sign and they tell you about all the possible complications. It was painful during and after the procedure. I was supposed to rest that day, but I packed for school and spent time with a friend. Nobody can describe what it's like to know something's inside of you—something independent of you but dependent on you.

NONSURGICAL ABORTIONS

RU-486, a.k.a. "the abortion pill," is effective in ending pregnancies that have not gone beyond seven weeks. The woman actually takes one kind of pill (mifepristone) and then vaginal suppositories of another drug (misoprostol) forty-eight hours later. RU-486 has been available all over Europe for years. In the fall of 1996, the Food and Drug Administration (FDA) issued an Approvable Letter for the drug—which means that the abortion pill is closer to being available in the U.S.

METHOTREXATE

This is a legal mix of a couple of different drugs that work together to induce abortion. Unlike RU-486, the ingredients of methotrexate are fully FDA–approved. Methotrexate consists of a chemotherapy drug (normally used for cancer patients) plus a uterine-contraction–inducing drug. The result is an at-home miscarriage. The disadvantages: There are many messy side effects, such as bleeding, nausea and discomfort. Although methotrexate is legal, it's still a prescription drug that not every doctor is comfortable giving out. If your doctor does prescribe it, he or she should keep you under watchful eye to make sure everything goes okay.

PREGNANCY AND YOUR PARENTS

You might be thinking that your parents are the last people on earth you want to tell about your pregnancy or your partner's pregnancy. But with some parents, there may be much to gain from talking with them. As parents, it's their job to watch out for your health and happiness and to help you plan your future. A pregnancy can definitely affect your health, happiness and future. Your mom and dad can probably help you out with a shoulder to cry on, a wise viewpoint and maybe an insurance plan or a few dollars. They also deserve to know. Even though times have changed, unplanned pregnancy was certainly an issue in your parents' day and long before that. If, however, you think news of a pregnancy will get you physically abused, kicked out of the house or cut off financially at a time you can't afford to be, or if there is sexual abuse in the family, then you might want to lean on someone else you trust.

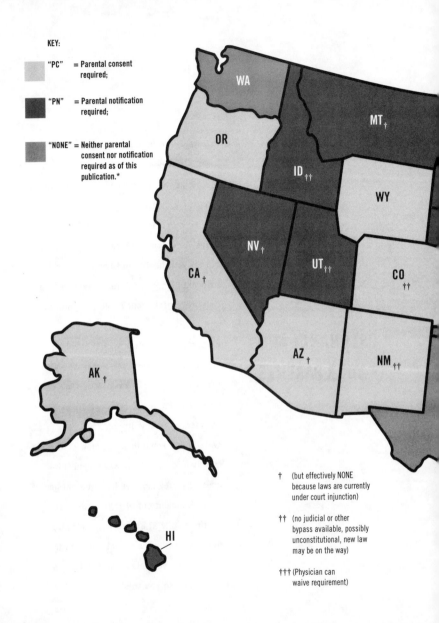

KEY:

"PC" = Parental consent required;

"PN" = Parental notification required;

"NONE" = Neither parental consent nor notification required as of this publication.*

WA

MT †

OR

ID ††

WY

NV †

UT ††

CO ††

CA †

AZ †

NM ††

AK †

HI

† (but effectively NONE because laws are currently under court injunction)

†† (no judicial or other bypass available, possibly unconstitutional, new law may be on the way)

††† (Physician can waive requirement)

STATE-BY-STATE ABORTION LAWS FOR MINORS

(as of September 1997)

†††
ME

MN

WI

MI

IA

IL †

IN

OH

KS

MO

KY

VT

NH

NY

MA

RI

CT

PA

NJ

DE

WV

†††

MD

VA †††

OK

AR

TN †

NC

SC

MS

AL

GA

LA

FL

Unplanned pregnancy is an enormous issue in this country. You can do your part to reduce the problem by educating yourself about preventive measures and using them in the bedroom. But no birth control method is fail-safe—so if you don't think you can handle a pregnancy, you should hold off on sex.

*Parental Consent means that you need to get permission from a parent if you're a minor (under 18 in most states). Parental Notification means that you have to tell a parent, but you don't need their permission. In some states a grandparent, counselor, or older sibling is an acceptable substitute for a parent. Unless otherwise noted, these laws can be bypassed by judicial or other means.

If you are thinking about an abortion and live in a state where there is a parental consent/notification law, it's a good idea to call a clinic and have someone explain your options. Some girls travel to a nearby state with different laws—although this can get expensive and difficult. Virtually all states with parental consent/notification laws give minors the option of avoiding parental involvement by explaining their situation to a judge. Most family-planning and adolescent-health clinics will know your local laws and how to put you in touch with a judge if you need one. Or they can at least put you in touch with a social worker who can help you find a judge. (Note: If you live at home and are calling nearby states to find clinics, keep in mind that the calls will show up on your family phone bill.) The chart on the previous two pages shows the current legal situation for each state, but remember that these laws change very often.

12 | SEXUAL HARASSMENT AND DATE RAPE

While sexual contact can feel great, unwanted sexual contact can be scary and painful. But there's so much gray area and miscommunication in human relationships (especially when it comes to sex) that it's sometimes hard to figure out whether you're dealing with a creep. Or maybe you're acting like a creep but you don't even realize it. Sexual harassment and rape are more about throwing around power than showing love. Check out the tips on how to avoid, recognize and deal with the ugly side of sex.

It happens all of the
time, walking up the street or in the
workplace, whatever. I gauge what
sexual harassment is by my reaction
to it. Some s**t people say just tears
me up. Like men who sit next to me
on the subway and demand that I
talk to them for no apparent reason.
I think that's sexual harassment
because I wouldn't ever do that to
them—why would I want to? It's
unwanted sexual attention. In some
ways it makes you feel like you're
luring these people. Like you wore
a short skirt and that's the reason
they came up to talk to you.

Smart Sex Poll

46 percent of young women and 14
percent of young men say they have
been sexually harassed at work.

DISRESPECT IS NOT AN APHRODISIAC

Sexual harassment is any unwanted sexual
attention, and it's usually an attempt at
intimidation. Though men can get sexually
harassed, it most often happens to women.

When guys go around grabbing girls,
hissing at them on the street, leering at
them in office hallways, pressuring them
for dates, casually throwing around words
like *bitch* and *ho,* it indicates a total lack of
respect. It communicates to girls that they
are sex objects before they're people—an
idea that does not fit into the 20th century.

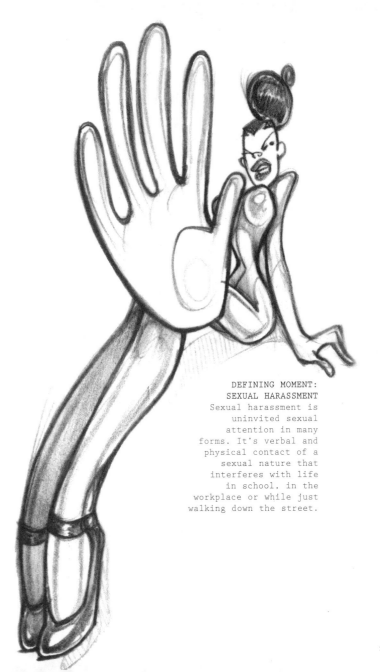

**DEFINING MOMENT:
SEXUAL HARASSMENT**
Sexual harassment is
uninvited sexual
attention in many
forms. It's verbal and
physical contact of a
sexual nature that
interferes with life
in school, in the
workplace or while just
walking down the street.

COERCION AND BRIBERY:

A person in power (or who thinks he or she's in power) gives or denies a benefit based on sexual behavior. Examples: A college professor offers you a good grade in return for sexual contact or threatens a bad grade if you refuse sexual contact; the parent of a kid you baby-sit promises a bigger tip in exchange for a goodnight kiss.

MOST ACTS OF SEXUAL HARASSMENT FIT INTO ONE OF THE FOLLOWING CATEGORIES:

HOSTILE ENVIRONMENT:

The workplace or school halls are unpleasant, uncomfortable places to be because of sexual innuendo, sexual comments, pictures, unwanted advances. It's hard to function properly and get work done. Examples: catcalls when you go down the hall, smutty posters of naked people in a communal area, lewd graffiti all over your locker, two guys in the next cubicle who talk all day long about who they want to bone or who has great breasts, a guy who calls another guy "wuss" and "faggot" on a regular basis, a boss who regularly comments on how sexy you look in certain clothes, the women in your dorm who rate you on a scale of one to ten when you walk down to the bathrooms.

AGGRESSIVE ACTS:

This kind of harassment is usually easier to spot. It includes unwanted touching, kissing, grabbing, embracing, fondling or more. Examples: Guys at school who snap your bra strap and then laugh, someone who feels your butt in a crowded elevator, an acquaintance who insists on hugging you when you'd rather not.

THIRD-PARTY EFFECTS:

This is more complicated, but it's sexual harassment nonetheless. It's when two people are in a sexual relationship and a third person is affected. Examples: The person next to you in your Melville seminar is sleeping with the teacher and getting an easy A, while you knock yourself out for a B; your coworker is having an affair with the boss and gets a raise even though you've been doing the same job a year longer.

If you feel you are being harassed, get out of the situation. Clearly ask the person to stop. Describe the behavior that upsets you. The offender may not even realize that he or she is out of line. If you don't get immediate results, go to a higher authority and make a report. Schools and workplaces often have a system in place to handle such complaints. Include as many details and examples as you can remember.

There might be pressure to dismiss your complaint. You might be told that "it's no big deal" or "it's just part of life." But sexual harassment is a big deal, and it shouldn't be part of life. You have every right to fight back, and maybe get the offenders to rethink their behavior. You will also be helping others in the same environment. If no one speaks up, how can it stop? You deserve respect, and your sexuality deserves respect. You have a right to pick and choose whom you give your good stuff to.

They Fought Back

Sexual harassment cases do not always need to go to court, but here are some examples of girls who did not stand still for harassment:

• In 1991 Katy Lyle (19 years old) won a $15,000 settlement from her school district in Duluth, MN, for failure to remove obscene graffiti about her from the boys' bathroom, despite the fact that she had made numerous complaints.

• In 1992, in Petaluma, CA, Tawnya Brawdy won a $20,000 settlement from her junior high school because no one had stopped the boys who mooed at her like a cow and teased her about her breast size.

• In 1992, Christine Franklin's $6 million sexual harassment suit against her Gwinnett County, GA, school went all the way to the Supreme Court and won. Judge Clarence Thomas (once accused of sexually harassing Anita Hill) was among those who sided with Franklin.

DATE RAPE

- Acquaintance rape or date rape is the most common type of rape, accounting for 70 to 80 percent of all rape-crisis-center contacts.
- The highest incidence of acquaintance rape seems to occur during senior year in high school and freshman year at college.
- Recent surveys in the U.S. found that up to 14 percent of all college women have experienced date rape.
- In a large college study, 73 percent of all assailants and 55 percent of the victims had used drugs or alcohol immediately before the sexual assault.

DEFINING MOMENT: RAPE/DATE RAPE

Rape: Sexual intercourse against the partner's will. Date rape (also called acquaintance rape): Sexual intercourse against the partner's will. Occurs between two people who know each other. Can occur on a date that began in a friendly manner. Date rape can also be sex that occurs when one partner cannot give consent—if he or she is superdrunk and passed out, for example.

Often a woman says yes to messing around up to a certain point and then starts saying no. If a guy uses physical or verbal intimidation to go ahead and have sex, that's date rape. Some guys still think that if a girl says no, it's possible she's simply being coy and might really mean yes deep in her heart (and loins). Note to guys: Even if your gal is breathing heavily and seems to be turned on, she might have reached her limit. If a girl is drunk, her judgment may be clouded, and you might want to stop for the night. If you two were destined to have sex, you can do it another time, when you're sure. Women may wait until the last possible minute to say something or take action because it can be difficult and embarrassing to put on the brakes. Please respect any resistance you get—whether she's pushing away your hand or just saying, "Enough" or "Let's wait." Remember you, too, have to live with your behavior the next day. Wouldn't you rather err on the safe side?

Date Rape Prevention Checklist

- Avoid drugs and alcohol. They cloud judgment.
- Communicate your sexual desires and limits clearly.
- If you don't want to have sex, be assertive
    in saying no. Your partner might interpret
    passivity for permission.
- Don't go to a setting where sexual activity is expected.
- Make sure someone knows where you're going
    and when you are expected back.
- Make sure you have money and a way to get home.
- Know your sexual desires and limits.
- Be aware that your dress and nonverbal actions
    send a message. Sexy clothes and flirtation
    may make a partner assume that you want
    to have sex. This doesn't make your clothes
    or behavior wrong, but you need to be aware
    of the miscommunication they can spark.

- Accept your partner's decision.
    No always means no.
- Do not assume that sexy clothes and
    flirtation are an automatic invitation for sex.
- Know that being turned down for sex is
    not a rejection of you personally. It means
    the other person doesn't want to participate
    in a physical act.
- Don't assume that previous sexual contact
    means permission for sex anytime thereafter.

Note to women: Lay out the boundaries beforehand (for example, "I'm not ready to do it, but I'd love to get you alone for a while"). Once you're in a sexual situation, speak up if and when you feel uncomfortable, and be clear. Even if you do say yes to something, you are certainly allowed to change your mind at any point. Get out of the scene if it feels out of control. It's far more empowering to say "stop" than to keep quiet and go along halfheartedly. Better to feel awkward for a moment than to feel like crud the next day. It's not worth it.

Note to guys: Lay out your own boundaries beforehand as well. Sometimes a partner will push to have sex, and you will acquiesce just to prove that you're not a wimp, or because you feel it's expected. Don't go along with sex just because you think that is what your partner wants or because you feel it's proof of your masculinity. There's no glory in having sex if you don't really want to. You aren't a wuss if you say no. You've got nothing to prove.

These issues are not exclusive to male-female encounters. Men can pressure and victimize other men. Women can do the same to other women.

RYAN P., 20: There was one time when I almost got raped. That was really weird. The guy was physically really big. I didn't realize until I was totally in the situation. I was like, Oh, my God, this is really scary, I'm really helpless here. Boys can usually get away from situations when it comes to sex, they never get dominated like that. But for once it actually happened to me, and I was like, "Holy s**t." It was analogous to a girl who was pressured by a big male; it's the same thing. So I said to him, "I'm gonna throw up. I need to go to the doctor." I made this big excuse. Then I just got my clothes on and said, "I can't believe I came here," and I burst into tears and ran out.

Date or acquaintance rape cases are very hard (but not impossible) to prosecute. If you think you have been raped, it helps to act quickly. Evidence collected within seventy-two hours can play a key role. Plus, you can begin to get the medical and emotional attention that you will need.

WHAT TO DO IN CASE OF RAPE

If you have been raped by an acquaintance or stranger, whether on a date or in a violent attack, please take the following steps:

1 Do not bathe, and do not change clothes (or at least save what you were wearing).

2 Tell a trusted friend, doctor, family member and/or the police immediately.

3 As soon as possible, go to a hospital emergency room or clinic. There, a doctor and nurse will tend to you with a standard sexual-assault kit so that they can collect any evidence that would help prosecute the attacker. It's a short, unscary procedure that includes:

•getting a saliva sample by having you put a special kind of paper in your mouth
•cleaning under your fingernails
•combing your pubic hair for evidence
•taking your underwear
•if necessary, photographing any cuts or bruises
•conducting a pelvic exam
•talking about what happened (the doctor will write down your story)

They will offer you emergency contraception (see page 236) to prevent pregnancy, and a dose of antibiotics to help fight off any STDs.

You have the right to keep this visit and report confidential (as in not telling your parents or regular family doctor), but you might benefit greatly from your parents' support in this tough time. And your doctor can better treat you if he or she knows your full medical history.

4 Talk to a counselor. If you are at a hospital, there is always a social worker on hand who is an expert, and who can also get you into follow-up care. The hospital can also help you contact anyone else you need (boyfriend, parent, sister, friend).

5 Go back for a visit two or three weeks later to make sure you're okay, and to get tested for pregnancy and STDs.

6 Get in touch with a counselor or support group for further counseling. You definitely will benefit by talking this through with others who understand.

7 After six months, get tested for HIV. Odds are that you are okay, but check just to be sure.

KATIE, 23: I think that if you feel strong enough to report a date rape to the police or to have a campus trial, then you should. If not, then at least join a support group or get counseling, because it's so important that you talk about it. If you try and keep the incident a secret or keep it inside, I think you never really heal.

Sexual response can take a leave of absence if you've endured a serious trauma like rape, assault or sexual abuse. If so, you have no reason to feel ashamed. If what happened is standing in the way of your establishing meaningful relationships, you might consider talking to a therapist. If the abuse is ongoing or you think another person is at risk, you really should speak out if you can. If you don't think you'll be believed, enlist support from others you trust. (See Resources, page 310, for rape and sexual-abuse survivor telephone numbers.)

TRAUMA

h

Hopefully, you won't experience
harassment or rape in your lifetime.
But if that's not the case, you (and
your love life) can survive. There
are many people out there who are
able to help you. It's important to
ask for support. It's important to
try to be there for others who
might be struggling with these
issues. Your voice makes it harder
to sweep sexual harassment
and assault under the rug.

INTERVIEW

INTERVIEW WITH STEVEN TYLER
Singer, Aerosmith

SMART SEX: HOW DID YOU FIRST LEARN ABOUT SEX? DID YOUR PARENTS TELL YOU ABOUT IT?

Steven: I don't think they were the first. I think I started picking up on it from little Nancy in the schoolyard: "You show me yours and I'll show you mine," you know? My uncle had *Playboy* magazines in the house, in the basement; I used to sneak down there and read them.

SMART SEX: DID YOUR PARENTS CREATE AN ATMOSPHERE IN WHICH YOU COULD TALK ABOUT SEX?

Steven: Yeah, yeah. Of course, I didn't, 'cause I was shy about it. Oh, God, when I look back on some of my girlfriends and how I would act with them now, as opposed to how I was then, I realize how shy I was.

SMART SEX: YOU ARE A PARENT TO OLDER KIDS, INCLUDING LIV [TYLER]. HOW DO YOU TALK TO THEM ABOUT SEX?

Steven: Well, I start off by saying that sex is sensory, sensual, it comes from being nursed by the breast, that sex is wonderful, a normal thing. But there is a big difference between that and being stuck in a moment of emotion, that one moment before you come. At that time, some people will do anything, caught in that emotion, that [*makes panting noises*], that's when they need to be the most careful; your brain disappears. That old joke about thinking with the wrong head—women can, too. I tell them that it's a wonderful place to get lost in, to drown in that sea of lubricity, and it's also a dangerous place, it needs to be looked upon with caution. A man and a woman can do something so detrimental for the rest of their lives, which is having a child that they don't want.

SMART SEX: HOW DO DRUGS AFFECT SEX?

Steven: I mean, certain drugs make you feel like a horse, like a stallion in a field, but I think that after a while, all of that wears off.

SMART SEX: SO HAVE YOU LEARNED TO APPRECIATE SEX WITHOUT DRUGS?

Steven: I do recall that one of the reasons I stopped taking drugs was 'cause I couldn't get a hard-on anymore. When you put the drugs down, you just get a chance to get a look at life on life's terms, and to make it work better naturally. I think that, on the natch, there are ways to milk it, to become a sexual being and enjoy it much more.

SMART SEX: WHAT IS THE DIFFERENCE BETWEEN SEX WITH LOVE AND SEX WITHOUT LOVE?

Steven: All right, let me speak for a man. A man wakes up in the morning, he's got this early-morning hard-on, the private is saluting the general, and it's more of an outside thing, an external thing. Sometimes it's easier for a man to get confused and think that sex without love is the same as sex with love—because it's there and it's erect, it's quick and it's over. But it'll be soft soon, and you'll have to deal with your shame or guilt at having sex, momentary sex with somebody you don't care about. But once you've done it with love, you look them in the eye, and you come together, you just learn after a while that with love, you could get off better than you ever could—I mean, to do it with love and understanding, it can be so much more rewarding. One of the things about being married, you have one partner, you learn how to be intimate, you can go way past masturbation and self-love or any of that stuff where you think you got off the best.

SMART SEX: DO YOU THINK THAT THERE IS ANY DANGER IN SEXUALLY EXPLICIT LYRICS?

Steven: I think, yes, there is some danger, but I think that if one doesn't take a risk, then there goes your art. Of course, it's important that the mind of the listener has been exposed to the love of knowing the difference between right and wrong. But I think that if you're a true artist, you really have to go down every avenue that your psyche, that your inside begs you to go down. And not that you shouldn't have a conscience, but yeah, for the sake of your art, you know, just kinda like get out there.

SMART SEX: TELL US ABOUT THE IMPORTANCE OF MASTURBATION.

Steven: It's like, in our society, you mention *jerk off* and it's like everybody gets red in the face, kind of stymied and their words get caught in the throat. The best thing about masturbation is you don't have to look your best!

I think that it's really important to learn how to love yourself, so that you can learn how to love others.

Steven: Yeah, you gotta get yourself good first so that you can be good to others. And I didn't really understand that for a while, it was just so many words. But I tried to study it, like I studied the phrase "One thing you can't hide is when you're crippled inside." It's fun to sing as a song, but if you ponder it, it's really got depth. So to get yourself good, so that you can be good for others. It kinda runs over into: If you can learn how to make love to yourself, then you learn how to make love to others. And to make love to others, it's all you'll really need.

Steven: I wrote "Love in an Elevator" because for years I'd stand in an elevator and get off big-time watching people look at the numbers. Why? Because they're too embarrassed to look at my face. It's too close quarters, and I'd look around, and I'd think, What a great place to make love.

Steven: Based on the urges I get, I would have to say no. But do you have to act out those urges? No. I mean, I would love to act out

on the whole front row of any Aerosmith concert, where they show me their tits and make out with each other, but I don't. I think it's wonderful sometimes to not masturbate, and to not make love or do anything for a couple of weeks, and then be with my wife and then do it slowly and get each other off, you know, slowly, and work our way up to it, and not just be a puddle of sweat in each other's arms.

Steven: Oh, no, they were big when I was a kid. If you had a round indentation, like most guys have Skoal in their back pocket, if you had a round ring in your wallet, that means you were way cool. You were having sex.

Tight jeans, with a round ring and a comb in your back pocket, meant that you were screwing.

SMART SEX: WHAT WOULD YOU SAY TO SOMEONE WHO RESISTS CONDOMS?

Steven: Well, it's true, they're a pain. When you roll it back down, it catches your pubic hairs. It desensitizes you. But you know the diseases that are around today. When I was a kid, if you got gonorrhea or something, you could take penicillin and get a shot.

Today you could get AIDS, and when you get that report from the doctor, it's all over, baby.

You know, how far could I run after telling my wife I had AIDS? So you gotta put up with condoms— it ain't that hard.

SMART SEX: WHAT WAS YOUR WAKE-UP CALL REGARDING THE REAL DANGER OF HIV AND AIDS?

Steven: The wake-up call for me was when somebody said, "You do it with a rubber, don't ya?" And I said, "Well, you know I can't ever seem to get it on. You know I can't ever seem to find the right moment—you know, 'Excuse me a minute, I gotta....'" That somebody said, "Oh, so you want to get AIDS? 'Cause you can get it. That's why we wear rubbers." So I thought about it for a minute, and I kinda started to cry a little bit, and it was enough to wise me up.

SMART SEX: WHAT'S THE BEST THING AND WORST THING ABOUT SEX?

Steven: The good thing about sex is that it can keep you young forever, and the worst thing about it is that it can kill you.

t

13

TROUBLESHOOTING

Like so many things, good sex is earned through
patience, practice, awareness and communication.
If your time under the covers is not cutting it, here
are some suggestions as to why, and some ideas on
how you can fix, improve and otherwise make sex
worthwhile. First, some basic complaints.

RYAN P., 20: Just being really, really rough. Or really, really gentle. Either way. Also expecting me to do all the work—or doing all the work themselves. It's a two-way street.

PRIY, 23: One of my pet peeves is when the person I'm in bed with is smelly. I hate when people are smelly. Usually I suggest that we take a shower together or that we bathe together.

LENA, 21: They concentrate too much on my breasts. If it gets too annoying, I say, "I do have the rest of the body."

CATHERINE, 19: Often, men don't know how to perform oral sex on a woman. I don't think most girls are willing to say, "No, do this." It's almost like you shouldn't know how to make yourself feel good. It helps to physically manipulate what he's doing.

ESTHER, 17: I hate a bad kisser. That won't turn me off, though. I'll teach 'em how. I'll teach by example. "Why don't you do it like this?" If someone's kissing sloppy, I say, "Pretend you're taking a bite out of me, you're tasting me, you're sampling me. I'm a delicious dish."

BRADFORD, 21: I've been in relationships where as soon as sex is over, they cover themselves. But as far as I'm concerned, if I didn't like a girl's body, I wouldn't be in bed. For me it's a huge turn-on for a girl to gallivant around the room nude. And another thing: Girls need to know that there are no teeth involved in oral sex. Guys talk about that. For guys, that hurts.

Smart Sex Poll

When asked if they were satisfied with their sex lives, these men and women gave the thumbs up:
68 percent of guys between the ages of 16 and 20
58 percent of girls between the ages of 16 and 20
76 percent of guys between the ages of 21 and 24
68 percent of girls between the ages of 21 and 24

Even great communicators can clam up when it comes to talking sex with a partner. When speaking of the nuts and bolts of sex—what feels good, what you're curious about, what's bugging you—words can suddenly become absent from your brain. Courage can be scarce, too. But then you end up putting off the very thing that will make your sex life better.

THE LANGUAGE OF LOVE (AND LUST)

Admittedly, timing can be very tricky. Talking before things get hot is always good—your head is clearer and your diplomacy skills are a bit better. Talking about things right after you fool around can be good if you two are feeling close and cuddly; just try not to sound like a movie critic giving a review ("That'll be two thumbs down").

ESTHER, 17: Sometimes it's better to talk about it after, not during. You don't want to wilt someone's flower. Having coffee the next day, you say, "You know what I like? You know what I don't like?"

Giving nonverbal guidance while you're getting busy is a help to everyone involved: Try giving a guiding hand or leading by example, and then say, "Try that on me." Talking can also get very heated and sexy. Saying "that feels good" or "mmmm" when your partner does the right thing is positive reinforcement (like giving Rover a dog biscuit). Sometimes the best time to talk is a neutral, nonsexual time, like when you're taking a walk or having a quiet brunch. Communication is vital to getting what you want (and avoiding what you don't want) in bed.

RYAN P., 20: I make it comical. If you put tension there, it's just going to ruin it. Like, "Ease up, dude, calm down." Because if you do handle it too negatively, that's not being fair. You don't know how that person feels. That person may be really into you. You've got to be tender about it.

BRADFORD, 21: The more open, the better. My girlfriend and I pride ourselves on going to a bar and quietly talking about sex. She'll lean over and whisper in my ear what she wants to do when she gets home. It's our little joke that no one knows what were talking about. It keeps the flame going.

VIRGINIA, 20: I've gotten a whole lot better at answering questions like, "Do you like it when I do this or when I do this?" Then saying, "Yeah, I like this and I like that."

DEFINING MOMENT: ORGASM
An orgasm is a series of muscle contractions in the genital area that releases sexual tension. In males, the orgasm is usually accompanied by ejaculation. For both women and men, orgasms can be either mild or strong, but generally quite pleasurable.

THE WILY FEMALE ORGASM

Guys' plumbing makes it much easier for them to have orgasms, and it's not difficult to tell when the male love-geyser blows. The female orgasm is more elusive. Many women don't have orgasms through vaginal sex at all. They need direct stimulation of the clitoris if they're going to come. The clitoris is the roundish, smooth nub above the urethra (see anatomy illustration in the Glossary); it sometimes hides a bit under some folds of skin that form a protective hood. Females may prefer to get this direct stimulation through oral sex or through manual attention. Other women find that indirect stimulation—touching everything above, below, near, but not right on the clitoris—is the key. In either case, the more foreplay, the better for everyone involved. If you're female and coming is just not in your repertoire, don't get stressed about it. Many women don't even start to have orgasms until they're in their twenties (or later!). Many gals are perfectly happy to have vaginal sex without having an orgasm at all—the intimacy and touching can be rewarding in itself.

PRIY, 23: I think that orgasms are not as vital as people might think. One of the big differences between men and women is that men must come—like it's not sex if they don't have an orgasm. I certainly don't orgasm every time I have sex with a man or woman. It's kind of cool, because if you don't orgasm, you could be at it for hours, so it lengthens the whole experience.

KIM, 20: I've never had an orgasm, so it's not really that important to me. I enjoy sex, so it's not really an obstacle for me that's stopping my enjoyment or anything. I'm curious about it, but I figure it'll happen when the time is right.

BRADFORD, 21: If you want to have an orgasm, don't bitch unless you help a guy out, because it's not easy. You're gonna have to talk about it. It's different from girl to girl. If something worked with the previous girl, it might not work with the next.

TODD, 22: It's not like having an orgasm is a goal. One of the main aims of sex is pleasure—but it's not the sole aim. I try to make sure that she is having as good a time as I am. If you set up having an orgasm as a goal, you're trying too hard. It shouldn't be a goal; it should be a bonus.

Faking it may solve problems in the short term—the guy can feel proud, the girl can feel pleased that she pleased him. But, Miss Theatrics, you are 1) reinforcing the idea that it's not good sex unless everybody comes, 2) teaching him that he thrilled your every cell when he really didn't, 3) not communicating clearly, which doesn't help for long-term sexual joy. Guys, you can help break this cycle by letting your female partner know that it's okay to not come every time as long as fun is being had by all. Women, you can reassure him that it's okay for you to not have an orgasm every time or not have one simultaneously with his.

FAKING IT

Some men and women treat the female orgasm like the holy grail and the gold medal of sex. This thinking can lead to a single-minded obsessiveness that is truly counterproductive. This thinking can also explain why many women fake it. Like Meg Ryan says in *When Harry Met Sally,* most women fake it at least some of the time. She also demonstrates that some well-timed moans and exclamations can convince a guy that his lady friend is having a moment of absolute bliss. But why pretend?

THAR SHE BLOWS! (PREMATURE EJACULATION)

While some women have trouble coming, many guys have trouble *not* coming. That is, they ejaculate too soon. Premature ejaculation is loosely defined as spurting your love potion less than two minutes after penetration. This can be embarrassing and leave both partners frustrated, thinking of what might have been.

Sometimes a guy will just lose his load quickly because of extreme sexual excitement. A second go-around will allow him to last longer. Premature ejaculation is not uncommon for teenagers and younger men. It rarely means that there's anything wrong with you, and the problem will probably get better with practice and experience. If climaxing early is a regular thing for you, try masturbating until you feel yourself on the brink of orgasm, then stop. Wait for the feeling to die down a bit. Then bring yourself close to the edge again and stop. Repeat this cycle for fifteen minutes or so, then deliberately let yourself come. After some practice, you can incorporate this method into partner sex. If you don't see improvement over time, you should mention it to your doctor.

PRIY, 23: One boyfriend came too soon sometimes, but it was always when he hadn't had sex for a couple of weeks. And that's when it's most frustrating, because you really want everything to go well.

SIMON, 17: It's happened. I was embarrassed. But my partner was cool. I just cleaned up, waited awhile and started all over again.

NOT GETTING OR KEEPING IT UP (IMPOTENCE)

Impotence means failure to get an erection strong enough to complete the sex act. In other words, a hard-on that doesn't stay hard. Or just plain wilt-city the whole time. All guys have moments of impotence. Usually it's anxiety-related, or just a bad day (see "Mind over Matter," below). But if you're having trouble in the woody department more than 25 percent of the time, take heed. Alcohol and pot are both proven boner-stoppers—a good reason to remove mood-alterers from your game plan. Other drugs (illegal or prescription) can be to blame, too. If these things don't seem to be the culprits, talk to your doctor. If you think you are completely erection-free—like you don't even get them when you're alone, when you wake up or when you read a dirty mag, you should chat with your doctor. And then you'll be one step closer to treatment.

PENIS SIZE: IS MINE OKAY?

It's easy to worry about penis size when that organ plays such a key role in sex and pleasure. Sometimes it gets treated like a third party in sex play ("Is it ready yet?" "Guess who's saluting?"). But since we go so far out of our way to hide our private parts, there's not much of a chance to compare. And even if you do get a glimpse of other units belonging to brothers or locker-room buddies, you probably don't see too many other erect penises (or if you do see them, it is likely in the context of adult mags or movies, where penises tend to be way bigger than the average).

THESAURUS MOMENT: HAVE AN ORGASM
Come, climax, bust a nut, encounter the big O, cream, explode, do the little death, get off, make indoor fireworks, get your rocks off, howl at the moon. *For guys especially:* jizz, spooge, spunk, spill seed, ejaculate, make love juice, shoot your wad.

This kind of privacy can lead to insecurity over the big question—is mine normal? The answer is most likely yes. There is a very wide range of normal sizes out there. Without a hard-on, anywhere from two to six inches in length is common. Erections can be the great equalizer—that is, smaller penises tend to get much bigger when erect, and larger penises only get somewhat bigger when erect. But for the number crunchers out there, the size range for normal erect penises is roughly three-and-a-half to twelve inches, averaging around six inches in length and one-and-a-half inches in circumference. (By the way, narrower penises tend to gain more girth when hard.) Though some partners report liking bigger penises—probably more for the visual appeal—the smaller brand should be just as good at bringing pleasure (and, when the time is right, at making babies).

Lots of penises curve one way or the other when erect (sort of a banana effect). This is also normal and shouldn't hinder performance. If something about your love organ's appearance makes you self-conscious, you might want to mention it before you get intimate, so that your partner can help you feel more at ease.

VAGINA SIZE:
IS MINE OKAY?

The whole idea of vagina size is a misconception. The vagina is made up of muscles that rest against each other. These muscles can expand during labor to allow something as big as a baby to come through. And they can hold something as small as a tampon firmly in place. During sexual excitement, the inner two-thirds of the vagina expand (see "The Anatomy of Sex," page 64), but the muscles near the vaginal opening actually close a bit to embrace the penis. Plus, women can actually contract their outer vaginal muscles voluntarily (the same muscles that allow you to stop peeing midstream). The bottom line? Though vaginas can vary widely in appearance (color, size of inner and outer lips, amount of pubic hair, etc.), yours is probably normal.

Note: There is a condition called vaginismus, in which the outer muscles of the vagina contract so tightly that neither a penis nor any other object can enter the vagina. If you are experiencing this, please mention it to your doctor. The cause could be physical, or it could relate to some fear, incorrect information or bad experience from your past.

WHAT A PAIN

If sex is consistently uncomfortable or painful, *do not ignore it*. Your body is waving a red flag, and you need to investigate the problem. Here's a list that might help you identify what's wrong. However, if in doubt, see a doctor!

ACHES AND PAINS: FEMALE AND MALE

Pain during intercourse for gals can be caused by the stretching of the hymen. A woman who is having sex for the first time—or even the first several times—can expect some pain from the stretching of her hymen (the membrane that partially covers the vaginal opening). The solution is not to force the issue. Stop if it hurts, and try another time. After enough gentle tries, the pain should lessen, then disappear.

Burning sensation and discomfort in your genitals during sex and immediately after can be caused by lack of lubrication. Either partner can feel pain from sex when there is not enough lubrication to soften the friction. The easiest solution is: Do not rush. Allow plenty of time for the woman's natural moisture in her vagina to do its job. Note the best-kept sex secret: Keep water-based lubricant nearby (KY Jelly and Astroglide are good choices, both available at drugstores).

An irritated, burning feeling in your genitals can be caused by a reaction to products you use. The vagina or the penis might feel irritated by your spermicide, the gel on a lubricated condom or even the latex rubber of the condom. The solution may be to switch brands or switch products. Gals, keep in mind that many women are sensitive to vaginal deodorant sprays, scented tampons and many commercial douches. Unless you are otherwise instructed by a doctor, you will probably never need to douche.

An aching in the genitals can occur after fooling around but not having an orgasm. This can occur because when you are in a state of major sexual stimulation, extra blood flows to your genitals and fills up the spongy tissue. If not released by orgasm, this can cause pain. Guys know this as "blue balls" but it can happen to gals too: constant sexual stimulation results in a darkened, swollen vulva and clitoris. Orgasms send this blood back to the rest of the body. If you don't orgasm, the extra blood and swelling down there can cause some pain—and guys, it might not just be balls; your penis can hurt, too. The fastest way to ease the feeling is to masturbate. Otherwise, the ache will dissipate if you just wait.

If you're a gal, a pain and/or burning sensation when you pee, possibly accompanied by a constant feeling that you need to pee, possibly even blood in the urine, may be a urinary tract infection (UTI). Guys, if you have this feeling, burning pee usually signals an STD more often than a UTI. Both of you should see a doctor. An untreated UTI can become a kidney infection. Some tips on preventing UTIs include urinating before and after sex (especially after) to help flush out germs that might bug you later. Showering before and/or after sex is also a help (and can be a fun team activity).

Itching and burning sensation in your genitals might be a yeast infection. This is mostly a gal thing. See your doctor the first time you feel these symptoms. If it is indeed yeast, he or she will probably prescribe an over-the-counter medication which will clear things up. If it clears up with medication, but you experience the same symptoms months or years later, try the over-the-counter treatment. If infection persists, you should see your doctor.

An open sore in the genital area is a sign of a possible STD. Definitely see your doctor right away.

Pain during intercourse that doesn't seem to be for any of the reasons listed above could be a sign of STD. Remember that most STDs are fairly straightforward to treat when caught early on. If you have any inkling that things don't feel right, see a doctor. You'll be glad you did; STDs do the most damage when left untreated.

Pain particular to gals can be for other reasons besides STDs. The following are a couple of conditions that can contribute to abdominal pain. Fibroids and cysts are growths that can develop in the uterus or on the ovaries. Ovarian cysts can make your period irregular, make you have to urinate often or even give you constipation. They can cause great pain or no symptoms at all. Endometriosis is when the lining of your womb, the stuff that you shed every month as your period, starts to gather in odd places—like on your ovaries, bladder or bowel. It can give you painful, long-lasting, or more frequent periods. Pelvic inflammatory disease (PID) is a blanket term for many different kinds of infections around your internal genitals (uterus, fallopian tubes, ovaries) and their surrounding tissues. Many STDs, if left untreated, can lead to PID. All these conditions must be treated by a doctor. If untreated, you risk really big problems, including serious illnesses and infertility. So don't panic, but check out anything suspicious with a pro.

Pain particular to guys that is cause to go straight to the doctor is testicular pain. A cause could be testicular torsion. In rare cases, a testicle can twist around at the base and strangle its blood supply. This will cause pain in one testicle. Testicular torsion is a medical emergency. If you are aching down there, see a doctor as soon as possible that day. If the testicle is twisted, the blood supply could get cut off and you could lose a family jewel. Pain in one or both of the testicles could be epididymitis, which is an inflammation of the epididymis, the tube that conducts sperm to the urethra. This needs to be diagnosed and treated by a doctor.

Women should get in the habit of checking for unusual lumps every month. There are reportedly 175,000 new cases of breast cancer every year. In recent years, almost all lumps (85 to 90 percent) have been discovered by women or their partners, which has led to diagnosing cancers at early stages. Here's a minicourse in breast exams. Try to do this checkup each month at the same point in your cycle.

MORE PREVENTION: CHECK IT OUT

1) As you undress for your shower, look in the mirror to check that both breasts look similar. Some women normally have asymmetric breasts, but look for *new* unevenness.

2) While in the bath or shower, raise an arm over your head and check every square inch of your breasts with the fingertips of your free hand. Start at the outmost part of the breast and move inward in a spiral pattern, feeling for lumps. When you reach the nipple, feel it for lumps, then gently squeeze. There should be no discharge. Finally, feel in your armpits.

3) That evening, repeat the breast exam while lying in bed with one hand behind your head and a small pillow under your shoulder.

4) If you feel anything unusual, see your doctor. Keep in mind that most lumps are not cancer, especially for younger women, but it is very important to get them checked.

Men: Testicular cancer is the most common kind of tumorous cancer in young male adults. If caught early, it is much more treatable. Once a month, take this self-exam after a hot bath or shower:

1) Feel each testicle (one at a time) with the forefinger and middle finger of each hand on the underside of the testicle and the thumbs on top.

2) Roll the testicle gently between the thumbs and fingers.

3) Feel for any changes, lumps, abnormalities or pain.

4) If you find anything irregular, see your doctor.

AU NATUREL, OR NOT

Bonus Fact
The word *testes* (which means the male reproductive glands) in its singular form is *testis*, which comes from the root word for "witness." In ancient times, a man would show he was taking an oath by placing a hand on his genitals. Hence, "testify."

Most men in America are circumcised. This means they have had the foreskin of the penis surgically removed (usually just after birth). In men who aren't circumcised, the foreskin covers almost the whole tip of the penis—sort of like a turtleneck. An uncircumcised man should pull his foreskin back when washing and putting on a condom. Women take note.

Once you've ruled out some of the physical causes for sexual snarls, examine the mental side. The mind-body connection is an important one in bed. Sometimes your body doesn't cooperate because it's trying to tell you something. Sex can be painful or impossible because of feelings, memories or issues that you are trying to avoid. For women, anxiety can prevent lubrication and relaxation. Ouch. For guys, this most commonly means not getting or keeping an erection. And by the way, it happens to *every* guy at some point. Sometimes the situation can snowball. Like, you have trouble once, so the next time you try to get it up you feel even more pressure to perform, and then you get so self-conscious that no one alive could give you a woody.

MIND OVER MATTER

Underlying issues, for either sex, might be: It's too soon. It's the wrong person. It's the wrong gender. You feel guilty. You are worried about performing. You have body-image issues (you're convinced you're too fat or scrawny or ugly or unendowed to be attractive). You are stressed about pregnancy and/or STDs. You are worried about privacy. You're posing too hard (there are entire conversations on the Internet about holding your stomach in during sex). You have trust issues (you are too wary of the other person to really let yourself go). You're afraid of losing control.

Step one is probably to stop having sex at that point. Step two is to cut yourself some slack. Sex is not going to be amazing every time. Talk about it, so your partner doesn't feel like it's his or her fault. Take this time to explore and enjoy all the ways you can give each other pleasure without having sex—massaging, talking, tickling, nuzzling. Take the emphasis off sex. Sometimes that will be all the solution you need. Or try to figure out where the pressure or anxiety is coming from. Your bedmate might have some reassurance, some insight to offer ("I don't think your breasts are at all too small," "Hey, maybe you're still sad about your breakup with Mr. Last Guy," "Let's not sweat it, and I'll give you a backrub instead," etc.). If it's your partner who's having the difficulty, try to be compassionate.

Sex isn't always fireworks and symphonies. But learning is part of the fun; being understanding and patient is part of maturing. One test of a good lover is how he or she handles disappointment in bed.

TRIAL AND ERROR

MELISSA, 23: There's nothing wrong with occasional bad sex. It's normal. I think this illusion that every time you get in bed your body all of a sudden turns perfect, and everything works properly, and you look great, is just ridiculous.

RYAN P., 20: When I have disappointing sex, I just view it as a step on my way to better sex. It will get better and better and better.

Hopefully, the *Smart Sex* panelists have offered up some insight and given you notes to compare to your own experiences. But if you're still seeking wisdom (and who isn't?) , here are their thoughts on the hardest lessons they've learned about sex:

LAST WORDS

ESTHER, 17: Sex is a good thing, a positive thing. I've had to strip from it the dirtiness that women are made to feel—lesbians especially.

GINA, 24: I've learned honesty and responsibility; also, what someone else thinks really doesn't matter. You know what else? You can't go back and do it right.

TODD, 22: It can put up a barrier between people. You share this very personal thing, but sometimes it can put up a wall.

LENA, 21: You have to really work hard at it. You have to know this is the person you want to do it with.

And on how they would like to improve their sex lives in the future:

MELISSA, 23: I have to figure out how not to bring all the stuff that happens in the outer world home. I'd like be able to go in my room, shut the door and have great sex with my boyfriend, and not have somebody pop into my head, or something that I want to do. Sometimes it works. You can totally lose yourself in sex, and lose all the stuff that's going on in your life. After I've had good sex, my head's eased. I'm like, Oh, this is great. This is how it's supposed to be.

CHARLIE, 17: Nothing. I mean, it can only get better, but I guess when I get older it will be cool to have had more experience.

KARLEY, 17: I don't want to just go out and hop into bed with the next guy who walks by. I've had my fill of one-night stands or whatever you want to call them. Also, to be on birth control, use some sort of contraceptive method to prevent another pregnancy, STD, AIDS, whatever.

PRIY, 23: I want to work on relationships. I'm at the point where I want to make a relationship work and fit sex into the context of it, more so than being driven by being attracted to somebody and then having the relationship be tacked on at the end.

RYAN S., 19: Being more confident about myself. I have a lot of pet peeves about myself, and I just gotta, like, let them go if I'm ever gonna be comfortable with myself. That's what I do want to work on for now, just being comfortable with myself. I can't say I love myself now, but I like myself a lot more than I used to.

LENA, 21: I want to work on finding the person I can share sex with without ever regretting it, who I can form a spiritual, emotional and physical bond with. And just once know it's possible.

GINA, 24: I want honesty. I want to have one lover who shares everything. A most awesome mental and physical relationship. I wouldn't want the physical without the emotional connection.

DAVID, 20: I want to have discipline about safe sex. If I can train myself to use a condom and still make sex as much fun as it can be, I'll be happy. When I use condoms, they prolong sex and I don't have any worries. It takes a strong person to stick to the rules.

THOMAS, 18: I want to think about the girl more, I totally want to learn how to please girls more.

VIRGINIA, 20: Definitely to be more aggressive and more assertive in what I want and what I need. Not being demanding, because I definitely think it's give-and-take. Just making sure that I can handle everything that comes along with it and making sure there are no regrets anywhere.

PROTECT YOURSELF.
RESPECT YOURSELF.

Smart sex is making your own decisions, knowing full well the consequences. It's having the information you need and the conviction and confidence to apply it. Your brain is your most sensitive erogenous zone. So think and enjoy. And remember that the learning never stops.

RESOURCES

If you need help, be sure that there is someone out there for you. It might take some digging, but somewhere, someone cares.

If an injustice pisses you off, do something about it. The best first step is to be informed. Read the paper; if your local school board is fighting over condom availability and you feel strongly one way or the other, call an administrator and offer your support. Call a local AIDS organization and ask if you can deliver food to sick people's homes. If there's a peer counseling group at a local youth center, check it out. If there isn't, start one.

IF YOU WANT HELP OR WANT TO HELP— OR BOTH—HERE ARE SOME SUGGESTIONS.

HOTLINES

Centers for Disease Control National AIDS Hotline
Advice on AIDS prevention, testing, and resources. Open 24 hours.
>**1-800-342-AIDS**
Spanish   **1-800-344-SIDA**
Deaf   **1-800-243-7889**

Emergency Contraception Hotline
Information about emergency contraception (the "morning-after" pill) and providers in your area.
>**1-800-584-9911**

National Domestic Violence Hotline
Advice and counseling for anyone who is concerned about domestic violence.
>**1-800-799-SAFE**
Deaf   **1-800-787-3224 (TDD)**

National Drug and Alcohol Treatment Routing Service
Drug and alcohol abuse information. Referrals to counselors and treatment options in your area. Open 24 hours.
>**1-800-662-HELP**

National Herpes Hotline
Callers can speak to counselors and/or order reading materials (which will be mailed in a privacy envelope).
>**1-800-230-6039**
>**1-919-361-8488**
Open M–F, 9 A.M. to 7 P.M. EST

National Runaway Switchboard
Provides crisis intervention, counseling, message services and referrals. Open 24 hours.
>**1-800-621-4000**

National STD Hotline
Provides free publications on
STDs and gives referrals for
diagnosis, treatment and follow-up.
1-800-227-8922

ORGANIZATIONS

Alcoholics Anonymous (AA)
Offers pamphlets and refers
callers to AA meetings in their
communities. Approximately
56,000 AA groups in the country.
P.O. Box 459
Grand Central Station
New York, NY 10163
1-212-870-3400
1-212-647-1680
(Volunteer Counselors)

**American Social Health
Association (ASHA)**
A national nonprofit organization
that educates about STDs. It has
a pamphlet for any sexual danger
you can name. Each costs a buck.
P.O. Box 13827
Research Triangle Park, NC 27709.
For free publications about
sexual-health communication:
1-800-972-8500
For publications about herpes
and HPV:
1-800-230-6039
For more information regarding
contraception and sexual health:
1-919-361-8400

Body Positive
For people who test HIV-positive.
Publishes monthly magazine
Body Positive in English and *Cuber
Positivo* in Spanish. Drop in support
groups for HIV-positive people and
their loved ones. Call for information
about weekly events.
19 Fulton Street, Suite 308B
New York, NY 10038
1-800-566-6599
Fax: 1-212-566-4539

ChildHelp, USA
Confidential information for anyone
whose life is affected by sexual
abuse—victims, parents, abusers.
Offers referral numbers, counseling
and help to abusive parents with
disciplinary action.
1-800-4-A-CHILD

The Hetrick-Martin Institute
For gay, lesbian, bi or
questioning teenagers who need
support coming out. Unfortunately,
it's only in New York City.
2 Astor Place
New York, NY 10003
1-212-674-2400

Herpes Advice Center
For many publications and patient
counseling, write or call:
51 East 25th Street
New York, NY 10010
1-888-ADVICE-8

Just Say Yes (also available in Spanish, as ¡Di Que Sí!)
A totally smart, totally laid-back, totally pro-woman and pro-gay guide to sexuality. Hip, cartoony illustrations. It's free if you're under 18, $3 if you're older.
3712 N Broadway, #191
Chicago, IL 60613
1-773-604-1654

National Black Women's Health Project
A self-help and advocacy group for African-American women and girls.
1237 Ralph David Abernathy Blvd SW
Atlanta, GA 30310
1-404-758-9590

The National Council for Adoption
For helpful booklet on adoption, write or call:
1930 Seventeenth St, NW
Washington, DC 20009-6207
1-202-332-0935

Other organizations and agencies that can help to arrange an adoption:
· United Community Services
· Catholic Charities
· The Federation of Protestant Welfare Agencies
· The United Federation Jewish Philanthropies
· Adoption agencies (listed in the Yellow Pages)
· The department/bureau of child welfare in your state

New York State Coalition Against Sexual Assault
Offers telephone numbers to Rape Crisis centers in each state. A great source for research material and advice on legal action.
1-518-434-1580

PFLAG (Parents and Friends of Lesbians and Gays)
A great source of information and support for all your coming-out needs.
1-202-638-4200

Planned Parenthood
Referral to clinics near you.
1-800-829-7732
Will put you directly through to a clinic near you.
1-800-230-PLAN

Right-to-Life Committee
Political group fighting to stop abortion, has any information on present and past legislation concerning abortion.
1-202-626-8800

True Love Waits
International campaign that challenges young adults to remain sexually abstinent until marriage. Sponsored by the Baptist Sunday School Board of Nashville, TN.
1-800-LUV-WAIT
To order resources, call
1-800-458-2772

ONLINE

If you are jacked in, your computer can provide you with all kinds of lifestyle, sex and health information that you can absorb anonymously and at your leisure. Here are some Web sites worth visiting.

AIDS

Information on AIDS, AIDS testing, demographics of the disease, safer sex and prevention, treatment overview, financial and legal issues, counseling and more.
http://www.thebody.com

AIDS

Q Action, the young person's part of the Stop AIDS Project.
http://www.stopaids.org

Alcoholics Anonymous

The official AA homepage.
http://www.alcoholics-anonymous.org
See also: **http://www.recovery.org/aa**

Condoms

To order condoms and find all about the different brands.
http://www.condomania.com

Gay Issues

Young people come out and talk to other folks who've been there.
soc.support.youth.gay-lesbian-bi

Youth Action Online

A great gay-youth organization.
http://www.youth.org

Oasis

Gay-youth magazine.
http://www.oasismag.com

Queer Resources Directory

An excellent general reference.
http://www.qrd.org/qrd

PlanetOut, LLC

An excellent general reference.
The Web: **http://www.planetout.com**
AOL: Keyword: PNO or PlanetOut
MSN: Go Word: PNO or PlanetOut
Suite 550
584 Castro Street
San Francisco, CA 94114
1-415-252-6285
Fax: 1-415-252-6287

Herpes

Information about prevention, resources, new medications and more.
http://www.racoon.com/herpes

Just Say Yes

Guide to sexuality (see above).
E-mail: mur2@midway.uchicago.edu,
or check out the Web site,
http://www.webcom.com/~cps

Pregnancy

Information on planning, contraception, adoption, abortion, prenatal care, nutrition, fitness, birth defects, sex problems.
http://noah.cuny.edu/pregnancy/
pregnancy.html

Safer Sex

Vast amounts of information on every safer-sex-related issue known to humanity, with links to other health and sexuality sites.
http://www.safersex.org

BIBLIOGRAPHY

Bell, Ruth. **Changing Bodies, Changing Lives.**
New York: Vintage Books, 1988.

The Boston Women's Health Book Collective.
The New Our Bodies, Ourselves.
New York: Touchstone, 1992.

Dorland's Illustrated Medical Dictionary. 28th ed.
Philadelphia: W.B. Saunders Company, 1994.

Kelly, Gary F. **Sexuality Today:**
The Human Perspective. 4th ed. Guilford, CT:
The Dushkin Publishing Group, Inc., 1994.

Neinstein, Lawrence, M.D. **Adolescent Health Care:**
A Practical Guide. 3rd ed. Baltimore:
Williams & Wilkins, 1996.

Orenstein, Peggy. **SchoolGirls:**
Young Women, Self-Esteem, and the Confidence Gap.
New York: Anchor Books, 1995.

Sex and America's Teenagers.
New York: The Alan Guttmacher Institute, 1994.

Winks, Cathy and Anne Semans.
The Good Vibrations Guide to Sex.
San Francisco: Cleis Press, 1994.

GLOSSARY

CROSS SECTION OF
FEMALE REPRODUCTIVE SYSTEM

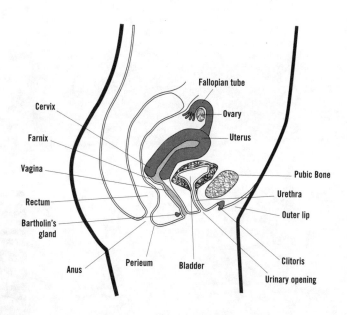

Fallopian tube

Cervix

Farnix

Vagina

Rectum

Bartholin's
gland

Anus

Perieum

Bladder

Ovary

Uterus

Pubic Bone

Urethra

Outer lip

Clitoris

Urinary opening

CROSS SECTION OF
MALE REPRODUCTIVE SYSTEM

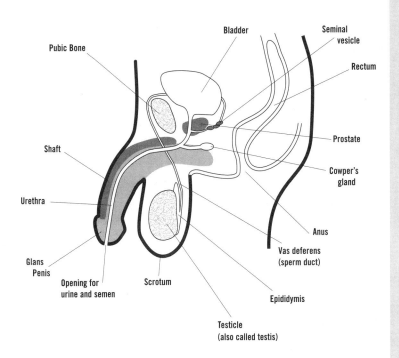

Bladder

Seminal vesicle

Pubic Bone

Rectum

Shaft

Prostate

Urethra

Cowper's gland

Glans Penis

Anus

Opening for urine and semen

Scrotum

Vas deferens (sperm duct)

Epididymis

Testicle (also called testis)

abortion:
The expulsion of a fetus from the uterus before it is sufficiently developed to survive outside of the uterus, resulting in the end of a pregnancy. An induced abortion is brought about intentionally while a spontaneous abortion occurs without apparent cause.

abstinence:
The act of voluntarily refraining from something. The term is often used to mean the act of voluntarily abstaining from vaginal or anal sex.

acquaintance rape:
Sexual intercourse against one partner's will, taking place between two people who know each other. Acquaintance rape can also occur when one partner has sex to which he or she cannot competently consent, as when he or she is drunk, under the influence of drugs, unconscious or being threatened with physical danger. Date rape is a form of acquaintance rape, which can occur on a date that began in a friendly manner.

acquired immunodeficiency syndrome:
See AIDS.

adoptive parents:
The people who legally take over parental rights of a child put up for adoption by that child's birth or biological parents.

AIDS:
A syndrome, also known as acquired immunodeficiency syndrome, that is caused by a slow acting virus, HIV (human immunodeficiency virus), which is transmitted through semen, vaginal fluid, breast milk or blood. There are many diseases that make up this syndrome, including opportunistic infections and cancers. A person who is HIV-positive and showing symptoms is said to have AIDS.

anal sex:
Sexual activity that involves the anus. Most commonly, the phrase refers to a man inserting his penis into someone else's anus.

anesthesia:
The loss of the ability to feel pain, caused by a medical intervention, such as giving the patient an anesthetic, or pain-killing drug. A local anesthetic, or "local," makes one part of the body unable to feel pain while the person who receives it remains conscious. A general anesthetic, or "general," causes unconsciousness.

antibody:
A protein made by the immune system to help fight infection. There are specific antibodies against specific infections. An example is the HIV antibody, which is tested for in the most common HIV test.

anus:
The end of the gastrointestinal tract, lying in the fold of the buttocks, through which feces leave the body.

aphrodisiac:
Anything that increases or intensifies sexual desire and/or improves sexual performance.

asymptomatic:
Showing or causing no symptoms. Some diseases are asymptomatic, meaning that a person is infected, but shows no symptoms for a period of weeks, months or even years.

bacterium (plural, bacteria):
A single-celled microorganism, which can be seen under an ordinary microscope. Although many bacteria are harmless or even necessary to life, some bacteria cause disease. Diseases caused by bacteria can be treated with antibiotics.

barrier protection:
Devices that help prevent the exchange of bodily fluids during sexual activity, including sexual intercourse, cunnilingus, fellatio, anal sex, and mutual masturbation. Barrier protection can be a form of birth control. Types of barrier protection include the cervical cap, condom, dental dam, diaphragm, and latex gloves. No form of barrier protection will protect you 100% from acquiring a sexually transmitted disease.

bimanual exam:
Part of a pelvic exam, in which the doctor examines the uterus and ovaries by inserting one or two fingers in the vagina and gently pressing on the abdomen with the other hand.

biological parents:
The man and woman whose sperm and egg resulted in the birth of a child, also known as birth parents.

biopsy:
The removal of a small piece of living tissue to be examined for signs of disease.

birth control:
Anything that prevents conception or keeps a woman from becoming pregnant. Common forms of birth control include the cervical cap, condom, diaphragm, female condom, IUD and the Pill, as well as spermicide, Depo-Provera and Norplant.

birth control pills:
A form of birth control that consists of pills containing hormones. The pills, which must be taken daily as prescribed to be effective, prevent pregnancy by suppressing ovulation. There are many different types of birth control pills (BCPs), also known as "the Pill" or OCPs (oral contraceptive pills). The Pill is extremely effective against pregnancy.

birth parents:
See biological parents.

bisexual:
A person who is consistently sexually attracted to people of both genders.

bodily fluids:
Fluids produced by the body. The term can be used to refer to the fluids that can transmit the AIDS virus: blood, breast milk, semen and vaginal fluids.

cervical cap:
A small rubber device, resembling a large thimble, that fits just over the tip of the cervix and blocks sperm from entering the uterus. The cap should be used with spermicide.

cervix:
The lower part of the uterus. The cervix connects the uterus with the vagina.

cesarean section:
A procedure in which a baby is delivered by the doctor cutting through the woman's abdomen and uterus, so that the baby is lifted out, rather than delivered through the woman's vagina.

chancre:
The usually painless ulcer caused by syphilis that forms at the place where the infection entered the body, from nine to ninety days after the infection occurs. Most chancres appear on the external genitalia, but may appear on the cervix, mouth, anus, lips, face, breast or fingers. Even though the chancre heals without treatment, the infected person still has syphilis and the disease will progress if he or she is not treated.

chlamydia:
An infection caused by a bacterium called *Chlamydia trachomatis*; one of the most common sexually transmitted diseases. Chlamydia is spread through vaginal, anal, and oral sex. At least half of the women and one-quarter of the men who get it show no symptoms, but for others, symptoms include vaginal or urethral discharge, a burning sensation during urination, mild abdominal pain, rectal pain or discharge, and for men, pain or tenderness in the scrotum. Untreated chlamydia can cause serious damage to the urinary tract in men, PID in women, and infertility in either sex.

circumcision:
An operation in which the foreskin is cut away from around the top of the penis; usually done in the hospital when a baby is one or two days old.

cirrhosis:
A chronic disease of the liver that may be caused by many conditions including alcoholism, hepatitis B, and syphilis. In its early stages it is asymptomatic but later can progress to liver failure with abdominal swelling and pain, the vomiting of blood, jaundice (yellow skin), hypertension and central nervous disorders that may end in coma.

climax:
Another word for orgasm.

clitoris:
The most sexually sensitive female sex organ; a small bud-shaped nub that protrudes slightly where the labia minora come together. Like the penis, the clitoris is capable of erection.

coitus interruptus:
When a man removes his penis from a woman's vagina before ejaculation. Coitus interruptus is a highly ineffective and unreliable way to prevent pregnancy or sexually transmitted diseases.

cold sore:
A kind of lesion usually around the mouth, caused by herpes simplex virus type 1. This is not the type of herpes virus that usually causes genital herpes. However, if a cold sore is brought in contact with the genital area, it may cause genital infection. (See also herpes.)

come (also spelled cum):
The fluid produced by a man ejaculating during orgasm, technically known as semen. (See also precome.) The phrase "to come" is also a slang term meaning "to achieve orgasm."

conception:
The beginning of pregnancy, marked by the implantation of the fertilized egg in the endometrium, or inner lining of the uterus. Also used to mean the moment an egg is fertilized by a sperm.

condom:
Thin sheath made of latex, polyurethane or animal parts that fits snugly over an erect penis to help prevent pregnancy and sexually transmitted diseases.

consensual:
Done by mutual consent; consensual sex is the opposite of rape, which is nonconsensual or forced sex. (See also acquaintance rape and date rape.) For sex to be consensual, both parties must agree to it; in addition, both parties must be old enough to make the decision, mentally and emotionally competent, sober, awake and not subject to any physical threat or danger.

contraception:
See birth control.

contraction:
A shortening or coming together, often used to refer to the shortening of the muscles of the uterus. Repeated contractions of the uterus are part of the process of delivering a baby.

crabs:
Pubic lice, *Phthirus pubis*. Yellow-gray insects about the size of the head of a pin. Infection with crabs is a common sexually transmitted disease. They feed on blood, and may be found in moist, hairy regions of the body, including the pubic region, armpits, belly, thighs, chest, anal area and sometimes in beards or eyelashes.

cunnilingus:
Using the mouth, lips or tongue to stimulate any part of the female genitalia.

date rape:
Sexual intercourse against a partner's will that occurs between people on a date. Date rape can also occur when one partner is unable to give consent, such as when he or she is drunk, under the influence of drugs, unconscious or being threatened.

dental dam:
A sheet of latex that can be placed over a woman's vagina. This is especially useful for safer oral sex.

Depo-Provera:
A birth-control hormone given in the form of a shot. The hormone, synthetic progestin, gradually enters the woman's bloodstream, preventing pregnancy for three months by inhibiting ovulation and making the cervical mucus unfriendly to sperm. Although Depo-Provera is extremely effective in preventing pregnancy it offers no protection against sexually transmitted diseases.

diaphragm:
A shallow, cup-shaped form of barrier protection. The diaphragm is made of soft rubber and should fit comfortably over the cervix, where it prevents pregnancy by blocking sperm from entering the uterus. It must always be used with a spermicide.

dilate:
To make wider or expand. During childbirth, a woman's cervix dilates so that the baby can be delivered.

discharge:
Substance that is released or excreted. Discharges of various types from the vagina or penis are often symptoms of sexually transmitted diseases. Some types of vaginal discharge also occur normally throughout the menstrual cycle and when a woman is sexually excited.

douche:
Method for washing out the vagina. Contrary to the popular notion that douching prevents vaginal infection, douching can force organisms that cause disease further into the uterus, actually increasing the risk of infection, and it may disrupt the vagina's natural cleansing mechanisms. Douching is also not an effective way to prevent or reverse pregnancy.

ectopic pregnancy:
A pregnancy in which the embryo implants outside of the uterus—most commonly in the fallopian tubes. Symptoms include bleeding about seven to fourteen days after the last menstruation and sharp one-sided lower abdominal pain. This is a medical emergency, and if an ectopic pregnancy is suspected immediate medical evaluation is essential. The use of IUDs and previous PID are major risk factors for having an ectopic pregnancy.

egg:
The female reproductive cell (also known as ovum) that is fertilized by the male's sperm.

ejaculation:
The release of semen from the penis during orgasm. (See also come.)

embryo:
In humans, the second to the eighth week of development after fertilization of the egg. (See also fetus.)

epididymis:
A small organ lying next to the testicles, composed of tiny tubes, to which the sperm travel after they are made, and

where they ripen into mature sperm.
(See also semen.)

epididymitis:
Inflammation of the epididymis,
which can be caused by some sexually
transmitted diseases. Symptoms are
pain in the groin, fever and chills.

erection:
When the penis or clitoris gets hard
and swells. This is caused by the organ
engorging (filling with blood), generally,
during sexual excitement, sleep or
physical stimulation.

erogenous:
A term that refers to those parts of the
body that are particularly sensitive to
sexual stimulation or excitement.

erotic:
Having to do with sexual love,
feelings or desires.

fallopian tubes:
The channels through which
unfertilized eggs descend from the
ovaries into the uterus. (See also
ectopic pregnancy.)

fellatio:
Using the mouth, tongue or lips to
stimulate the penis; a form of oral sex.

female condom:
Thin, loose polyurethane sleeve, closed
at one end, and with a ring at each
end. The closed end goes inside the
vagina, covering the cervix, while the
open end rests outside the vagina.

This form of barrier protection helps
block semen, bacteria and viruses
from contacting the vagina.

fertility observation:
A system of observing and carefully
tracking changes in cervical mucus,
basal body temperature and the cervix
in order to predict one's fertile phase.
Different versions of this system are
used by people who are trying to
become pregnant, those who wish to
increase the effectiveness of their use
of barrier contraception, and those who
use it exclusively to avoid pregnancy
(note: this is not the rhythm method).
As an exclusive method of birth control, this system can only be used after
training, requires rigorous record-keep-
ing, has a relatively high failure rate,
and offers no protection from sexually
transmitted diseases.

fetus:
After the second month of
pregnancy until birth, the
developing human is called a fetus.

fingering:
Literally, touching or handling with
the fingers; used to refer to using
the fingers for sexual stimulation.

foreplay:
Sexual activities shared by partners
at the early stages of sexual arousal.

foreskin:
Skin covering the head of the
penis on an uncircumcised male.

gardenerella (also known as bacterial vaginosis or BV):
An infection in women caused by overgrowth of the bacteria *Gardenerella vaginalis*. Gardenerella can be sexually transmitted, or it may develop from other causes. Half the women with this bacteria are asymptomatic; others experience a grayish-white discharge with a fishy odor, as well as burning discomfort, abdominal pain and long or irregular menstrual periods. The presence of gardenerella in an asymptomatic woman does not necessarily require treatment.

gay:
Term that refers to a homosexual of either sex.

gender:
The sex of a person, male or female.

general anesthetic:
See anesthesia.

genitals (also called genitalia):
The reproductive organs. The female external genitals include the mons, labia, clitoris and vaginal opening, while the internal genitals include the vagina, uterus, fallopian tubes and ovaries. The male genitals include the penis, testes and scrotum.

genital herpes:
See herpes.

genital warts:
Warts in the genital area brought on by the human papilloma virus (HPV). A common sexually transmitted disease, genital warts may be transmitted through vaginal, oral or anal sex with someone who either has warts or is carrying the virus without symptoms.

gonorrhea:
A common sexually transmitted disease, gonorrhea is transmitted through vaginal, anal and oral sex.

hepatitis B:
A virus that causes liver infection and can lead to cirrhosis. It lives in all the body fluids of infected persons, including saliva, and is transmitted through contact with body fluids. It may also be passed through shared needles. Many of those infected are asymptomatic.

herpes:
A virus called Herpes simplex that has two strains, types 1 and 2. Herpes simplex virus type 1 usually appears as a cold sore on the mouth, although it may also appear as a painful outbreak in the genital area. Herpes simplex virus type 2 usually appears as one or many painful, blister-like sores in the genital area.

heterosexual:
Person with a primary romantic and erotic attraction to people of the opposite gender, with few or no erotic feelings for people of the same gender.

HIV:
A slow-acting virus, also known as the human immunodeficiency virus, that attacks the human immune system and causes AIDS. In order to infect

a person, this virus must penetrate the body, most often during sex or intravenous drug use. (See also AIDS.)

HIV-negative:
Term used to describe a person who has had a negative HIV test. In the most common test this means that HIV antibody has not been detected. In the first six months after infection with HIV, a person may test HIV-negative but actually be infected with HIV because antibodies to HIV have not yet developed.

HIV-positive:
Term used to describe a person who has had a positive HIV test showing that that person has been infected with HIV, the virus that causes AIDS.

home test:
Test to diagnose a medical condition that can be taken at home, without a doctor's supervision; usually refers to a pregnancy test.

homoerotic:
Term used to describe something that stimulates or refers to sexual or erotic feelings for people of one's own gender.

homophobia:
Irrational fear or hatred of homosexuality.

homosexual:
Person with a primary romantic and erotic attraction to people of the same gender, with few or no erotic feelings for people of the opposite gender.

hormones:
Chemical substances made by the body's glands to regulate the growth, development and behavior of different parts of the body. Hormones regulate the growth of the male and female genitals, the menstrual cycle, the development of such sexual characteristics as breasts and body hair, and the process of pregnancy.

HPV:
See genital warts.

human immunodeficiency virus:
See HIV.

human papilloma virus:
See genital warts.

hymen:
The thin piece of skin tissue that partially covers the vaginal opening. The hymen can be stretched or broken during sports, masturbation or sex.

immunity:
Resistance to or protection from a disease.

implantation:
The process of the fertilized egg establishing itself in the lining of the uterus, or endometrium. This usually happens about one week after fertilization.

impotence:
A man's inability to achieve or maintain an erection, so as to complete sexual intercourse. Impotence can be caused by physical factors, such as alcohol, drugs, fatigue or prescription medications.

It can also result from psychological factors, such as stress. Most men experience difficulty in achieving or maintaining an erection at some time in their lives.

incest:
Sexual intercourse or other sexual activity between closely related people, such as parents and their children, or siblings.

infertility:
Inability, or diminished ability, to produce children.

inflammation:
A condition of pain, heat, redness and swelling. This is a common tissue reaction to injury or infection.

intercourse:
See sexual intercourse.

intravenous:
Literally, within a vein; a term that can be used to describe a drug that is taken by injection into a vein. Sharing needles used to inject intravenous drugs can transmit the AIDS virus.

IUD (intrauterine device):
A small plastic or plastic and copper birth control device, which is placed inside the uterus. A string attached to the device is left emerging from the cervix to aid removal. The IUD prevents implantation by creating inflammation in the uterus and may prevent fertilization of the egg also. In the presence of infection such as

chlamydia or gonorrhea, this device poses a relatively high risk of PID, with a possible risk of future infertility. It offers no protection against sexually transmitted diseases.

labia:
Literally, lips, used to refer to the inner and outer lips of a woman's vulva. The outer lips are known as the labia majora and the inner lips are known as the labia minora.

latent:
Used to describe something that is present but invisible, inactive, hidden or undeveloped. A latent infection is one that is present but asymptomatic.

latex:
Synthetic rubber material used to make various types of barrier protection, including the condom, diaphragm, cervical cap, dental dam and gloves.

lesbian:
A homosexual woman. The term comes from the Greek island of Lesbos, the home of the woman-loving female poet, Sappho.

lesion:
An injury or other change in body tissue that may be caused by, among other things, infection, e.g., a chancre is a lesion associated with syphilis.

local anesthetic:
See anesthesia.

masturbation:
Self-stimulation of the genitals for sexual pleasure.

menstrual cycle:
A series of changes in the uterus and other sex organs that is regulated by hormones. It occurs in women from puberty to menopause. During the approximately four-week cycle, an egg matures and is released by the ovary during ovulation. At the same time, the lining of the uterus thickens in readiness to receive a fertilized egg. If a fertilized egg does not implant during the cycle, the lining sheds and is expelled during menstruation, and the cycle begins again.

menstrual period:
See menstruation.

menstruation:
The discharge of blood and uterine tissue through the vagina of a nonpregnant woman during her reproductive years (puberty through menopause). Otherwise known as a menstrual period, it is regulated by hormones and normally occurs about every four weeks for three to seven days. (See also menstrual cycle.)

miscarriage:
The natural ending of a pregnancy before the fetus can survive outside the uterus; also known as "spontaneous abortion." Most miscarriages occur during the first trimester, or twelve weeks, of pregnancy.

monogamous:
Sharing sexual relations with only one person.

Nonoxynol-9:
A form of spermicide that also gives some protection against sexually transmitted diseases, such as HIV.

Norplant:
A form of birth control consisting of match-sized capsules implanted under the skin of a woman's upper arm, under local anesthesia. Over a period of up to five years, the capsules slowly release a hormone into the body to prevent pregnancy. Norplant is an effective method of birth control, but it offers no protection against sexually transmitted diseases.

opportunistic infection:
A disease or infection caused by a bacterium or other microorganism that does not ordinarily cause disease but that does cause disease under certain circumstances, such as when a person's immunity is lowered due to disease or to drug treatment. HIV lowers a person's immunity, making him or her vulnerable to opportunistic infections.

oral contraception:
See birth control pills.

oral sex:
Using the mouth and tongue to stimulate a sexual partner's genitals. Contact between a mouth and a

penis is called fellatio. Contact
between a mouth and a vagina
is called cunnilingus.

orgasm:
Muscle contractions in the genital area
that release sexual tension and usually
bring pleasurable sensations. For both
sexes, actual orgasm lasts about
ten seconds, but subsequent muscle
spasms and other intense feelings may
make the process seem to last longer.

ovaries:
Pair of female sex organs that produce
eggs (ova) and female hormones. The
ovaries are located inside the body in
the abdominal cavity, on either side
of the uterus.

outercourse:
Term used to mean sexual activity
that includes everything except
sexual intercourse. Outercourse
might include foreplay, oral sex,
mutual masturbation, massage
and sharing fantasies.

ovum:
See egg.

Pap smear:
A medical procedure performed by
a doctor as part of a pelvic exam, in
which the doctor scrapes some cells
from the cervix using a small spatula.
The cells are then examined under
a microscope for signs of infection
(especially with genital warts) or for
changes that could lead to cancer.

pelvic exam:
A medical procedure in which a doctor
examines the inside of a woman's vagina.

pelvic inflammatory disease:
See PID.

penis:
The male organ of sexual
intercourse, ejaculation and
urination. When stimulated,
the penis becomes erect.

period:
See menstruation.

perineum:
In women, the area between the
anus and the vulva; in men, the area
between the anus and the scrotum.

PID:
Pelvic inflammatory disease; a severe
infection in the internal genitalia
(uterus, fallopian tubes and/or ovaries)
or their surrounding tissues in the
abdomen that may lead to hospitalization
and infertility; a common result of
the sexually transmitted diseases
chlamydia and gonorrhea.

the Pill:
See birth control pills.

polyurethane:
Synthetic rubber material used to
make various types of barrier
protection, such as the condom
and the female condom.

precome:
A clear or milky fluid, a few drops of which may appear at the tip of an erect penis before orgasm; this fluid may contain semen, and may also contain viruses. Therefore, contact with precome might result in pregnancy or contraction of a sexually transmitted disease. (See also coitus interruptus.)

pregnancy:
The state of having an embryo and then a fetus developing in the uterus. Pregnancy lasts approximately 280 days and is divided into three trimesters each lasting about three months.

pregnancy test:
A test used to determine whether a woman is pregnant. This involves testing a woman's urine or blood for hormones that indicate pregnancy. However, if a woman is pregnant but it has been fewer than six weeks since her last period, certain tests may not work. It may be necessary to test more than once. Home tests for pregnancy that measure the hormone level in urine can be purchased over the counter at a pharmacy.

premarital:
Occurring before marriage; often as in premarital sex—sexual intercourse that occurs before marriage.

premature ejaculation:
Difficulty that some men experience in controlling the reflex of ejaculation. As a result, the man ejaculates rapidly after erection.

prenatal:
Literally, before birth; the phrase "prenatal care," for example, refers to the care that a pregnant woman gets to help keep herself and the fetus healthy.

pro-choice:
Term used to describe people who believe that abortion should be legal, and, in most cases, easily available. The term comes from the notion that women's ability to choose should be the main consideration in making laws about abortion.

procreation:
The production of children.

prolife:
Term used to describe people who believe that abortion should be illegal, or that it should be restricted to a very limited number of circumstances. The term comes from the belief that the fetus, and in some views, the embryo, constitute human life, so that abortion consists not just of ending a pregnancy but also of ending a life.

prostate gland:
One of the male internal sex organs located next to the urethra and bladder. The prostate gland adds fluid to the semen.

pubic lice:
See crabs.

pulling out:
See coitus interruptus.

rape:
Sexual intercourse against one partner's will. Rape may also be considered to have occurred if one partner cannot give consent competently: If he or she is underage, drunk, under the influence of drugs, unconscious or being threatened.

rectum:
The portion of the large intestine that leads into the anus.

rhythm method:
A means of birth control that involves tracking the length of a woman's menstrual cycles to predict times to have vaginal intercourse that will not result in pregnancy. This method of birth control has a notoriously high rate of failure because previous cycles are not good predictors of current or future cycles. This method should not be confused with systems of fertility observation.

safer sex:
Forms of sexual activity that reduce the possibility of contracting a sexually transmitted disease. Safer sex involves using various forms of barrier protection and birth control, but no method makes sexual activity risk free.

scabies:
A small insect that lays its eggs under the human skin. Scabies seek warm, moist folds of skin, such as beneath the female breast, around the penis, in the webs of fingers, and in the bends of wrists and ankles. They cause intense itching and red sores.

scrotum:
The sac below the penis, containing the testicles and epididymus. The circulation of air around the scrotum keeps it slightly cooler than the rest of the body, which is necessary for sperm production.

semen:
The thick, whitish fluid that the male ejaculates, composed of sperm and fluids from various glands, including the seminal vesicles and the prostate gland.

sex:
Primarily, the act of the penis penetrating the vagina, although the term can also refer to oral sex (fellatio and cunnilingus) and anal sex or anything related to reproduction or erotic pleasure.

sexual abuse:
Sexual activity that a person is powerless to stop or does not comprehend; including incest, or unwanted sexual attention from a person who is in a position of power. The sexual activity may include exhibitionism or genital viewing, fondling or any penetration.

sexual harassment:
Uninvited sexual attention in any form that interferes with life in school, the workplace, or any public place. Sexual harassment might include unwanted comments about one's appearance, inappropriate physical contact, repeated invitations to sexual activity,

promises of job advancement if sexual favors are offered, or threats of job loss or demotion if sexual favors are not offered

sexual history:
A person's past sexual practices and partners, as well as information about those partners' practices, state of health and previous partners. Many people may not be fully aware of their own sexual histories: They may have failed to question their partners, or their partners may not have been completely truthful.

sexual intercourse:
Describes genital sexual contact between individuals. See also vaginal sex and anal sex.

sexual identity:
Generally used to mean sexual orientation, although the term can refer to a person's sexual feelings and behavior.

sexual orientation:
A person's erotic and emotional attraction to members of a particular gender, or of both genders. For example, if a person is attracted to members of the opposite sex, his or her sexual orientation would be heterosexual; if the attraction is to members of the same sex, the sexual orientation would be homosexual; if to members of both sexes, the orientation would be bisexual.

sexually transmitted disease (STD):
An infection that is passed on through sexual contact.

sodomy:
A general term for types of sexual acts regarded as abnormal. While often used to refer to anal sex, the term also includes oral sex as well as sexual contact between humans and animals of other species. There are laws forbidding sodomy, even between consenting adult partners, in many states.

solo sex:
See masturbation.

sonogram (also called ultrasound):
The use of ultrasonic waves to project a picture of the internal structure of the body; uses include examination of the fetus during pregnancy, as well as diagnosis of possible maladies in nonpregnant women.

sperm:
Reproductive cells that men produce within the testicles. The sperm combines with the egg, usually in the fallopian tubes, to produce an embryo.

spermicide:
A substance used to kill sperm. Spermicide may take the form of jelly, cream, foam, a thin tissue-like square or a waxy suppository that melts with body heat. Spermicides are used alone or with some form of barrier protection to prevent pregnancy. Many spermicides help fight sexually transmitted diseases, including HIV.

statutory rape:
Sexual intercourse with a female below the age of consent (sixteen in most states).

STD:
See sexually transmitted disease.

sterilization:
This term has two meanings: (1) Making a woman unable to conceive a child or making a man unable to impregnate a woman; sterilization generally makes the woman or man permanently infertile. However, occasionally the procedure can be reversed. (2) Making something free from living organisms, such as bacteria or viruses.

symptom:
A change in the body or its functions that is noticeable to a person and suggests the presence of a disease. (See also asymptomatic.)

syphilis:
A sexually transmitted disease, caused by bacteria that infect the bloodstream. It is transmitted through open syphilis sores or open syphilis-related rashes, as well as through sexual contact. (See also chancre.)

T cell:
A kind of white blood cell that helps the body fight infection. HIV causes AIDS by infecting T cells, and decreasing their number.

testes:
Another word for testicles.

testicles:
Pair of male sex organs that produce sperm and male hormones. They are located inside the scrotum.

toxic shock syndrome (TSS):
A disease that is almost always associated with tampon use, especially if the tampon is not changed often. This is not a sexually transmitted disease and is caused by a bacteria called *Staph. aureus*. Symptoms include high fever, vomiting and diarrhea, followed by the appearance of a sunburn-like rash.

trich:
See trichomoniasis.

trichomoniasis:
A sexually transmitted disease caused by a one-celled parasite, *Trichomonas vaginalis*. It is spread through manual and genital contact with the vagina or the male urethra; it may also live outside the body for over an hour, causing infection via someone else's bathing suit, towel or damp clothes.

trimester:
Three-month period of time, used to refer to one of the three periods into which the nine months of pregnancy are divided.

tumor:
An abnormal swelling or mass that is composed of cells that multiply out of control.

tumorous:
Having the characteristics of a tumor.

ulcer:
A kind of open sore on the surface of an organ or of body tissue, produced by the sloughing off of dead, inflamed tissue. As an opening into the bloodstream, an ulcer may be an entry point for a sexually transmitted disease; it may also be a symptom of an STD and produce fluid that will transmit an STD.

unsafe sex:
Sexual activity undertaken without adequate birth control or barrier protection, and without full consideration of the potential risks of sex. (See also safer sex.)

urethra:
In men, a tube in the center of the penis through which sperm and other seminal fluids travel on their way out of the penis during ejaculation; urine from the bladder also travels through the urethra during urination. Just before ejaculation, a valve closes off the bladder so that urine can't enter the urethra while sperm is there. In women, this tube is for urination only, and its opening is located between the clitoris and the vaginal opening in the perineum.

urinary tract:
The portion of the body in which urine is produced and through which urine passes, primarily the bladder and urethra.

urinary tract infection:
An infection of the urinary tract, most commonly caused by bacteria that normally live in the gastrointestinal tract. These infections are much more common in women than men. Lower urinary tract infections, also known as cystitis or bladder infections, may cause frequent urination, pain with urination, blood in the urine and fever. Upper urinary tract infections, also known as kidney infections or pyelonephritis, are associated with back pain, shaking chills and high fever. It is important to have these infections treated as soon as possible so as not to damage the urinary tract. The symptoms of pain with urination and frequent urination are also associated with infection of the urethra by chlamydia.

uterus:
A female genital organ, also known as the womb; a thick-walled, muscular organ in whose lining the fertilized egg is implanted at the beginning of pregnancy. As the egg develops into an embryo, the uterus creates a nourishing environment for it. During pregnancy, the uterus expands to accommodate the developing fetus. During childbirth, the walls of the uterus contract to force the fetus out through the cervix and into the vagina. If a woman is not pregnant, the uterine lining is enriched and then sloughs off every month in the menstrual cycle.

UTI:
See urinary tract infection.

vagina:
Female sex organ; a muscular canal within the woman's body that connects the cervix with the labia. The vagina is sensitive to sexual arousal.

vaginal lips:
See labia.

vaginal sex:
A term that usually refers to the process of a man inserting his penis into a woman's vagina.

vaginismus:
Painful contraction of the vagina, which makes penetration difficult or impossible. This may be due to vaginitis, lack of lubrication, a problem with the anatomy or fear of intercourse.

vaginitis:
An inflammation of the vagina which can be caused by infections, such as Candida (see yeast infection) or Trichomonas (see trichomoniasis) or chemical irritation such as could be caused by douching.

virgin:
Person who has never experienced sexual intercourse. Although definitions of this word vary, most people consider themselves virgins if they have never experienced vaginal sex, even if they have had oral sex or experienced other types of sex play.

virus:
An infective agent too small to be seen with an ordinary microscope that causes disease in humans, animals or plants. Viruses can multiply only in connection with living cells. They are regarded both as living organisms and as complex proteins. There are many different types of viruses causing different infections, from the common cold to AIDS. Antibiotics are not effective therapy against viruses.

vulva:
Female external genitals, which include all the female sex organs except the vagina. The vulva includes the labia, the clitoris and the vaginal opening.

warts:
See genital warts.

womb:
Another name for uterus.

yeast infection:
Also known as candidiasis. An overgrowth of Candida, usually *C. albicans*, a yeast-like fungus that is normally present in the vagina, mouth, intestinal tract, skin and anus.

INDEX

Picture Credits